Maryland and Delaware Canoe Trails

By Edward Gertler

A Paddler's Guide to Rivers of the Old Line and First States

Seneca Press

1983

First Edition Copyright ©1979 by Edward Gertler
Second Edition Copyright ©1983 by Edward Gertler
ISBN 0-9605908-1-1 All Rights Reserved
The Seneca Press
Silver Spring, Maryland
Printed in the United States of America
By the George Banta Company

Preface

This book was written to answer a question so frequently forwarded to me; "Where's a good place to go canoeing around here?". "Here" usually meaning somewhere within reasonable driving distance of Washington, Baltimore, Wilmington, and Philadelphia. That is not an easy question to answer, particularly since boaters' tastes vary so widely. As a result, I have taken the approach of presenting as completely as possible the entire selection of free-flowing creeks, runs, and rivers and many of the most scenic tidewater paddling routes in the Maryland-Delaware region with sufficient information to allow any and all paddlers to find the right river. Then armed with this guidebook plus a few excellent available guides to canoe streams in neighboring Virginia and West Virginia, the eager paddler should never again be able to claim ignorance as an excuse for staying home.

I have not included information on boating technique, design technology, river safety, and consumer advice in this book. Such information is already plentifully available from books and periodicals and from a large, knowledgeable, and educationally oriented paddling community.

The scope of this guide book can only be rationalized as a reflection of my own tastes and prejudices. Although identified as a Maryland and Delaware guidebook, I have included streams in southern Pennsylvania, since snipping off a river description just because the river strays across a political boundary seemed artificial and unfair. On the other hand, restraint was necessary on the Susquehanna, Youghiogheny and Casselman rivers.

This book concerns itself mostly with free-flowing streams. While there are hundreds of miles of beautiful tidewater paddling in Maryland and Delaware, the author has not developed the discipline necessary to fight wind, adverse tides, bloodsucking insects, and motorboaters to explore them. Further, this book is aimed mostly towards the tastes and perceptions of the intermediate whitewater paddler, be they in kayak or canoe, decked boat or open, so as to be meaningful to the widest range of paddlers. Of course, the trip descriptions and classification of rapids are my own, and since it is impossible to share everybody's outlook, it is expected that some novices will consider the descriptions underrated and that some experts will consider them overrated. Novices and experts are not the only groups that see things differently, for decked boaters and open boaters also never seem to agree on very much either. Therefore, when warranted, I have attempted to tailor the trip descriptions to satisfy the specialized needs and tastes of paddlers of both craft.

Finally, I have paddled all streams in this volume. Be assured that if I recommend carrying a dam or falls, it is because I carried (or wished that I had); and if I say that you will see no houses in a certain gorge, it is because I saw no houses when I was there. And so on. Of course, rivers are dynamic and ever-changing; trees fall, houses are built, dams wash out, and fences are strung. I am sure there will be differences in the rivers as I saw them and future paddlers will see them. I welcome any and all comments and inputs for future editions. In the meantime, have a safe and enjoyable trip.

Ed Gertler

Acknowledgements

I have found that it is much easier soloing a canoe through whitewater than soloing the production of a book, so a few unsung heroes shall now be sung about. First of all thanks go to Roger Corbett who was the logistical mastermind behind this volume. Roger helped me plot and plan, offered advice, gave guidance and generally shared the fruit of years of experience gained in assembling his own guidebooks. He also guided me to Don Rau of Word Design who was responsible for converting piles of dogeared smudgy-typed manuscripts into the readable print and format that follows. Errors have no place in a guidebook so credit is due to Mimi Hayman for donating a perfectly healthy pair of eyeballs to the tedious drudgery of proofreading.

I wish to acknowledge the numerous paddlers who have helped me explore these streams but most notably praise goes to Pete and Barb Brown and Tom and Paulette Irwin. These poor souls have suffered through countless mismeasured mileages, mistimed and mislocated take-outs, misread gradients, misinterpreted weather forecasts and other such abuse all in the name of exploring one more new river. And when the going got too tough they still would be kind enough to run my shuttles. Also besides being good paddling companions the Browns are fine photographers, Barb having contributed the back cover photo. Since much of my exploring was done alone I shall take this opportunity to thank the scores of motoring strangers who were kind enough and brave enough to stop, pick up and shuttle the funny bearded hitchhiker clad in black rubber longjohns and with purple paddle in hand. I want to thank the personnel of the U.S. Fish and Wildlife Service, Blackwater and Prime Hook National Wildlife refuges who were so helpful to my exploration of their refuge waterways. Lastly, praise goes to the personnel of the Delaware Department of Transportation whose promptness in filling out map orders is amazing.

Finally bibliographical credit goes to the amazing American Guide Series books for Maryland, Delaware and Pennsylvania that were produced during the 1930's by the Writers Program of the Work Projects Administration and the more recently published *Maryland A New Guide to the Old Line State* by Papenfuse, Collins, Stiverson and Carr, references that have proved a bountiful source of interesting historical and cultural background information. Also recommended is *Delaware's Outstanding Natural Areas And Their Preservation* by Lorraine M. Fleming, a mind-boggling in-depth inventory of Delaware's natural assets.

Contents

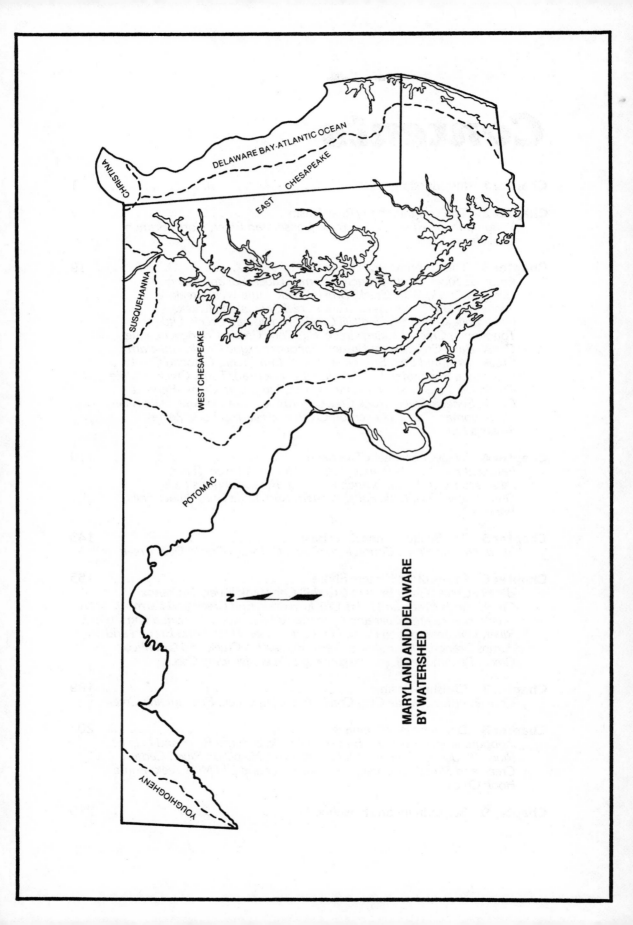

DELAWARE BAY-ATLANTIC OCEAN

CHRISTINA

EAST CHESAPEAKE

SUSQUEHANNA

WEST CHESAPEAKE

POTOMAC

YOUGHIOGHENY

N

MARYLAND AND DELAWARE
BY WATERSHED

Chapter 1

Introduction

In order to fully acquaint you with the many streams in Maryland and Delaware the waterways are described and organized in the following manner.

Introduction

An introduction starts each description by locating the stream, pointing out any notable peculiarities, dredging up a little historical background, and briefly noting any redeeming values or the lack of them.

Section

Following the introduction, the stream is divided into sections and each section is identified; as a rule, the criteria for the sections was based on the general character of the river or sometimes just what comprises a reasonable day's run. Often, if a stream is short or is of a fairly uniform nature, one section will cover the entire distance. The vital statistics for the sections include gradient, difficulty, distance, time, width, scenery, and map number.

The first statistic, gradient, is expressed in feet per mile and was developed by dividing the total drop of the segment by its length. Gradients range from zero on tidal streams to in excess of 100 feet/mile on the upper Youghiogheny. If the gradient is unevenly distributed, then the gradient of the steepest stretch has also been included. The gradient is a general indication of the likelihood of rapids; the higher the gradient, the more rapids or riffles are likely to be found. However, high volume and/or uneven distribution of drop can produce difficult and dangerous whitewater even with very low gradients, as in the case of Little Falls of the Potomac. Conversely, an even distribution of a steep gradient on a small stream can result in surprisingly easy whitewater as on upper Big Cove Creek.

Difficulty is expressed in the international whitewater rating scale that runs from 1 to 6 and a smooth water scale that goes from A to C. The rating scale is intended to be quite descriptive and objective and can be interpreted as follows.

A. Smooth Water. This is a condensation of the regular smooth water scale which is supposed to run from A to C, thus lumping together all flatwater, both swift and dead. Most whitewater paddlers consider all flatwater dead and dull anyhow.

1. Easy. Short straightforward riffles usually formed by gravel bars, low ledges or constrictions of the river. Waves are less than one foot high and little maneuvering is required. Routes are easy to determine and all riffles are followed by adequate rescue opportunity.

2. Medium Difficulty. Rapids are more frequent, comprised of waves less than two feet high and in regular patterns and with easy eddies. There are more rocks and obstructions, but manuevering is still easy and rescue spots are still plentiful.

3. Difficult. Rapids are long and require extensive manuevering. Both

1

ledges and waves are up to three feet high and waves are often irregular. Course is not always easily recognizable. Rescue opportunities are spaced farther apart.

4. Very Difficult. Long, pushy extended sets of rapids with high irregular waves. Boulders and ledges block the course and along with powerful cross-currents require abrupt and intricate turns. Course is often difficult to recognize and scouting is often necessary. Rescue is difficult.

5. Exceedingly Difficult. Long heavy rapids with high irregular waves and powerful cross-currents or steep, complex, boulder-clogged rapids with poor visibility. Big drops and powerful hydraulics are unavoidable and ability to catch small fast eddys are essential for control. Rescue is very difficult and scouting is often unavoidable.

6. Utmost Difficulty. All of the difficulties stated in class 5 carried to the extreme. Running such water involves an unusual risk of life.

Unfortunately this classification system can be influenced by subjective assessments that may include variables such as the experience of the rater, the volume of water, the effect of adverse weather, and the number of wipeouts/swampings/rolls associated with a particular trip. For example, the Savage River has been rated anywhere from class 3 to class 6. Nevertheless, most paddlers will agree that the Savage is harder than the Gunpowder, which in turn, is harder than the Antietam. And this is where the numerical system still retains its usefulness: it provides a basis for the comparison of streams on a relative scale. Hence, if one is familiar with one stream in this guide, it is possible to relate the difficulty of all others. Finally, please note that this is a whitewater rating system only and thus only addresses the conditions encountered on an ideal unobstructed stream. In reality many of the small streams in these states are complicated by fallen trees, fences, and other strainers that greatly increase the difficulty and risk involved in paddling those rivers.

Distance is expressed in statute miles and is rounded off to the nearest half mile. The number given describes the distance from one end of the stream section to the other. Remember that on some of the tidal creeks which possess only one access point and thus require a round trip itinerary, you must double the distance given. Sometimes distance does not tell the whole story. For example, to battle through six miles of log-choked Zekiah Swamp Run will consume as much time and energy as paddling thirty miles of the North Branch Potomac above Bloomington. So time is also included, expressed in hours and rounded off to the nearest half hour. This represents paddling and portaging time only. Be sure to allocate extra time for lunch, scouting, and rescue.

Width, in feet, and scenery are self-explanatory. Finally a map is referenced that will clarify the description and aid in the difficult art of shuttling.

Trip Description

A trip description provides a brief narrative of what the paddler can expect to find, encounter, or confront on that section. Where practical, all difficulties are described, points of interest are acknowledged, and more historical background is presented.

Hazards

Next hazards are enumerated. Although hazards are mostly objects that pose a threat to the paddler, major annoyances are also included.

Water Conditions

Water conditions describe the best time of year and under what hydrological and meteorological conditions one can expect to find adequate water in the stream. Since the author detests driving long miles and endless hours wasting gallons of precious gasoline to find an empty river, the time spans recommended for catching a stream up are fairly conservative. Probably most creeks retain water longer than indicated but do not count on it.

Gauge

Most streams have some point of reference from which to establish the adequacy of the water level. Sometimes it consists of just a joint in a bridge pier or the depth of an indicative riffle. However, a fair number of streams are graced with the presence of at least one USGS (United States Geological Survey) stream-flow gauging station which usually possess an outside readable staff gauge. The gauge scale is set so that the stations never record a negative level. Hence zero canoeable water may still read 2.0 feet on a USGS gauge. Gauging stations are usually recognized as tall rectangular concrete structures that are most often located near a bridge. Generally one has to personally inspect a gauge for a reading, but, in a few lucky cases on the North Branch Potomac River, the Potomac River, and the Monocacy River, daily readings are available as part of a recorded Weather Bureau forecast. The forecast can be heard by phoning 301-899-3210 after 11:30 a.m. or by tuning in to the NOAA weather broadcast on vhf frequency 162.55 mh. Finally, on some popular streams canoeists have painted simple gauges, usually at foot or half foot increments, on bridge piers or abutments. This system, developed and refined by Randy Carter, a renown and widely travelled whitewater canoeist, usually establishes zero as the minimum possible level of navigation. However, you must realize that paddlers possess varying ideas of what constitutes "too low" depending on such variables as the gauge-painter's skill, boat materials and construction, and degree of aversion to repair and maintenance. So, the boater who runs a river with an unfamiliar canoe gauge that indicates zero may be a real gambler.

Maps

Maps accompany each river description most importantly to answer shuttle and access questions. The maps are drawn to varying scales but are proportionally accurate. The little numbers along the rivers are river mileages and they denote the distances between the little arrowhead-shaped ticks. These marks do not necessarily indicate an access point. However in general you can assume any bridge shown affords some degree of access while on tidal rivers I generally have only included those dead end roads that terminate at public landings.

Geography and Geology

Rivers do not just happen but rather are a product of the environment through which they flow. If the paddler has a general understanding of this environment, in particular the geology and geography of that area, then he can more easily find the streams best suited to his tastes.

Although Maryland and Delaware combined still do not encompass a whole lot of area, their unusual wedge-shaped configuration manages to pack a wonderfully varied collection of topography into those meager boundaries. Geologists neatly divide the states into three "provinces"; the Appalachian, Piedmont and Coastal Plain. Furthermore the Appalachian Province is subdivided into the Allegheny Plateau, Valley and Ridge, and Blue Ridge districts.

Starting in the far west, the Allegheny Plateau extends from Dans Mountain, west of Cumberland, to and beyond the West Virginia Line. This is a rolling upland punctuated by a series of long, gently rising ridges and underlain by fairly flat alternating layers of sandstone, coal, shale and limestone. Streams in this region tend toward the extreme; either meandering peacefully about high, fairly open valleys or plunging violently through steep deep v-shaped canyons. Often the transition between the extremes occurs quite abruptly. This area also holds title to Maryland's most rotten weather. The high ridges are buffeted by the cold winter storm systems that roll out of the northwest and, in the process, scrape out copious quantities of moisture. It is not uncommon to lose 10-15 degrees F and go from sunshine to snowfall in the ten mile drive from Cumberland to Frostburg.

Next comes the Valley and Ridge District which extends from Cumberland east to Hagerstown. A drive down U.S. Rte 40 between these two towns will no doubt convince you that this is a very descriptive name. As a general rule, the valleys evolve from narrow, rugged, and semiwild in the west to wide, fairly flat, and well-cultivated in the east. The streams in this region wind about like drunk snakes but within the confines of very straight valleys. Occasionally these streams will cut through a ridge to get to another valley and it is here that one can best expect to find whitewater in this district. Finally, huge quantities of limestone underlying this area make it a caver's delight.

The Blue Ridge District is a narrow strip occupied by South Mountain, Catoctin Mountain, and the valley in between. There is only one stream, Catoctin Creek, that flows entirely within this region whose scenery in Maryland, while very pretty, does not look much different from the Ridge and Valley District to the west. Geologists will blanch at this callous assessment.

Next, extending from the Blue Ridge east to an imaginary line connecting Washington, Baltimore and Wilmington is the Piedmont Plateau. This is a very rolling land dominated by beautiful old farms on the west, sprawling cities on the east, and transition in between. The rivers of this region flow in every direction, sometimes straight, sometimes crooked, but almost always flat. However, on the eastern edge of this district, where the Piedmont meets the Coastal Plain all eastward flowing rivers drop over a band of old hard rock referred to as the fall line. The nature of the fall line can vary from stretches of gentle riffles to the violent cataracts of the Great Falls of the Potomac.

All lands to the east of the fall line fall in the Coastal Plain. The plain on Maryland's western shore (of the Chesapeake Bay) is rolling and sometimes even rugged while, in contrast, the land of the eastern shore and most of Delaware is as flat as a pancake. One thing is for sure; streams of the coastal plain are invariably flat. Most of the stream mileage here was flooded out by the ocean thousands of years ago, creating hundreds of miles of tidal estuaries, the largest and most spectacular example of which is the Chesapeake Bay which fills the former lower Susquehanna River Valley. This watery area is heaven on earth for sailboaters, powerboaters, waterfowl watchers, fishermen, seafood lovers, etc. but has little to offer the river paddler. The remaining free-flowing segments of these rivers are very small, fairly swift and twist a lot through usually a swampy environment.

The Importance of an Education

Believe it or not, the hapless fellows in the movie "Deliverance" (the suburbanites, not the perverts) are a real and common phenomenon of our nation's rivers. For it seems that a dumb myth persists in this land, a myth in which many individuals believe that the ability to masterfully handle a canoe is instinctive. Unfortunately too many of these people venturing forth to demonstrate their born-to-canoe theory become the clients of the local rescue squad, mortician, etc. If you are a raw novice contemplating using this book, you will enjoy it much more if you first accumulate a little education. Now if you go to the local library or book store and obtain a "how to canoe" book, that is better than nothing at all. But you will find it much more effective and enjoyable to be taught by a real live paddler.

It is very easy to learn to paddle, especially if you live in or near the area covered by this guidebook. First of all you can contact your local Red Cross chapter which usually conducts a schedule of basic canoeing classes each summer. These courses teach you details of the canoe and its equipment, basic flat-water handling skills and rescue. Next contact any of the local clubs listed on page 107. Most of these conduct basic flatwater and whitewater paddling classes and offer trips to join where you can practice your newly acquired skills in the presence of more experienced individuals. Note that even if you do not aspire beyond smooth water paddling, the knowledge gained in boat handling and understanding currents from a basic whitewater course will be of great value to you elsewhere. Finally, if you have lots of money to spare, there are a fine selection of private paddling schools located around Washington, D.C., Ohiopyle, Pennsylvania and up and down the Appalachians, where you can receive more intense, advanced and more personal instruction. They also have the advantage of providing your equipment and other logistical needs. So as you can see, the opportunities to become a master of your craft are there. Please use them.

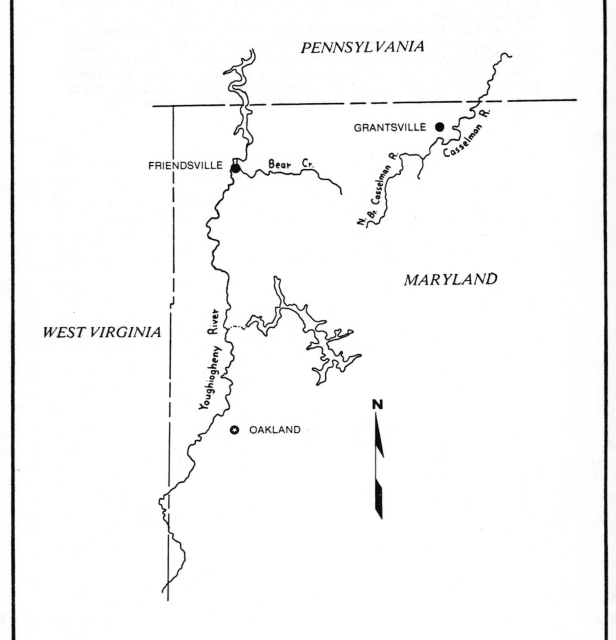

PENNSYLVANIA

GRANTSVILLE

Casselman R.

N. Br. Casselman R.

FRIENDSVILLE

Bear Cr.

MARYLAND

WEST VIRGINIA

Youghiogheny River

N

OAKLAND

YOUGHIOGHENY RIVER TRIBUTARIES

Chapter 2

The Youghiogheny River Basin

The Youghiogheny and its tributaries drain 1748 square miles of rugged plateau country in West Virginia, Maryland and Pennsylvania. Roughly 400 square miles of that area is in Maryland. This is the only basin in the state that drains to the westward-flowing Ohio River system. The Youghiogheny watershed in Maryland is a thinly populated territory, possessing no cities or even large towns, with light agriculture, coal mining and recreation being the major activity in the region. Most of the basin's waterways, navigable or otherwise, are deeply incised into the landscape, rushing at the bottom of steep-walled, rhododendron-clothed gorges. This is a wild and lonely corner of the state and the rivers truly reflect this character.

The following streams are described in this chapter:

Youghiogheny River
    Bear Creek
    Casselman River
      North Branch Casselman River

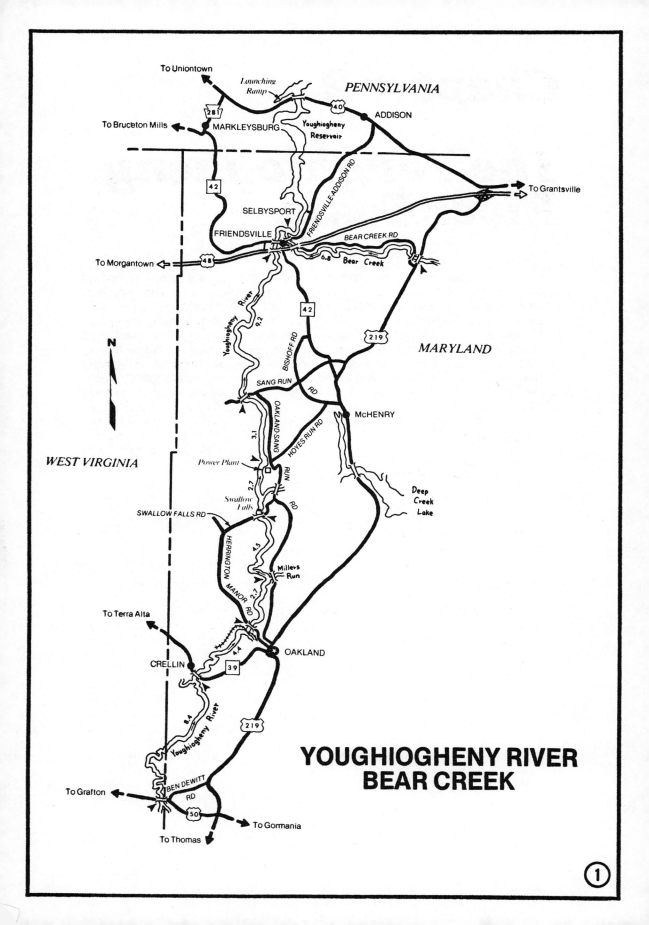

YOUGHIOGHENY RIVER
BEAR CREEK

Youghiogheny River

Introduction

A lot of nice things can be said about the Maryland section of the Yough but to 99% of the paddling community it is known for only one thing; it is the big white-water challenge. Probably no section of river in the East is so famous and sought after to test one's technical ability as this river from Sang Run to Friendsville. Unfortunately the Yough, as of this writing, is also a troubled river. The State of Maryland has designated the segment of river from Millers Run to Friendsville as a Wild and Scenic River, a status which regulates land use in the canyon in order to preserve the natural qualities of the river corridor. Local landowners and residents have not received this very restrictive legislation well and some of those people living in the stretch from Hoyes Run to Sang Run have chosen to express their distaste for it by posting their land and denying access to the river to all outsiders. This includes fishermen, hunters and hikers as well as paddlers. Boaters putting in at Sang Run have been harrassed, threatened and their vehicles vandalized. Hopefully the situation will cool off in another year or two and it is recommended that you contact some of the local paddlers in Ohiopyle, Pa. to assess the current conditions. In the meantime if you insist on running sections 2 or 3, as far as we know you can legally put in directly off the county right-of-way (specifically off the east bridge abutment). You should not risk leaving a vehicle at Sang Run, unload and put in fast to avoid attracting attention and if approached by an irate local please keep it cool and courteous, no matter how hard it hurts. Finally as a last resort paddlers have called on the State Police at Oakland for escorts so if necessary call 301-334-3001 for assistance.

Section 1. U.S. Rte. 50 to Millers Run

Gradient	Difficulty	Distance	Time	Width	Scenery	Map
4	A-1,2	15.5	5.0	10-40	Good	1

Trip Description: This section makes it possible for a status-conscious novice to go out and spend a lovely, safe day on the river and then go home and brag to all his friends about how he ran the Upper Yough. To Crellin it is an initially tiny brook that twists and turns through a woodland or pastoral setting in a fairly remote upland valley. The water is mostly flat but swift. The town of Crellin is an eyesore of riverbank trash heaps, the remnants of which festoon the riverbank trees for miles downstream. Below Crellin the Yough begins passage through an attractive wooded gorge that more or less brackets the river all the way to its mouth at Mckeesport, Pa. There is one fairly long boulder-studded rapid (class 2) a few miles below Crellin to challenge the novice but the river is otherwise flat with an occasional riffle. The trip can be shortened by three miles by taking out at Herrington Manor Road.

Hazards: One low-water bridge between Rte. 50 and Crellin, possible fallen trees above Crellin and raw sewage from Oakland coming in via the Little Yough above Herrington Manor Road.

Water Conditions: Runable within few days of hard rain or during a thaw.

Gauge

None. For winter and spring correlations, Kitzmiller gauge on the North Branch Potomac should be reading over 4.0 feet.

Section 2. Millers Run to Sang Run Road

Gradient	Difficulty	Distance	Time	Width	Scenery	Map
36*	1-5	10.5	4.0	30-50	Excellent	1

*3.5 mi. at 90fpm

Trip Description: This section is commonly referred to as the Top Yough and is for top paddlers only. One starts with a relaxing 3.5 mile paddle down fairly placid waters through quiet woods before the bottom drops out of the river. Here the river plunges over a few high scary ledges followed by a relatively easy slalom through the boulders for one mile down to Swallow Falls Road. Swallow Falls is about a hundred yards downstream where you can land on the left brink and carry both the falls and a vicious eight foot ledge just downstream. For about the next two miles the river is characterized by long steeply dropping boulder-clogged rapids. Most rapids can be scouted from the eddy except for a nasty one about a mile below Swallow Falls where all the water funnels steeply down a complex route on the left. Things calm down toward Hoyes Run and the final three miles to Sang Run allow you to cool down on riffles and easy rapids through a more open valley. Finally, do not get so engrossed with the whitewater that you miss the beautiful falls just up Muddy Creek from its confluence with the Yough just below Swallow Falls.

Hazards: Swallow Falls which is about a hundred yards down easy rapids from the Swallow Falls Road bridge. Just below is a jagged eight-foot ledge with a deceptively powerful hole at the bottom.

Water Conditions: Winter or spring within few days of hard rain or during thaw.

Gauge

Staff gauge on downstream side of right pier of Sang Run Road bridge. On weekends it should read about two feet for a good run. During weekdays, water releases from the power plant at Hoyes Run render this gauge very unreliable. Look for at least 4.0 feet at Kitzmiller for winter and spring correlation.

Section 3. Sang Run Road to Friendsville, Md. (Rte. 42)

Gradient	Difficulty	Distance	Time	Width	Scenery	Map
52*	2-5	9.0	4.0	30-50	Excellent	1

*exceeds 100fpm at times

Trip Description: This section is referred to as the Upper Yough and has the whitewater that made this river famous. Specifically what makes it so special are four miles of unrelenting boulder piles, ledges, blocked views, unobvious passages, menacing undercuts and technical difficulties. At lower levels the typical rapid is tight, has poor visibility, requires quick and precise maneuvering and has an eddy or small pool at the bottom. At higher levels the passages open up but are still complex, visibility is still poor, waves and holes become big and vicious, strength, a good brace and a roll is essential and rescue possibilities are few and far between. The seriousness of this section is reflected in there being only a two foot difference between being too low and too high to run.

One has over two miles of riffles and flat water to warm up on before confronting Gap Falls, a sloping five-foot ledge that is run on the left. From here it is all down-hill through too many rapids to describe in detail. Just remember, everything is runable. It is entirely possible to eddy-hop down this river doing all of your scouting from your boat. If you are going to need to get out and scout then start very early for it is going to be a very long day. A better option though for most first timers is to run with someone who knows the way down. If you do not know any such person, during the summer wander over to nearby Ohiopyle, Pa. where four commercial rafting companies have guides who on their days off on weekdays often run the Upper Yough and might be willing to take you under their wing. The final two and three-quarter miles from Kendall, where the rough stuff ends, are a soothing coast over continuous riffles and easy rapids.

You probably will not notice it on your first run but this is a very beautiful tour. People's recollections from their first trip generally tend to omit trees, boulders, sky and other normally obvious scenery. But there are cliffs, graceful hemlocks, falls on side streams, rhododendron gardens and beautifully sculpted boulders. It is a true wilderness river.

Hazards: The entire four miles from Gap Falls to Kendall may be hazardous to your health. Besides the normal bumps and abrasions inherent to such a rocky stream the boulders on this river are very round and undercut, so it is not a good place to swim. On the other hand it is not necessarily a safe river to get out of either. During the summer watch out for rattlesnakes which find the numerous boulders a splendid place to sun themselves; one more reason not to scout from shore.

Water Conditions: Found up during winter and spring within few days of rainfall or during a thaw. During summer it can be run on weekdays, when water is released from a hydroelectric station at Hoyes Run. Water is usually released in the morning and afternoon, the noon water arriving at Sang Run usually around 1:00 to 2:00 P.M. Can also be caught up on summer weekends sometimes after heavy rains.

Gauge

Staff gauge on Sang Run Road Bridge should read 1.7 feet for minimal level and consider 3.0 feet as maximum although it has been successfully run as high as 3.5 feet by a few. On weekends when the power plant is not running one can call Pittsburgh Weather (412-644-2890) and ask for Friendsville reading. Three feet corresponds to roughly two feet at Sang Run.

Section 4. Friendsville (Md. Rte. 42) to U.S. Rte. 40

Gradient	Difficulty	Distance	Time	Width	Scenery	Map
27*	A,2	10.5	3.5	50-1600	Good	1

*gradient to reservoir

Trip Description: The last section of Maryland's Yough belongs again to the novice. There is about one mile of free-flowing river over mild gravel bar and rock garden rapids to the backwater of Yough Reservoir. The reservoir is relatively narrow and fringed by high slopes that are just about free of any development. It is really a pleasant place to paddle if you go early in the season when it is full and early in the morning when it is calm and unpopulated. If you do not go at such times you can look forward to slogging through disgusting mudflats to get in and out and being buzzed by power boat jockeys while fighting aggravating headwinds. Take out at the public launching ramp off Rte. 40 about a half mile west of bridge over the reservoir. If water is too low at Friendsville go two and a half miles north from center of Friendsville on the Friendsville-Addison Road to Selbysport where a short steep road decends on left to the lake.

Hazards: Being run over by a water skier on Yough Lake.

Water Conditions: Spring and early summer except after a dry spell or freeze. The lake is best in late spring or early summer when the drawdown is minimal.

Gauge

None. Judge riffles at Rte. 42 bridge.

Mine Over Matter

The plateau that the Yough drops off of is underlain by vast deposits of coal, most of it being the semi-bituminous variety, which is a high grade product preferred for use by the steel industry. The coal lies in several seams, the largest and most worked being the fourteen foot thick Pittsburgh Seam. Coal was discovered in Maryland as far back as 1782 near Georges Creek but mining did not really pick up until the railroad arrived about seventy years later. Since then the coal industry has operated on cycles of boom or bust. Currently, with the decline in petroleum supplies, coal has been enjoying a comeback and new mines are sprouting up everywhere.

Traditionally the boater could always tell if there was mining in the area by a dead river with orange rocks and water that tasted like a rusty nail. The acidic river also did a number on concrete bridge piers and the paint on nearby houses. Strip mines meant scarred and denuded hillsides and deep mines meant smoldering tailings piles. The paddler could only be thankful that there was not coal under more of the state.

Today mining is becoming less of a trauma to the landscape. Tough environmental regulations in Maryland on surface mining, which comprises most of the mining done here, now regulate the methods of mining, require control of acid drainage and sediments and require complete reclamation of the site when the mining is completed. An extra benefit has been realized when new mines open on top of old unreclaimed mines since the newer mine still has responsibility for reclamation of the site. Another fringe benefit of the new boom is that the price of coal has now made it economical to go back and sift the coal from the old tailings (gob) piles, resulting in the disappearance from the landscape of many of these eyesores. With coal mining continuing on the upswing we will soon find out whether coal mining can really be kept compatible with a good environment. One thing is for certain; the paddler will be the first to know.

Bear Creek

Introduction

Bear Creek is an attractive little trout stream that gushes into the Yough at Friendsville. It is not easy to catch up so do not pass it up if you have enough water and daylight to do it. If you like hairy ledge rivers, this one will turn you on.

Section 1. U.S. Rte. 219 to Friendsville (Friendsville-Addison Rd.)

Gradient	Difficulty	Distance	Time	Width	Scenery	Map
81	2-4	7.0	2.0	15-25	Good	1

Trip Description: The first three miles are suitable for the intermediate paddler, rushing swiftly over gravel bars and small boulder patches through a gorge-like valley. You can count on some fallen trees and other woody hazards, usually in fast spots. About three miles above Friendsville the stream hits the highway and the gradient begins to grow and grow. This is where the advanced paddlers take over. After a bouldery introduction the creek begins to flush over sandstone ledges up to five or six feet high. Some of these have technical sloping configuration that requires expert boat handling.
Hazards: Trees and the whitewater.
Water Conditions: Canoeable only after a heavy rain or thaw.

Gauge

None. Judge as you scout from highway.

Fun and Games Off the River

Most paddlers head to the Youghiogheny Basin to get away from it all and find paddling and just enjoying the great outdoors sufficient recreation. But even out here in the sticks there are occasional interesting diversions in the form of happenings, events and festivals to occupy your time. Take Friendsville, for example, that quiet little town at the confluence of Bear Creek and the Yough. On the third Saturday of every July the air fills with the sweet sounds of the Annual Fiddler's Contest featuring the finest and some not so fine regional artists. Just across the West Virginia line from Garrett County is Preston County, a cold rugged plateau land that has at least found success in growing buckwheat. The county is so proud of this that every September they celebrate a weekend-long Buckwheat Festival at Kingwood, the county seat. Fanciers of buckwheat cakes will go hog wild at this extravaganza. When spring arrives the rivers begin to rise and so does the sap, especially in the sugar maples. Sugar maples are common trees in these cold high elevations and tapping them for their sweet sap is vigorously pursued. Meyersdale, Pa., a small town on the Casselman River just north of Salisbury, Pa. celebrates with an annual Maple Sugar Festival. It sure would be nice to coordinate this with the Buckwheat Festival.

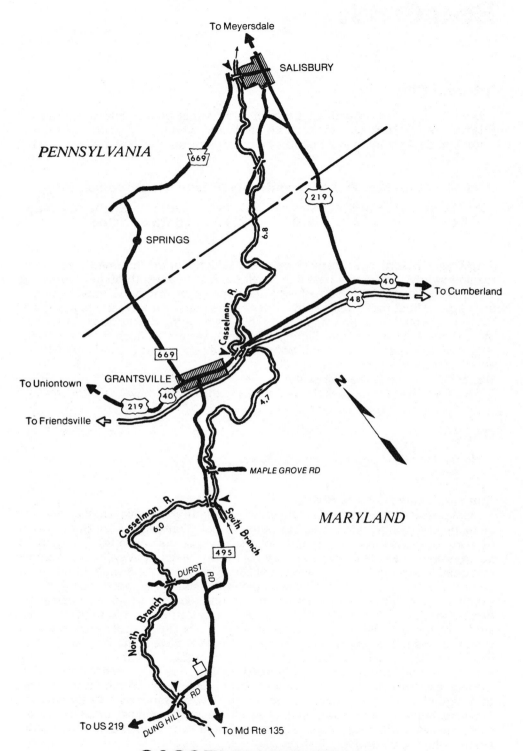

CASSELMAN RIVER
NORTH BRANCH CASSELMAN RIVER

②

Casselman River

Introduction

The Casselman is the Youghiogheny's largest tributary, born at the junction of the North and South branches and joining the Yough about ten river miles north of the Mason-Dixon Line at Confluence, Pa. As it cuts down into the Yough gorge it creates miles of good scenery and intermediate whitewater but the initial miles in Maryland are relatively tame and a fine place for novices when the weather is warm enough. The stream flows through a Mennonite and Amish enclave, the influence of which surfaces, among other places, in some of the valley's attractive barn architecture and in the fine eateries around Grantsville (closed on Sundays).

Section 1. Md. Rte. 495 to Salisbury, Pa. (Rte. 669)

Gradient	Difficulty	Distance	Time	Width	Scenery	Map
15	1-2	11.5	3.5	15-35	Good	2

Trip Description: The put-in at Rte. 495 is on the North Branch a few yards above the confluence with the South Branch. Initially the stream flows flat, deep, and narrow, winding through a pretty pastoral valley close by Rte. 495. After about a mile and a half it leaves the road and cuts into a wooded gorge and in the process rushes over almost continuous riffles formed by cobbles and small boulders. When it leaves the gorge it passes under in quick succession Rte. 48, Rte. 40 and the big graceful stone arch of the old Casselman Bridge. Built in 1816 to carry the National Road across the river, it was the largest bridge of its kind in the country at that time. Building such an innovative project apparently did not inspire the bridge's contractor to confidence for legend has it that he was so worried that the bridge would not stand that the night before the formal grand opening he had his workmen remove the supporting framework just to make sure of its integrity and avoid a lot of embarrassment. Below Rte. 40 riffles and easy rapids still occur with great frequency though the gradient decreases with each mile and by the time it reaches Salisbury the stream is mostly flat. Views from the river are of woods, pasture and some big lovely farm houses and barns. On the negative side, coal mine acid drainage also appears here and there, so do not bother to bring your fishing pole.
Hazards: None
Water Conditions: Canoeable winter and spring within few days of hard rain or during a thaw.

Gauge

USGS gauge about a half mile downstream of Rte. 40 at deteriorating bridge (turn north off Rte. 40 a quarter mile east of bridge onto River Road and follow about half mile to bridge) should read at least 1.9 feet. For just eyeballing it, the riffles at the put-in should all be passable. Also for a winter and spring correlation Kitzmiller gage on the North Branch Potomac (call 301-899-3210) should read at least 4.0 feet.

North Branch Casselman River

Introduction

The North Branch of the Casselman River drains the high plateau valley between Negro and Meadow mountains in Garrett County. This is the heart of Maryland's icebox so it is best to shoot for this gem during spring thaw. In spite of the presence of three strip mines it affords a very pretty run through a rather isolated corner of the state.

Section 1. Dung Hill Road to Md. Rte. 495

Gradient	Difficulty	Distance	Time	Width	Scenery	Map
44	1-3	6.0	1.5	10-25	Very Good	2

Trip Description: The fun starts immediately as one can shoot the metal culvert tubes under Dung Hill Road (only in Garrett County can the high peak baggers ascend such prizes as The Dung Hill, Pee Wee Hill, Roman Nose Mountain, Snaggy Mountain, Monkey Lodge Hill or Contrary Knob). Initially the clear stream is flat but very swift, rushing through escape-proof alder thickets at the base of a pastoral valley. In spots these alders arch completely across the creek and though passable, should be approached with utmost caution. It then enters a gorge filled with easy rapids of boulders and small ledges. Things calm down above Durst Road but below it enters another gorge, filled with long rock gardens and a few exciting boulder patches. Both gorges are lush with hemlock and rhododendron. **Hazards:** Fallen trees aggrevated by narrow island formed channels and alders. **Water Conditions:** Canoeable after a hard rain or big thaw. Since the stream drains bogs and swamps it holds its water better than most streams this small.

Gauge

There are joints in the concrete piers of the Rte. 495 bridge. The fourth below the top represents a minimal but enjoyable level. If the Casselman looks runable from bank to bank at the rapid below U.S. Rte. 40, go up and check out this gauge.

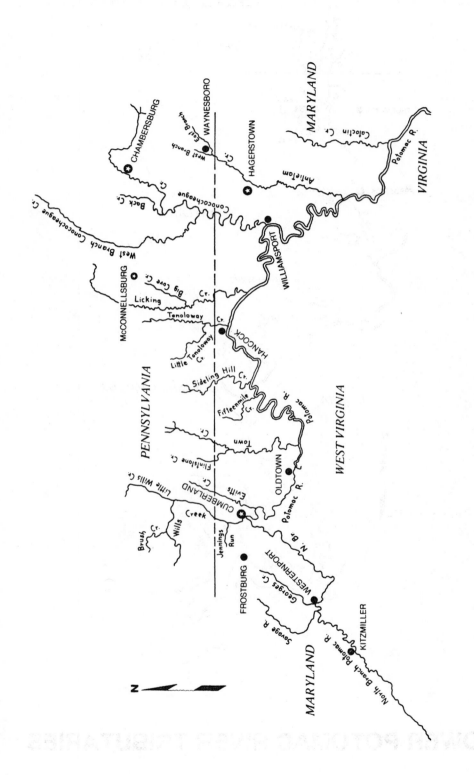

UPPER POTOMAC RIVER TRIBUTARIES

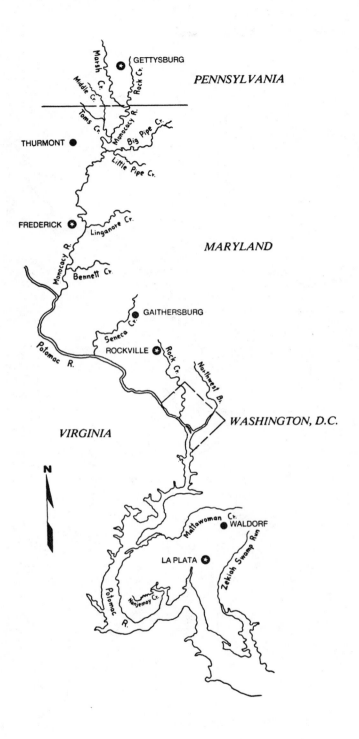

LOWER POTOMAC RIVER TRIBUTARIES

Chapter 3

The Potomac River Basin

The Potomac is the longest and most diverse river system in Maryland. The basin includes altogether over 15,000 square miles of Maryland, Pennsylvania, West Virginia and the District of Columbia. It ranges from the cold high plateau of the Alleghenys to the broad waters of the Chesapeake Bay and tidewater. The Potomac and its tributaries flow through wild mountain gorges, open farm country, lush swamps, past heavy industry and through the nation's capital. Its waters range from fresh to foul to brackish and their temperament varies from the raging cataracts of Great Falls to rushing mountain torrents like the Savage to the peaceful meanderings of the Antietam. One can fish for trout in its mountain headwaters, for bass in its broad main stem and go crabbing in its tidal reaches. You can spend a day just playing the rapids in the Mather Gorge or spend two weeks floating and camping the long lazy Potomac, Monocacy or Conococheague. One can be buzzed by swallows under the C&O aqueduct over Seneca Creek or buzzed by jet airliners under the approach path to National Airport. The variety of experiences are infinite and you can always count on some good boating to be enjoyed somewhere in the basin.

The following streams are described in this chapter:

Potomac River
   North Branch Potomac River
     Savage River
     Georges Creek
     Wills Creek
       Brush Creek
       Little Wills Creek
       Jennings Run
     Evitts Creek
   Town Creek
     Flintstone Creek
   Fifteenmile Creek
   Sideling Hill Creek
   Tonoloway Creek
     Little Tonoloway Creek
   Licking Creek
     Big Cove Creek
   Conococheague Creek
     Back Creek
     West Branch Conococheague Creek
   Antietam Creek
     West and East Branches
     Antietam Creek

Catoctin Creek
Monocacy River
   Marsh Creek
   Rock Creek
   Toms Creek
     Middle Creek
   Big Pipe Creek
     Little Pipe Creek
   Linganore Creek
   Bennett Creek
Seneca Creek
Rock Creek
Northwest Branch Anacostia River
Mattawoman Creek
Nanjemoy Creek and Hill Top Fork
Zekiah Swamp Run

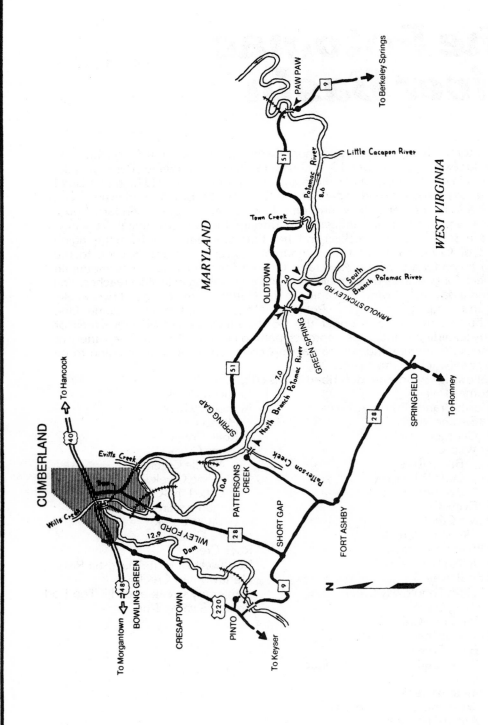

POTOMAC RIVER
NORTH BRANCH POTOMAC RIVER

Potomac River

Introduction

If any river in the state can be called "Old Reliable" it is unquestionably the Potomac. When the Potomac, on those very rare occasions, gets too low to float then it is time to go to the Bay or the Ocean. When it gets too frozen to paddle then it is time to go skiing. Reliable flow means reliable whitewater. When most other streams in the state are a jumble of wet rocks, the rapids at Harpers Ferry and on the lower Potomac are still interesting. But most of the Potomac is rather docile and as such always provides plenty of opportunity for novice paddling and leisure canoe camping. Much of the left bank of the river is protected by the C & O Canal National Historical Park thus alleviating to a large extent the problems of trespass inherent with camping on most streams and providing reliable camping with its thirty-two hiker-biker campsites between Oldtown and Washington. Finally if you are poaching, running from the law or have any other reason to be concerned with the location of political boundaries, you can rely on the Potomac to never float you out of Maryland as the whole river, right up to the right bank belongs to "The Old Line State."

Section 1. Oldtown, Md. to Paw Paw, W. Va. (Md. Rte. 51, W. Va. Rte. 9)

Gradient	Difficulty	Distance	Time	Width	Scenery	Map
4	A-1	11.0	3.5	100-500	Good	3

Trip Description: One can start a Potomac cruise right at the junction of the North and South branches but putting in at the low-water toll bridge over the North Branch at Oldtown, Md. is much more convenient. The river follows a relatively straight eastward course as it cuts through the lovely low hills and ridges of Allegany and Hampshire counties. Except for a short stretch of highway near Town Creek the impression from the river is one of remoteness. The river runs mostly flat with a few riffles formed by tiers of low ledges. Unfortunately the water often still suffers some odor and discoloration from upstream pollution on the North Branch. If this presents a problem on a hot summer day, the wilting paddler in search of a swimming hole can find excellent refuge by paddling a few yards up such clear and clean sidestreams as Town Creek (left) or the Little Cacapon (right). The take-out is reached by a dirt road branching off of W. Va. Rte. 9 at Paw Paw just before the bridge over the Potomac or if you also need room to leave several cars, there is a Park Service Access Area off of Md. Rte. 51, north side, just west of the railroad overpass a half mile west of Paw Paw.
Hazards: None
Water Conditions: Canoeable most of summer except after a prolonged drought.

Gauge

USGS gauge at Hancock (301-899-3210 after 11:30 A.M.) should read at least 2.8 feet and Paw Paw gauge at least 3.6 feet.

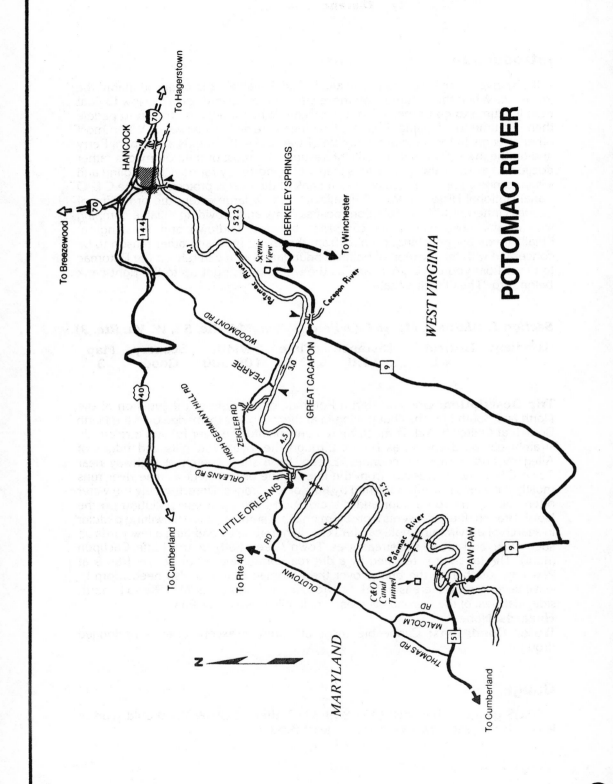

POTOMAC RIVER

WEST VIRGINIA

MARYLAND

HANCOCK

To Hagerstown

To Breezewood

To Cumberland

BERKELEY SPRINGS

To Winchester

Scenic View

Potomac River

9.1

WOODMONT RD

PEARRE

3.0

Cacapon River

GREAT CACAPON

HIGH GERMANY HILL RD

ZEIGLER RD

4.5

ORLEANS RD

LITTLE ORLEANS

21.5

Potomac River

C&O Canal Tunnel

OLDTOWN

To Rte 40

RD

THOMAS RD

MALCOLM RD

PAW PAW

To Cumberland

N

70

70

144

522

40

9

9

51

④

Section 2. Paw Paw, W. Va. to Little Orleans, Md.

Gradient	Difficulty	Distance	Time	Width	Scenery	Map
3	A-1	22.0	7.0	200-400	Very Good	4

Trip Description: If John Smith had first set eyes upon the Potomac from the top of Sideling Hill he probably would have named it the "Snake River." For about twenty-five miles, from Paw Paw to Sideling Hill Creek the river coils down a serpentine path as it cuts an almost-canyon through the foothills between Town Hill and Sideling Hill. The valley is thinly inhabited and except for the presence of some well-traveled railroad lines it is a fairly wild river that has long been very popular with canoe campers. Although this section can be easily covered in a day at most levels, the favorite procedure is to make it an overnighter with a camp stop at the Sorrel Ridge canal campsite. Even if you do not camp here, it is worth a stop to hike up the towpath to explore the old C&O Canal Tunnel. The current through "The Paw Paw Bends" is usually strong and though most of the way is flat there are lots of riffles formed by low ledges. Take out at the launching ramp at the mouth of Fifteenmile Creek.
Hazards: None
Water Conditions: Runable all year except after exceptional drought.

Gauge

USGS gauge at Hancock (call 301-899-3210 after 11:30 A.M.) should read at least 2.6 feet.

Section 3. Little Orleans, Md. to Hancock, Md.

Gradient	Difficulty	Distance	Time	Width	Scenery	Map
2	A-1	16.5	5.0	300-600	Good	4

Trip Description: This section makes an ideal canoe camping extension to the Paw Paw Bends cruise. To Great Cacapon, W. Va. the atmosphere is mostly wild (except when the trains roar by) and dominated by beautiful Sideling Hill and Cacapon Mountain. Below Great Cacapon the mountain views are still pretty but the river banks are marred by miles of often shoddy summer homes and shacks. The river glides swiftly over a rocky bottom with occasional riffles formed by tiny ledges and one strong straightforward riffle through the ruins of the old C&O Canal Dam No. 6 above Great Cacapon. The water quality seems to have recovered by now and is often fairly clear. A launching ramp at the mouth of Little Tonoloway Creek in Hancock allows easy exit.
Hazards: None
Water Conditions: Runable anytime.

Gauge

USGS gauge at Hancock (301-899-3210 after 11:30 A.M.) should read at least 2.6 feet and Paw Paw gauge at least 3.5 feet.

Section 4. Hancock, Md. to Williamsport, Md.

Gradient	Difficulty	Distance	Time	Width	Scenery	Map
2	A	28.0	9.0	400-700	Good	5

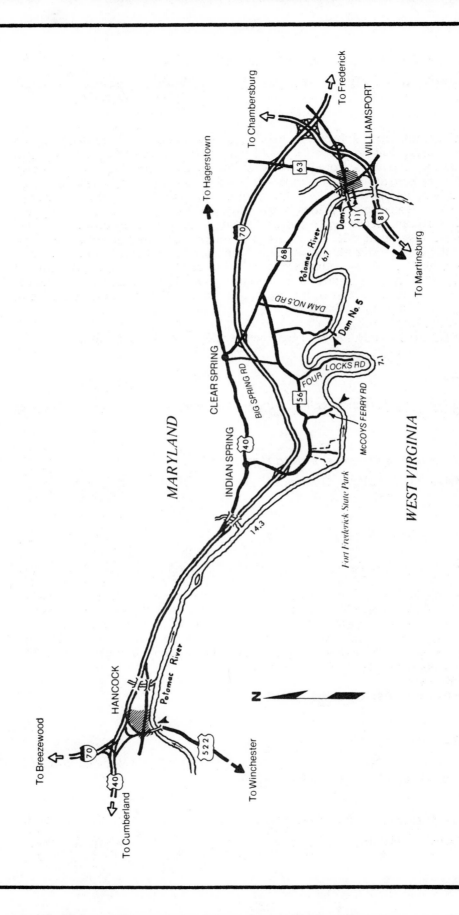

POTOMAC RIVER

MARYLAND

WEST VIRGINIA

To Hagerstown

To Chambersburg

To Frederick

WILLIAMSPORT

To Martinsburg

CLEAR SPRING

INDIAN SPRING

BIG SPRING RD

Potomac River

DAM NO.5 RD

Dam No. 5

FOUR LOCKS RD

McCOYS FERRY RD

Fort Frederick State Park

HANCOCK

Potomac River

To Breezewood

To Cumberland

To Winchester

N

70

40

63

68

111

81

56

522

Dam

6.7

7.1

14.3

0

⑤

Trip Description: This section can be divided into two comfortable runs of fourteen miles each by gaining access at the McCoys Ferry launching ramp. To McCoys Ferry the river is flat, flowing over a rocky bottom but with a strong current even at low water. The trouble with this section is that I-70 runs so close to the river that it sounds like one is paddling down the median strip. But the scenery of wooded hills and bluffs is attractive and with a good pair of earplugs this can be pleasant cruising. Seven miles of deadwater backed up by the C&O Canal Feeder Dam No. 5 begins at McCoys Ferry. The dam entails a rough carry with the left side being the lesser of the two evils. Below the dam are a few riffles formed by old fish trap weirs and micro-ledges. The best part of these last few miles is decorated by some beautiful towering white limestone cliffs on the right. Take out at the town park in Williamsport just below the junction of Conococheague Creek.

Hazards: Dam No. 5, carry either side.

Water Conditions: Runable anytime.

Gauge

USGS gauge at Hancock can read at least down to 2.5 feet.

Section 5. Williamsport, Md. to Dam No. 4

Gradient	Difficulty	Distance	Time	Width	Scenery	Map
2	A	15.5	5.0	400-700	Poor	6

Trip Description: The trip starts off with a short portage around a four-foot dam at the Potomac Edison Power Plant. At high levels (over 11.0 feet at Hancock) the dam washes out but at lower levels approach with caution. Then after two and a half miles of current begins thirteen miles of deadwater behind Dam No. 4. This would not be so bad except that most of this stretch is lined by a most distasteful display of summer dwellings. These include mobile homes, old school buses, trailers, shacks and anything else that someone thought of to keep the rain out, all often crammed together like a long parking lot. In warm weather count on competing with motor boats and water skiers for the right-of-way. Dam No. 4 is easily carried on the left but a better idea is to put in here and skip this section.

Hazards: A four-foot dam at the power station at Williamsport and Dam No. 4, both carried on the left.

Water Conditions: Canoeable all year.

Gauge

USGS gauge at Hancock (call 301-899-3210 after 11:30 A.M.). Late summer flows drop below 3.0 feet. While nothing is too low, high levels (over 5.0 feet) should be handled with care when approaching Dam No. 4.

Section 6. Dam No. 4 to Dam No. 3

Gradient	Difficulty	Distance	Time	Width	Scenery	Map
2	A-1	22.0	7.0	300-900	Good	7

Trip Description: This is an attractive section without too much second home development and on those stretches where it does exist the dwellings are better spaced and of a more tasteful design than those upstream. The first five miles below the dam include many easy riffles best enjoyed at low water levels (under

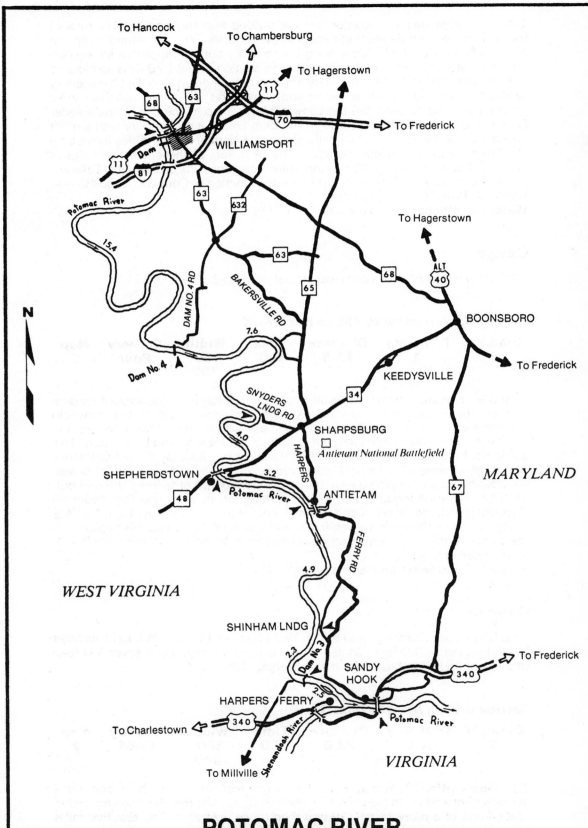

POTOMAC RIVER

3.0 feet at Hancock) which expose old fishtrap weirs and low ledges. One particularly interesting spot called the Horsebacks is found a few miles below Dam No. 4 where the river weaves through a staircase of tiny ledges that run parallel to the direction of the river. The rest of the way to Shepherdstown is flat. It is 11.5 miles from Dam No. 4 to Shepherdstown where it is possible to take out at the gauging station on the right about 500 feet below the Rte. 34 bridge. Below Shepherdstown wooded bluffs and the approaching Blue Ridge dominate the scenery. There are some small ledgy riffles down to Antietam Creek and a few isolated ledges further downstream but the rest of the way is flat. One can take out at Dargan Bend (Shinhan Landing) launching ramp on the Maryland side about eight miles below Shepherdstown or on the West Virginia side about 2000 feet above Dam No. 3. This point is reached by turning north off of U.S. Rte. 340 at the four way intersection 1.5 miles west of the Shenandoah River Bridge, following 1.5 miles to railroad underpass and turning right immediately beyond.

Hazards: None

Water Conditions: Always has enough water.

Gauge

None is necessary.

Section 7. Dam No. 3, Harpers Ferry to Point of Rocks, Md. (U.S. Rte. 15)

Gradient	Difficulty	Distance	Time	Width	Scenery	Map
4	1-3	13.5	4.0	1000-2000	Very Good	7

Trip Description: For these thirteen miles the Potomac cuts through the ancient Blue Ridge and its foothills and in the process forms the first whitewater since its headwaters. Start by carrying Dam No. 3 on the Maryland side or if the level is under five feet at Hancock, by lifting over the left end of the dam itself. The dam has some tempting runable looking breaches but they all bristle with old iron reinforcing rods. The following mile and a half, known as The Needles, is at moderate levels an intricate ledgy staircase that has long been a favorite novice whitewater run. Rocky as this section may be, only the most extreme droughts render this section unnavigable. On the other hand if the river is high, novices should skip this section altogether as bank to bank the broad river rolls along powerfully and is spotted with waves and souse holes that are always much larger than they look from the bank. A swim here would be a long one and in cold weather this could be potentially fatal.

If you have never been to Harpers Ferry before, be sure to stop and spend some time there. Besides being picturesque and historical this town benefits from the National Park Service's practice of not only restoring old shops, homes and businesses but also of peopling them with interpreters dressed in the garb of the times (and occupation) who will answer your questions, spin interesting yarns and offer you at least an approximate feeling of what it was like to be in Harpers Ferry 120 years ago.

The Shenandoah joins at Harpers Ferry and at summer levels often doubles the flow of the Potomac. About a half mile below the confluence, the river tumbles over a series of jagged ledges, the rocky spine of the Blue Ridge, which always carries enough water to run along the Maryland side. The ledges form two distinct rapids, the second and by far the bounciest of which is named Whitehorse Rapids. At medium to high levels boaters wishing to avoid heavy water can opt for a variety of more technical routes through the ledges on the right. Below Whitehorse and U.S. Rte. 340 the river glides through a beautiful maze of rocks

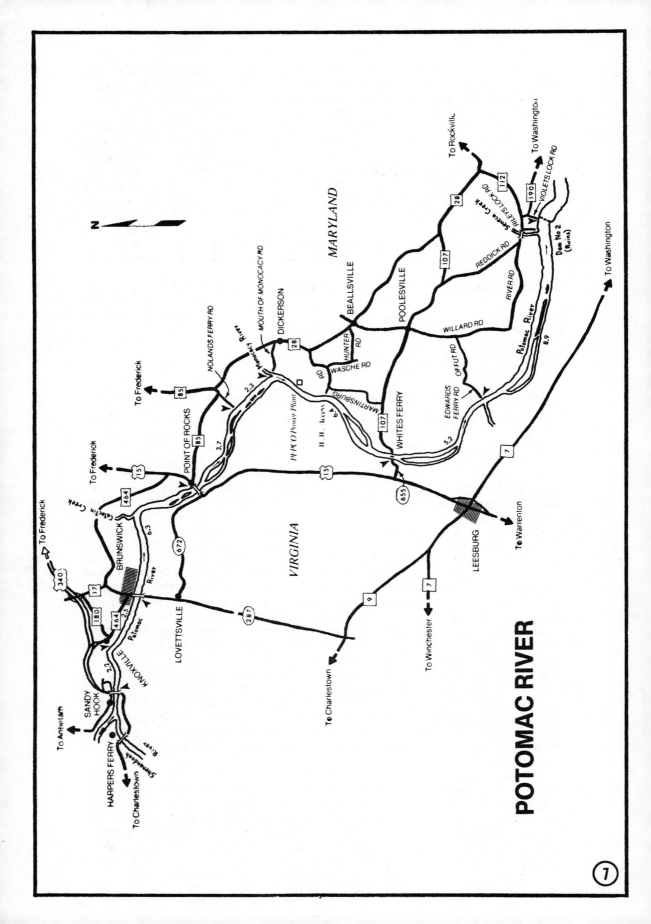

POTOMAC RIVER

and islets to another gap, this time through South Mountain (left) and Short Hill (right, now Virginia). Once again the Potomac tumbles over a staircase of ledges to form two short easy rapids. The remainder of the run is flat but swift past wooded bluffs, more rocks and islands and finally through a gap in Catoctin Mountain. Take out at the launching ramp under the Maryland end of the U.S. Rte. 15 bridge. Other popular access points to this section of river are about a hundred yards upstream of U.S. Rte. 340 at Sandy Hook, Md. or the wayside picnic area at the Virginia end of this bridge (mile 2.5) and Lock 30 under Md. Rte. 17 bridge, Brunswick, Md. (mile 7.0)

Hazards: Dam No. 3 at start and twisted debris of an old steel bridge that is strewn about the river bed immediately below Harpers Ferry.

Water Conditions: Always runable below Shenandoah, with Needles sometimes becoming marginal during late summer low flow.

Gauge

USGS gauge at Hancock should read at least 2.8 feet and Shepherdstown should read at least 1.8 feet for The Needles. Levels over five feet on Hancock gauge and/or Millville gauge (on Shenandoah) mean relatively high water conditions.

Section 8. Point of Rocks, Md. (U.S. Rte. 15) to Violets Lock

Gradient	Difficulty	Distance	Time	Width	Scenery	Map
1	A	26.5	8.5	1000-2200	Good	7

Trip Description: The Potomac leaves the mountains for good now and settles down to a leisurely coast across the Piedmont. The river now is wide, fairly straight and while flat still possesses a good current. There are some wooded bluffs here and there but the usual scenery is a uniform line of trees on each bank, silver maples, sycamores, willows and box elders as far as you can see. There are also some unusually long islands which along with the absence of railroads (below Monocacy) and highways make this a prime section for camping. The only significant civilized intrusion is the PEPCO power plant below the Monocacy which while not the most beautiful sight in the world has produced a synthetic whitewater gem. The huge volume of cooling water discharged down a short canal to the river creates a very playable chain of standing waves at low water levels (under 3.0 feet on Little Falls gauge). Higher levels destroy the necessary gradient and the phenomenon is inundated. The only catch to this wonder is that under optimal late summer low flow conditions the water is also very hot hence creating one of the rare situations where a soaking wet paddler could keel over from heat stroke. Access to the power plant discharge is best gained at Mount of Monocacy a mile and a half upstream or at the Dickerson Warmwater Access Area a mile downstream. Other access points to this section are Nolands Ferry Launching Ramp (mile 3.7), Whites Ferry (mile 12.4), Edwards Ferry (mile 17.6) and Seneca Creek (mile 26.2).

Hazards: None

Water Conditions: Canoeable all year.

Gauge

None necessary.

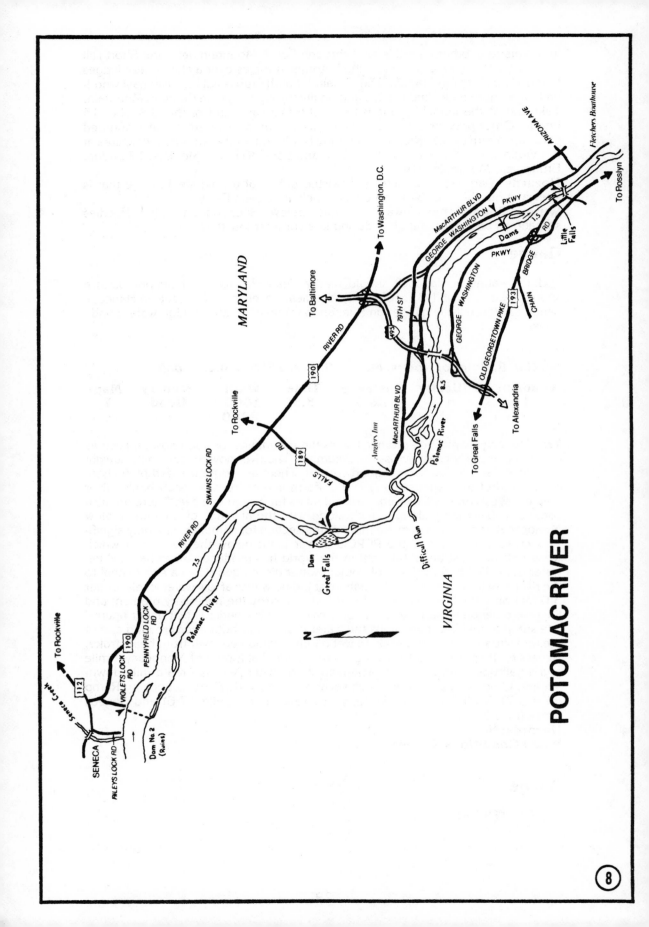

POTOMAC RIVER

MARYLAND

VIRGINIA

N

To Washington, D.C.

To Baltimore

To Rockville

To Rockville

To Great Falls

To Alexandria

To Rosslyn

SENECA

Spence Creek

112

190

WOLFS LOCK RD

PALEYS LOCK RD

Dam No. 2 (Ruins)

PENNYFIELD LOCK RD

Potomac River

7.5

RIVER RD

SWAINS LOCK RD

189

FALLS RD

190

RIVER RD

Anglers Inn

MacARTHUR BLVD

Dam

Great Falls

Difficult Run

Potomac River

8.5

Potomac River

495

79TH ST

OLD GEORGETOWN PIKE

193

GEORGE WASHINGTON PKWY

MacARTHUR BLVD

GEORGE WASHINGTON PKWY

Dams

Little Falls

1.5

CHAIN BRIDGE RD

ARIZONA AVE

Fletchers Boathouse

⑧

Section 9. Violets Lock to Great Falls

Gradient	Difficulty	Distance	Time	Width	Scenery	Map
4	A-2	7.5	2.5	1300-3000	Very Good	8

Trip Description: The Potomac now gently begins its 180 foot descent over the fall line to tidewater. A special feature of this section is that it is paralleled by the usually rewatered C&O Canal thus alleviating the paddler of the burden of setting up a car shuttle as on most other streams. The river starts by rushing over the rubbly ruins of the C&O Canal Dam No. 2 and then for the next mile through a maze of islands, rocks and easy riffles. If you prefer something more closed in, especially if the river is high and powerful, ferry over to the Virginia side from Violets Lock where you will find a small channel splitting off perpendicularly from the river just above Dam No. 2. This is the washed out remains of the old Patowmack Canal, part of a pre-C&O Canal navigational venture of George Washington's to bypass the fall line rapids. Below here the river is split in half by three and a half mile long Watkins Island and further subdivided by dozens of other islands. Except for a pair of riffles at a pipeline crossing the river drifts lazily all the way to Great Falls. Paddlers taking the left side of Watkins Island will in a few years probably encounter a proposed weir at the Potomac River Water Filtration Plant. This weir, which will form a drop of from five feet at low water to none at all at high levels, will include special runable chutes for boaters. Take out at Great Falls Park on left being sure not to get washed over the Washington Aqueduct water supply dam.

Hazards: Possible trees on the Potowmack Canal, a low weir on the Maryland side of Watkins Island about four miles below the start and Great Falls Dam at the trip's end. Do not mistake this little dam for the falls which is just downstream.

Water Conditions: Always runable though high levels (over 5.0 feet) can be risky for novices because of the falls downstream and at low levels (under 3.0 feet) Dam No. 2 will be scrapey.

Gauge

USGS gauge at Little Falls (call 301-899-3210 after 11:30 A.M.).

Section 10. Great Falls to Washington, D.C. (Chain Bridge)

Gradient	Difficulty	Distance	Time	Width	Scenery	Map
8	A-3,5	10.0	3.5	60-1500	Excellent	8

Trip Description: This final section is the Potomac's finest. It has the best whitewater, the most dramatic scenery and at least in the Mather Gorge below Great Falls possesses a wilderness character normally unthinkable in the heart of a major metropolitan area. Normal healthy people wishing to remain normal and healthy will want to portage Great Falls. This is easily accomplished by carrying down the C&O Canal towpath 800 yards to the second lock (Lock 17) below the old Great Falls Tavern and following a well-trod path that branches off to the right and winds about a hundred feet to a sand beach on a lagoon cut off from the main river by Rocky Island. This puts you at the bottom of a wild rockbound gorge that extends for over a mile downstream. If the level is under 3.8 feet paddle off to your right and carry or drag over the slippery slimey rocks to the main channel at a passage referred to as the S-Bend by local paddlers. It is possible to paddle and portage from here upstream to within sight of the falls. Going downstream is a turbulent flush through a short narrow rock gorge ending with a wavey but uncomplicated ride through Rocky Island Rapid. When the river rises above 3.8 feet water flows into the sand beach lagoon and it now becomes an arm of the river. At such levels it is now possible to paddle straight downstream from the put-in or off to the extreme left plunging over some small but twisting drops, a route preferable for undecked boats and paddlers uncomfortable in heavy water. The alternate route is the main, S-Bend, channel which becomes extremely turbulent at levels over 4.0 feet while Rocky Island Rapid just below develops into a long chain of big breaking waves. Below Rocky Island the river widens and after a short pool rushes over a short bouncy drop called Wet Bottom Chute. From here to the end of the gorge the river is flat in a turbulent sort of way, ending with a wide easy rapid on the left hand bend above Difficult Run. A mile downstream the river splits around Offutt Island, recognized by its rocky upstream face. Take the left side for the most exciting route except at low water when it almost dries up. Another half mile down and the river splits around two large islands. The most interesting passage is down the right channel over Yellow Falls, a three-foot double ledge. The other two channels drop more gradually and dry up in low water. Another mile through a long rock garden brings you to Stubblefield Falls, a short, easy, bouncy rapid. From here on down to Brookmont is mostly flat water gliding through rock gardens and dozens of small islands. These islands and the adjacent bottomlands, especially on the southern exposed Maryland side are a wildflower lover's paradise during April and May. Brookmont is recognized by a monolithic concrete pumping station on the left side of the river. The pumping station marks the location of Brookmont Dam, an insignificant-looking two-foot weir that has a reversal that will stop you and never let you go. Get out well above this trap and carry down the C&O Canal towpath to the pool below or if you are not comfortable in big powerful turbulent water then take out here. Below the river funnels down to a final narrow rocky plunge to tidewater called Little Falls. The rubble dam below Brookmont Dam is C&O Canal Dam No. 1 and can be run to the left of Snake Island, the narrow island at midstream. Below the dam the river filters through some rock gardens, narrows, rushes through some bouncy but uncomplicated chutes and speeds on toward Chain Bridge. Within sight of the bridge, where the river and downstream visibility appear blocked get out and scout. This is Little Falls, a steep heavy rapid split down the middle by a jagged rocky island. Depending on the level either side can be run with each choice having its special problem. At lower levels the Maryland channel is dependable but to get there you have to fight an awesome current that attempts to wash objects against the upstream face of the island. At medium levels (over 4.0 feet) the paddler can take the more straightforward Virginia side but in doing so risks being snared by a hole against the island that is almost as deadly as the roller at Brookmont Dam. Finally at high levels (over 6.0 feet) the island is buried and Little Falls is simplified to a long heaving mass of giant waves, boils and whirl-pools extending past Chain Bridge. The major hazard now is the center pier of Chain Bridge which forms a powerful recirculating eddy that will hold you and your boat for the rest of your short life. It is possible to take out at the new pump-ing station at the foot of Little Falls (easy and convenient if you are using the canal as your shuttle) where a straight concrete roadway leads back to the canal or con-venient access to your car is available by paddling a mile downstream to Fletchers Cove (left) where a boat livery provides easy exit. Other popular access points to this section are located opposite Anglers Inn on MacArthur Blvd., Carderock Recreation Area, Lock 8 (79th St., Cabin John), Sycamore Island and Lock 6 at Brookmont. Depending on water conditions much of this section can be handled as a circuit paddle using the rewatered C&O Canal.

Hazards: High water; surging high-speed current combined with vertical rock banks make escape for the swimming paddler extremely difficult in the narrow Mather Gorge or at Little Falls. On the wide stretches the shear distance from shore breeds the potential for a marathon swim. Either could be lethal when the water is cold. Brookmont Dam; this structure is to paddlers and other floating debris, as flypaper is to flies. Stay away from it, even from below, as at even medium-high levels the upstream pull of its reversal reaches thirty feet downstream. Little Falls; the power of a big river being constricted through a narrow rocky channel allows only a narrow margin of error. If there is any question about this section hike in and scout it first. If there still is doubt, skip it.

Water Conditions: There is always enough water for paddling and the problems arise when there is too much, a situation most likely to occur in winter or early spring.

Gauge

USGS gauge at Brookmont (Little Falls, call 301-899-3210 after 11:30 A.M.). For the river above Brookmont levels of 3.5 to 4.5 feet bring out the best in most rapids. For the Little Falls section levels under 3.2 feet provide a reasonable margin of safety for open boats. Above 4.5 only expert decked boaters with reliable rolls should venture down this last mile of whitewater.

State of the River Address

For a river that has been subjected to almost 350 years of civilization, the Potomac has held up quite respectably. Partly it remained this way because enough residents cared to protect it from pollution and dams.

The Potomac in recent decades has suffered a widespread reputation as an open sewer. This is unfortunate and unfair as most of the river flows quite clean with normally clear waters supporting healthy populations of bass and other cleanwater species, waters that provide a safe swimming and boating environment and waters that provide a safe drinking supply from numerous towns along the river. On the other hand the section passing through Washington, D.C., the portion most visible to the nation and the media, has suffered horribly in past years from discharges of raw sewage, combined sewers, street runoff and inadequate treatment plants, hence spawning its notorious reputation. However over the past 15 years sewage treatment plants have been built and upgraded, some storm runoff controlled, combined sewers separated and raw sewage discharges stopped. By 1978 conditions had so improved that the Interstate Commission on the Potomac River Basin, a basin watchdog agency, pronounced the river through Washington to be clean enough to swim in.

The Potomac has remained remarkably free of dams for such a major river. There are only two Corps of Engineers-built dams in the basin, Savage River and Bloomington and there are a few large municipal and industrial water supply impoundments. The Corps long ago drafted plans for a huge system of reservoirs across the basin, including one that would drown the Potomac from just above Great Falls on into Frederick County, a reservoir at Sixes Bridge on the Monocacy and one on Town Creek. Most of these proposals have been fought and defeated with Bloomington so far the only survivor. An even more encouraging development has been the construction by the Corps of a pumping station on tidewater below Little Falls. The pumping station represents an economical and viable alternative to upstream dambuilding, many of which were justified as water supply impoundments for Washington's insatiable thirst, by tapping a huge reservoir of fresh water that lies trapped between Little Falls and brackish water below Fort Washington.

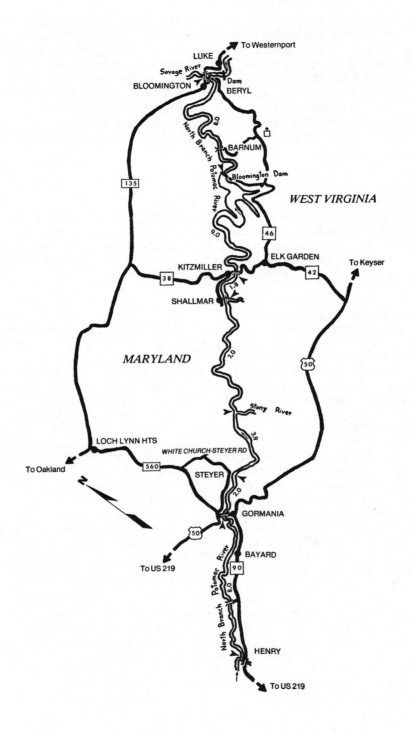

To Westernport

LUKE

Savage River

BLOOMINGTON

Dam

BERYL

8.0

North Branch Potomac River

BARNUM

Bloomington Dam

WEST VIRGINIA

135

9.0

46

KITZMILLER

ELK GARDEN

To Keyser

38

42

1.8

SHALLMAR

MARYLAND

2.0

US 50

Stony River

3.9

LOCH LYNN HTS

WHITE CHURCH-STEYER RD

560

To Oakland

STEYER

2.0

N

GORMANIA

US 50

BAYARD

To US 219

90

North Branch Potomac River

8.0

HENRY

To US 219

NORTH BRANCH POTOMAC RIVER

⑨

North Branch Potomac River

Introduction

The North Branch of the Potomac River, as a matter of historic tradition, is considered the headwaters of the Potomac. This is a rather embarrassing background for our "national river" for the North Branch has suffered decades of abuse, pollution and devastation, the scars of which are hard to ignore. In contrast with the agricultural valley and wild gorges of the South Branch, the North Branch has been a valley dedicated to industry. Its bottoms are sites for factories producing plate glass, tires, synthetic fibers and paper; its canyons provide passage for railroads to cross the high Allegheny ridges; and, its surrounding hills yield the coal to generate electricity for Eastern cities and to fire iron and steel furnaces from Pittsburgh to Japan. The price of this development has been half a river poisoned to death by acid mine drainage, mining and pollution-scarred hillsides and stinking air up and down the valley. Why go there then? Because in between the blights just mentioned are miles of beautiful and natural riverscape, miles of land that has healed over from past abuses, and besides, some of the best whitewater in the Potomac Basin is here (although it tastes like a rusty nail).

Section 1. Henry, W. Va. to Gormania, W. Va. (U.S. Rte. 50)

Gradient	Difficulty	Distance	Time	Width	Scenery	Map
38	1-3	8.0	2.5	15-30	Fair	9

Trip Description: The North Branch officially starts at Fairfax Stone, an ancient boundary stone marking the western limit of Lord Fairfax's enormous domain. The stone is located just beyond the southwest tip of Garrett County inside West Virginia (Virginia in Fairfax's day). Only six miles downstream the North Branch gathers enough water to consistently float a canoe. The put-in is about seven miles southwest of Gormania on W.Va. Rte. 90 where it leaves the river for good at Island Creek Coal Mine. Initially the stream meanders swiftly between alder-bound banks and rushes over easy rock garden rapids through less than spectacular scenery. But the North Branch soon comes alive, tumbling continuously over a bed of small boulders and ledges of all sizes. However when it is bank full all this technical nonsense transforms to a roaring flume that is short on eddys but overstocked with big waves and nasty diagonal holes, a run rivaling the Savage River for excitement and pushiness. The most interesting spot is located a short distance above Wilson where the river plunges over a sloping seven-foot ledge run to the right of center at low levels and left of center at high water. The stream returns to a sluggish state below Bayard and stays that way to Gormania. Take out on left bank below Rte. 50.
Hazards: None
Water Conditions: Winter and spring after heavy rain or thaw.

Gauge

USGS gauge at Kitzmiler (call 301-899-3210 after 11:30 A.M.) should read at least 5.0 feet.

Section 2. Gormania, W. Va. (U.S. Rte. 50) to Kitzmiller, Md.

Gradient	Difficulty	Distance	Time	Width	Scenery	Map
47	3-5	15.0	5.0	30-70	Good	9

Trip Description: If you are the kind of paddler who loves to bloat yourself on mile after mile of continuous wild whitewater, then you should have been here before they built the Bloomington Dam. From Steyer, Md. to Bloomington, Md. there were 30 almost unbroken miles of the splashy stuff or you could have put in on the Stony River at the VEPCO Dam near Mount Storm, W.Va. and made that 38 miles. Furthermore, it was not out of the question to complete either one of these runs in a day and in the process, on the Stony River option, drop a phenomenal distance of 2,140 feet from start to finish. Luckily the dam left the best of the North Branch's whitewater, this section from Gormania to Kitzmiller, intact. And rest assured that this section should be sufficient to satisfy all but the most demanding whitewater enthusiasts. The first two miles to Steyer, an alternate put-in, contain nothing more difficult than easy gravel bar rapids. The scenery is hilly but unspectacular and the water is tan from acid mine drainage. Below Steyer the stream begins dropping over more ledges and forming more hydraulics than you ever dreamed could exist. As you play these beautifully formed holes to exhaustion think of all the poor slobs lining up on a hot summer's day for a few paltry seconds in the famous Swimmers Hole on the lower Yough. Things get even more interesting at the junction with the Stony River as the river becomes noticeably more powerful and pushy. About a half mile below Stony starts a series of three big memorable ledges. The first is a sloping complex affair entered on the left and finished on the right; the second, you aim for the middle and shut your eyes; and, the third is a sloping, jagged complex drop run on the left, usually with a lot of scraping. Now begins mile after mile of nonstop small ledges, boulder patches, giant cobble bars and a lot of maneuvering to get through it all. If you take this at high water (over 6.0 feet) look forward to traveling at high velocity, bouncing down some big waves and having to avoid some terminal holes. Aside from the water quality and the railroad, which is certainly comforting as a rescue feature, the scenery is beautiful, comprised of cliffs, hemlock, rhododendron and big, forested canyon walls. At Shallmar, two miles above Kitzmiller, the natural beauty is displaced by massively stripmined hillsides and ramshackle dwellings and the natural river is replaced by a dredged channel that becomes tediously shallow at lower levels. Take out on either end of Md. Rte. 38 bridge in Kitzmiller.

Hazards: Three ledges described above and an inconveniently placed old bridge pier a few miles downstream on left.

Water Conditions: Winter and spring from two to four days after a hard rain and during snowmelt.

Gauge

USGS gauge at Kitzmiller, located about two blocks below Rte. 38 on left (call 301-899-3210 after 11:30 A.M.) should read at least 4.25 feet, is optimal for both open and decked boats at 5.0 feet and 6.0 feet indicates a big and hairy river waiting for you upstream.

Section 3. Kitzmiller, Md. to Bloomington, Md.

Gradient	Difficulty	Distance	Time	Width	Scenery	Map
38	3-4	17.0	5.5	40-70	Good	9

Trip Description: This former seventeen miles of almost continuous intermediate grade whitewater has now been cut in half by the new Bloomington

Dam Project. Few whitewater paddlers will care to bother with the first half of this section as only three miles of free river and good scenery remain below Kitzmiller. Because there is no access to the head of the reservoir, at least five and a half miles of deadwater paddling to either the dam or Howell Boat Launch Area is unavoidable. But on the bright side, much of the massive railroad relocation and old strip mining scars have been revegetated and in another ten or twenty years this reservoir should at least be an attractive place to paddle (providing of course that you do it when the pool is high and the mudflats are covered). Next comes the dam. Even the thought of portaging this nearly 300-foot high barrage would exhaust most paddlers but for those inclined towards tackling such challenges, a road up and down the right edge of the dam makes this grim goal semi-reasonable. As of this writing the option of starting your cruise at the dam is not very encouraging either as the Corps of Engineers does not allow private vehicles onto the road down to the tailrace area. Hopefully this will soon change. Until then, these restrictions leave the only vehicle access via that wretched excuse for a road into Barnum, putting you in about a mile and a half below the dam. Rapids on the sections both above and below the reservoir are long, dropping over huge bars of cobbles and small boulders, with a few low ledges thrown in. One set of ledges on the right side of an island below Barnum, because of their surprise element and because of one particularly deep and nasty hole, has long been the nemesis of less experienced paddlers, so keep an eye out. Take out at Bloomington on the left bank at the roadbridge to Beryl just above the mouth of the Savage River. Parking is no longer allowed on this side road at the bridge so look forward to a bit of a carry up to Rte. 135 where on the shoulder parking is still legal.

Hazards: A few hydraulics below Barnum, a hernia carrying the dam and getting run over by a truck at the bridge to Beryl W. Va. Rte. 46 may rearrange your car's front end.

Water Conditions: Runable above the reservoir winter and spring within week of hard rain. The Corps is trying to juggle the reservoir outflow to best address downstream water quality management, flood control and Washington, D.C.'s emergency water supply needs. Thus discharge from the dam depends on these needs versus how much water is in the reservoir that day. This management is still being fine-tuned. Roughly though, the best odds for favorable flows are late spring when the lake is full or late fall when they are drawing down the lake, combined with some wet weather. The Corps will probably also schedule some periodic recreational releases, so contact your local canoe club for more up-to-date details.

Gauge

USGS gauge at Kitzmiller (call 301-899-3210 after 11:30 A.M.) should read at least 3.8 feet to run down to the lake. Call Bloomington Dam at 304-355-2346 to find discharge out of dam. Consider flow of 380cfs about minimal.

Section 4. Bloomington, Md. to Keyser, W. Va.

Gradient	Difficulty	Distance	Time	Width	Scenery	Map
22	2	8.0	2.5	60-100	Fair	10

Trip Description: If you have a head cold or acute hayfever you may be specially qualified to run this river, for you will be the only member of your party not repulsed by the stench that fills this valley; a byproduct of the paper mill at Luke. The trip starts with a .7 mile paddle down a gentle rapid followed by a short pool to a small unrunable dam at the Westvaco paper mill with a short miserable portage up and

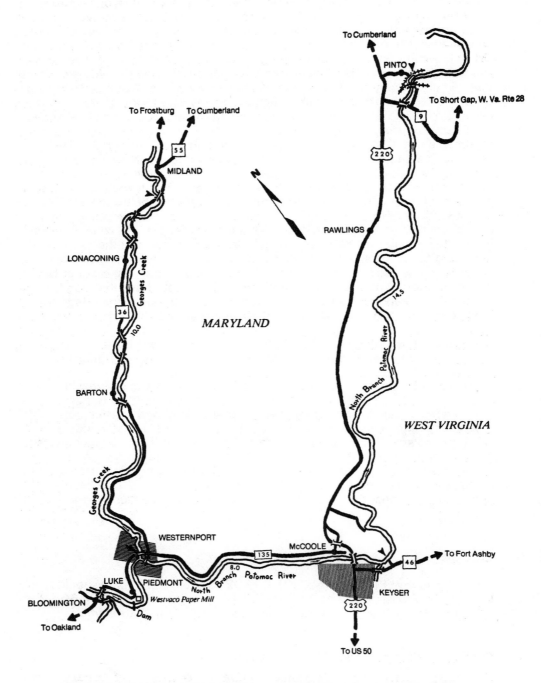

NORTH BRANCH POTOMAC RIVER
GEORGES CREEK

down steep slippery banks on the right. The paper mill if not beautiful is certainly interesting and immense. Easy boulder patch rapids carry one through the less than scenic Tri-towns of Luke, Westernport and Piedmont. Westernport was so named as it was the upper limit of navigation on the Potomac. If you have trouble with the rocks and holes on this section just think about trying to get a loaded coal barge down it. Below Westernport the river cuts a deep attractive gorge through Dans Mountain. The rapids are often fairly long, dropping over patches of small boulders and cobbles and a few ledges. The gradient levels off approaching Keyser and the scenery becomes junky again. There is no good take-out at Keyser so proceed below U.S. Rte. 220 about a half mile, just past New Creek (right) to a hard bend to the left with a striking rock outcrop on the right. Approach by road by heading east on W. Va. Rte. 46 from Keyser and a half mile east of the bridge over New Creek turn left and drive 200 yards to river.

Hazards: Carry dam at paper mill on right or at low levels, lift over crest on right. One surprise hole on left at bottom of long rapid below Westernport.

Water Conditions: Winter and spring within week of hard rain, during snowmelt and when there is a special release from Savage or Bloomington dams.

Gauge

USGS gauge at Cumberland (call 301-899-3210 after 11:30 A.M.) should read at least 3.0 feet or the combined outflow from the Bloomington and Savage River dams should be roughly at least 500 cfs. If you are utilizing a race release from the Savage, be sure not to outrun the water. Also the USGS gauge at Pinto (half mile downstream of Rte. 9 bridge, on West Virginia side, at railroad bridge) should read at least 3.0 feet.

Section 5. Keyser, W. Va. to Pinto, Md.

Gradient	Difficulty	Distance	Time	Width	Scenery	Map
9	1	14.5	4.0	60-100	Good	10

Trip Description: If the water, air and litter ever get cleaned up this will become one of the most popular novice trips in Maryland. The river winds back and forth through a seemingly isolated valley away from highways and even the ever-present railroad is usually set back from sight. The mountainsides are periodically lined by the biggest and most ornately beautiful shale cliffs in the Potomac Basin. The current through here is usually strong while the whitewater never amounts to more than straightforward gravel bar type riffles. Take out at Pinto at site of the old bridge (be sure you can recognize this spot from the river). To get there turn off U.S. Rte. 220 about half mile north of Rte.9 and follow three quarters of a mile to railroad underpass and dead end. Alternate access points are at the Rte. 9 bridge which is very steep and at the Pinto gauge on the West Virginia side, reached by turning off of W. Va. Rte. 9 just past the bridge, onto the road heading to Allegheny Ballistics Lab but then bearing left at the lab entrance.

Hazards: None

Water Conditions: Winter and spring except after long dry spell and during releases from the Savage or Bloomington dams.

Gauge

USGS gauge at Cumberland should read at least 3.0 feet and USGS gauge at Pinto should be at least 2.8 feet.

Section 6. Pinto, Md. to Wiley Ford, W. Va.

Gradient	Difficulty	Distance	Time	Width	Scenery	Map
4	A-1	13.0	4.0	80-100	Poor	3

Trip Description: The paddler who bypasses this section will not have missed much. After a pretty start, past more spectacular shale cliffs, the scenery slowly succumbs to the visual blight of the Cumberland area. With each mile the pools get longer and the riffles shorter. Four and a half miles from the start is a five-foot rubble dam at the huge Celanese Corp. plant (set back from river) that is runable with great care. Below that, houses, factories, railroads and trash become more frequent; and upon entering Cumberland, the river which is now a dead pool, enters a leveed flood channel. The pool ends at a fifteen-foot dam located directly under the Rte. 28 bridge between Cumberland and Ridgeley, W. Va. Carry on right. Below that the dredged out river flows straight and at low levels tediously shallow almost to Wiley Ford.

Hazards: Five-foot dam of large jagged rocks at Celanese Corp. can be run by experienced boaters. An unrunable fifteen-foot dam under the Rte. 28 bridge at Cumberland must be carried on right.

Water Conditions: Winter and spring except after long dry spell.

Gauge

Same as Section 5.

Section 7. Wiley Ford, W. Va. to South Branch Potomac River

Gradient	Difficulty	Distance	Time	Width	Scenery	Map
4	A-1	19.5	6.5	80-100	Good	3

Trip Description: Below Wiley Ford the impact of Cumberland dwindles and the river now flows by high wooded banks, bluffs and through some small mountain gaps. The water still has that papermill odor but it is tolerable. Most of the river is now flat with the only excitement being at a three-foot dam runable on the right about eight miles below the start. The confluence with the South Branch is two miles beyond the low-water toll bridge at Oldtown. To reach the take-out, cross the toll bridge into West Virginia, pass under the railroad and turn left 200 yards beyond at Arnold Stickley Road. Follow a mile and a half to the South Branch just above its mouth.

Hazards: Three-foot dam at Pittsburgh Plate Glass, run on right and the low-water bridge at Oldtown.

Water Conditions: Winter, spring and early summer.

Gauge

Cumberland gauge should read at least 2.7 feet.

Savage River

Introduction

The Savage is probably Maryland's most famous whitewater river, even more widely known than the Upper Yough. Much of this fame comes from being the country's premier racing stream. The combination of five miles of continuous, powerful and complex rapids backed by assured controlled reservoir releases has made this the site of national championship races in slalom and wildwater, the 1972 Olympic Trials and an international fall slalom race. And since these releases usually occur when most other small streams are low, they have proven to be a real boon to cruisers. Finally the river deserves credit as an educational aid for the one minute on and the next minute off character of its flow provides an ideal opportunity for the paddler to study just what makes whitewater so wild.

Section 1. Merrill (Westernport Road) to Savage River Dam

Gradient	Difficulty	Distance	Time	Width	Scenery	Map
34	2	8.5	2.5	10-20	Very Good	11

Trip Description: This is the unsavage part of the Savage River. From the bridge at Merrill to Big Run Campground it offers about five and a half miles of intimate rhododendron-fringed cruising down a narrow, thinly inhabited valley. The water is fairly clear and the rapids numerous and easy, dropping over a bed of cobbles and small ledges. The reservoir is short, narrow and has steep undeveloped shores so that if it is not drawn down it is quite pretty to paddle across. However, for those paddlers who are allergic to flatwater, Big Run Campground is an easy egress point.

Hazards: Fallen trees and overhanging rhododendron in fast spots.

Water Conditions: Up in winter or spring after a hard rain or good snow melt.

Gauge

None. Judge flow at put-in.

Section 2. Savage River Dam to North Branch Potomac River

Gradient	Difficulty	Distance	Time	Width	Scenery	Map
75	3-5	4.5	1.5	20-30	Good	11

Trip Description: To reach the put-in follow a narrow dirt road that branches off the Savage River Road at the left end of the new concrete bridge below the dam. Drive to the end of the grassy field and carry about a hundred feet to small pool at end of the emergency spillway channel. The next pool is one exciting mile downstream behind the five-foot high Piedmont Dam. One has the choice of running the dam via a semi-cylindrical metal flume on the left end (safe), a narrow breach located a few feet to the right which at levels over 1000 cfs starts forming a nasty hole (exciting) or the deteriorated rock-studded right abutment (not recommended). About a half mile below Piedmont dam is a narrow concentration of heavy turbulent whitewater known as the Triple Drop, the final drop of which has a

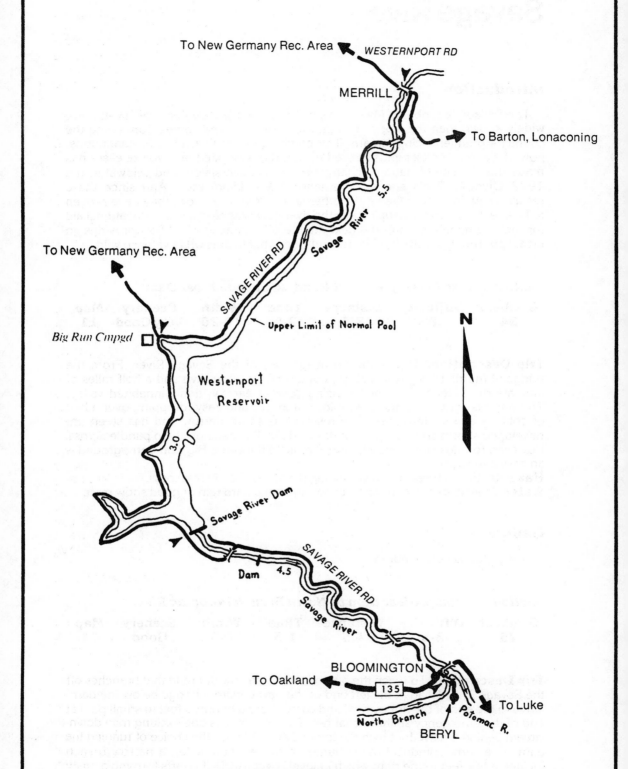

To New Germany Rec. Area

WESTERNPORT RD

MERRILL

To Barton, Lonaconing

5.5

SAVAGE RIVER RD

Savage River

To New Germany Rec. Area

Upper Limit of Normal Pool

Big Run Cmpgd

N

Westernport
Reservoir

3.0

Savage River Dam

Dam   4.5

SAVAGE RIVER RD

Savage River

BLOOMINGTON

To Oakland   135   To Luke

North Branch   BERYL   *Potomac R.*

SAVAGE RIVER

⑪

strong hole best run on the right. Just below is the worst problem on the river, Memorial Rock Rapid, recognized by a large pointed boulder sticking out of the water about ten feet off the left bank. Run just to the right of this rock to avoid a big submerged rock and mean hole or sneak on the extreme left. Below here the really big pressure is off and many conservative paddlers choose to start at the church just downstream of Memorial Rock. Take out on North Branch Potomac about a hundred yards above Savage.

Hazards: Piedmont Dam which is run as described above or easily carried on left.

Water Conditions: Winter and spring after hard rain or snowmelt and during scheduled race releases.

Gauge

None, but road runs along enough of the river to easily assess conditions. Race releases usually range from 900 cfs to 1400 cfs and a minimal level is probably about 350 cfs.

What's That I Smell?

Anyone who paddles the Savage or North Branch Potomac can not help but be aware of the presence of the Westvaco paper mill at Luke. Ugly as it may be it is a fascinating mass of technology that is worth a pause to study. The plant is one of the world's largest producers of fine paper, fine paper being the high quality smooth glossy paper used in magazines, picture books, etc.

To understand the mill one must understand papermaking which briefly is as follows. First, the raw material for this paper is hardwood which is stored in the woodyard along the last mile of the Savage. Before use, the logs must be de-barked. Nothing is wasted as the bark is shipped across the river to supply a charcoal plant in Beryl, W. Va. The wood is then chipped and the chips are "digested" under heat and pressure in a caustic brew. Digestion dissolves the lignin, a natural glue that binds the wood fibers together. The fibers are also physically agitated to break them apart, literally beating it to a pulp, a disgusting-looking slurry of cellulose fibers. The fibers are removed, rinsed, bleached and are now ready for papermaking which entails spraying the pulp evenly upon a large moving cloth conveyor belt called a "felt". As the felt moves along a finish that may contain clays, pigments or starch is also sprayed on. Excess water drains through the felt (called "whitewater" in the industrial jargon) and blasts of hot air complete the drying process. The result, voila, paper.

How much of this affects you paddling by? First the plant uses the huge volume of over 60 million gallons a day of water from the North Branch and at extreme low flow this exceeds the flow in the river. So the plant pumps its uncontaminated cooling water (about half the water used here) back to the head of the plant where it is sprayed into the air to cool it and into the river where it can reenter the plant's intakes. The strange metal pipes you see bristling along the banks upstream of the mill are for this recycling system. The wastewater from digestion, called "black liquor", used to go into the river but now is totally processed for reuse in the tall huge building next to Rte. 136 and at the rotary kiln across the river. All other contaminated wastewater flows to a treatment plant downstream. The plant removes most harmful pollutants but unfortunately the stink remains. Speaking of stink, most of the frightening looking white clouds billowing from the mill are just steam. With all of the drying, cooking and cooling over six million gallons of water daily go up the stacks as steam. Unfortunately this also still smells. The high stack was built so to disperse these gases, or else this would be one foggy valley. The dead mountainside across the river was Westvaco's doing, a result of past abuse, but now vegetation is reclaiming the slopes.

Georges Creek

Introduction

Georges Creek is the shame of Maryland. It flows through a valley whose mountainsides are scarred and tortured by decades of mining abuse. The narrow bottoms along the stream are crowded with roads, railroads and a chain of decaying towns while old cars, washing machines, torn plastic and all the other debris of civilization are strewn about its bed and banks. The water stinks of raw sewage and its rocks are yellowed from acid mine drainage. In fact the only reason that the stream is not a major health hazard is because at normal flows the water is so acidic that even the bacteria cannot survive. However, it is one heckuva good piece of whitewater (white?) so if you have had your typhoid shots, go to it.

Section 1. Md. Rte. 36 bridge halfway between Midland and Lonaconing to Westernport

Gradient	Difficulty	Distance	Time	Width	Scenery	Map
72	3-4	10.0	2.5	15-30	Poor	10

Trip Description: Georges Creek drains a six mile wide trough between Dans and Big Savage mountains. It is fed by numerous small streams so a put-in can be selected by driving upstream until the paddler considers it too small or too shallow for the prevailing water level. From the suggested put-in the stream tumbles continuously over gravel bars, rock gardens and small ledges. In addition there is such man-made excitement as cables, low bridges, retaining walls, debris, bridge piers and one sharp three-foot dam below Lonaconing. Run the dam to right of center. The volume grows noticeably with each mile and by the time it reaches Barton it is feeling powerful and pushy. Things then get increasingly interesting as the river begins dropping over sets of high (5 or 6 feet) sloping often complex ledges. Unless you intend to continue on to the North Branch, the best take-out is at the American Legion Hall located on the right bank about 100 yards upstream of Md. Rte. 135, Westernport.

Hazards: There is a three-foot high dam below Lonaconing, best run to right of center. Logs, low bridges and debris coupled with high stream velocity and poor eddys can be dangerous.

Water Conditions: Most likely caught up in winter and spring after a heavy rain. Steep and sometimes denuded slopes and small watershed means a quick and intense runoff.

Gauge

None. Judge conditions from road.

Wills Creek

Introduction

Most paddlers do not even know Wills Creek exists, even though if they are from Washington or Baltimore, they pass over it every time they travel to the Yough or Cheat or Savage. This is too bad, for given a good rain this watershed offers the advanced paddler one full weekend of exciting challenging whitewater in a setting ranging from the scenic to the strange. Besides the variety of the main stem, there are also three paddleable tributaries; Brush Creek, Little Wills Creek and Jennings Run. Together they comprise the best and closest whitewater package accessible to the Baltimore-Washington areas.

Section 1. Glencoe to Fairhope

Gradient	Difficulty	Distance	Time	Width	Scenery	Map
61	3-4	4.5	1.5	15-30	Very Good	12

Trip Description: Although this run is mostly of intermediate difficulty and considerably easier than Section 2, one should be over-qualified for it as there are two waterfalls encountered; one which could destroy your boat, and the other which could destroy your health. It is a zesty rush down continuous bouncy little rapids punctuated by sets of exciting ledges with individual drops of up to three feet. One can start at the highway bridge in Glencoe or better yet drive 2.5 miles upstream on a dirt road paralleling the creek and carry about a hundred yards down a gentle slope to the put-in. To reach this upper access point coming from Fairhope, take the first right in the center of town and then .1 miles beyond, turn left. Two and a half miles up this rough dirt road is a house, a road to the right, a small creek and a trail on the left down to the river. To Glencoe the tiny stream rushes over gravel bars and a few ledges in a mostly uncomplicated manner, which is fine since heavily vegetated banks make escape or rescue rather difficult. When you get to Glencoe begin counting railroad bridges. Directly beneath the fifth bridge, which if you lose count is recognized by a tunnel at its downstream end labeled Falls Cut Tunnel, is the first falls. It is a six-foot verticle drop that splats onto a rock. Scout and carry on the left or if the level is suitable and you want to live dangerously, you can eddy out on the right brink and drag over the slippery sloping rocks to the pool below. About a half mile below the confluence with Brush Creek is the Railroad Cut Falls. This is a man-made cataract blasted out by the railroad to bypass a hairpin loop of the river and thus eliminate the need for two bridges. Paddle down as far as your good sense and/or nerves allow you and carry on left.
Hazards: Trees above Glencoe and the two falls described above. Before setting up shuttle the paddler should hike up the railroad grade from Fairhope to establish some landmarks (most notably a black cliff on river right and a concrete retaining wall on the left) so as not to miss that last very important eddy.
Water Conditions: Canoeable only in the winter or spring after a good rain or snowmelt.

Gauge

There is a painted gauge on the retaining wall downstream right of the silver-painted truss in Hyndman. It is erased below 6 feet so you will have to extrapolate

45

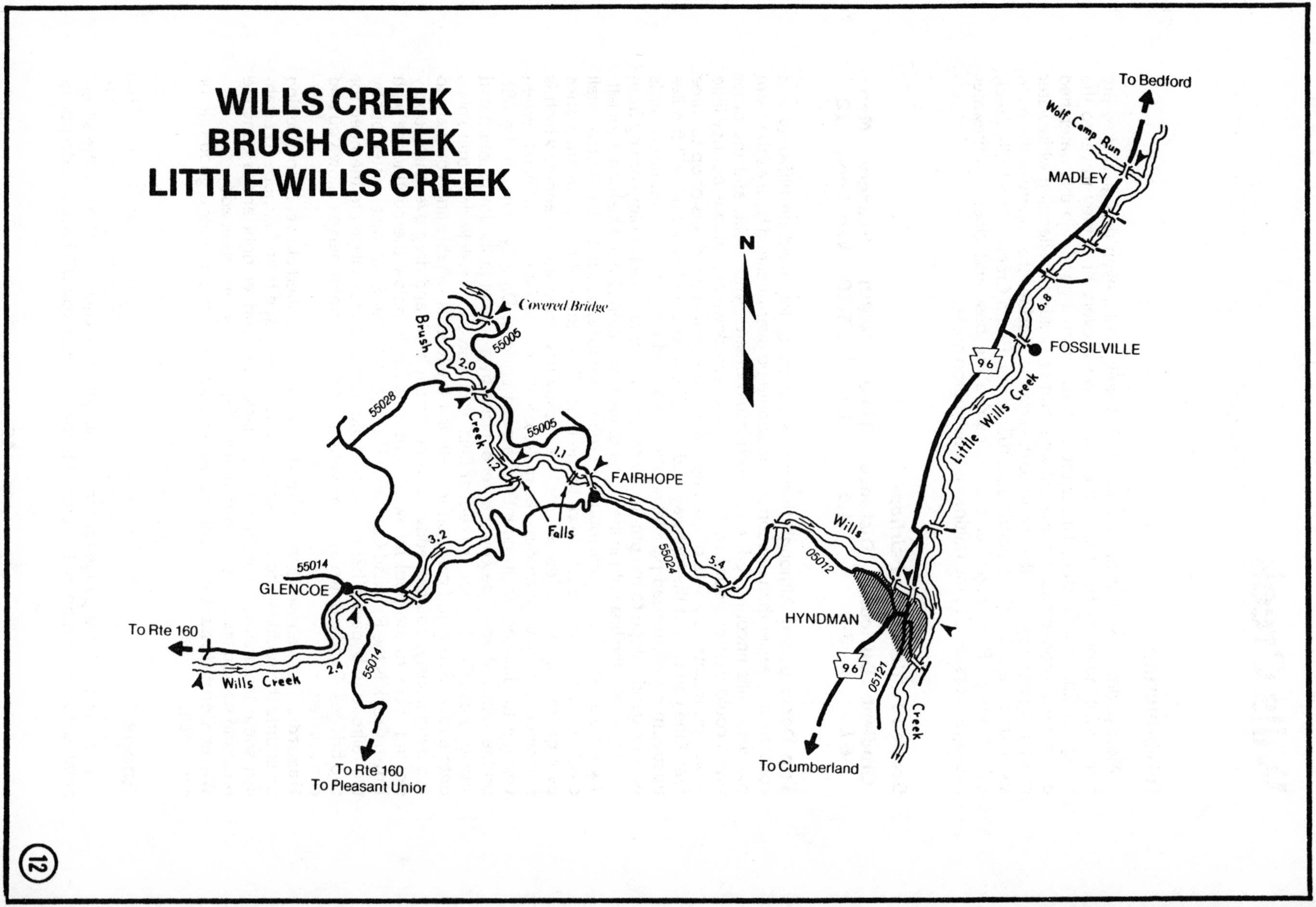

WILLS CREEK
BRUSH CREEK
LITTLE WILLS CREEK

To Bedford

Wolf Camp Run

MADLEY

6.8

96

FOSSILLVILLE

Little Wills Creek

Creek

05121

96

HYNDMAN

To Cumberland

Wills

05012

5.4

55024

FAIRHOPE

N

Covered Bridge

55006

55005

1.1

Falls

1.2

55006

2.0

Brush

Creek

3.2

55028

GLENCOE

55014

55014

2.

55014

To Rte 160
To Pleasant Union

Wills Creek

To Rte 160

12

a reading. About 2.5 feet is an ideal level for both open or decked boats though a few ledges will be scrapey. This level roughly correlates with about 5.5 feet at Kitzmiller.

Section 2. Fairhope to Hyndman (Pa. Rte. 96)

Gradient	Difficulty	Distance	Time	Width	Scenery	Map
73	3-5	5.5	1.5	20-35	Very Good	12

Trip Description: This is five miles of probably the most enjoyable and challenging whitewater in the Potomac Basin. The first few miles which cut through Big Savage Mountain are a memorable tumble over a mostly bouldery bed. At low levels it is an often tedious, incredibly rocky natural slalom suitable for both open and decked boats. At medium levels it becomes powerful and pushy with complexity that includes not only dodging boulders but also powerful holes. At higher levels the rocks are all covered, eddys gone and there is just one long rapid of big waves and huge holes.

The initiation rites on this beauty occur about 150 yards below the put-in bridge at Fairhope. There is a sloping four-foot diagonal ledge with a powerful stopper which if entered in the middle will grab you and then violently thrust you to the right before maybe letting you go. This can be traumatic to right-sided canoeists. The more timid can sneak on the far left or clunk over on the far right. About a mile downstream is a short boulder-choked rapid called Yo Yo (named for the tenacity of one hole) that is noticeable from the shuttle road. It is best run at moderate levels by entering left center and charging to the far right, then negotiating the lower drop by charging toward center. After the second bridge the stream bed widens and things begin to gradually calm down. At low levels this section becomes impassable before the upper does.

Most people do not notice the pretty scenery in this canyon for obvious reasons. The river flows through a deep gorge that is only civilized by the railroad, the shuttle road and some interesting old industrial ruins. Take some time and look around.

Hazards: Four-foot ledge at Fairhope that can be run anywhere at moderate levels depending upon your skill and nerve. Steep boulder-choked rapids about a mile below Fairhope with poor rescue below. At high levels this becomes a barrier of powerful holes so do not put in until you have scouted and figured a way through Yo Yo.

Water Conditions: Runable in winter or spring after rains or thaw.

Gauge

Painted gauge at Hyndman. Minimal level is about 1.5 feet; 2.0 feet would probably be reasonable for expert open boaters with quick bailing arms. Two to three feet is a moderate decked boat level and above three feet is big water boating for paddlers with sure-fire rolls. The USGS gauge at the head of The Narrows in Cumberland should read at least 3.0 feet and Kitzmiller 5.0 feet for a passable level on this section.

Section 3. Hyndman (Pa. Rte. 96) to Eckhart Junction

Gradient	Difficulty	Distance	Time	Width	Scenery	Map
22	1-3	13.0	3.5	30-50	Fair	13

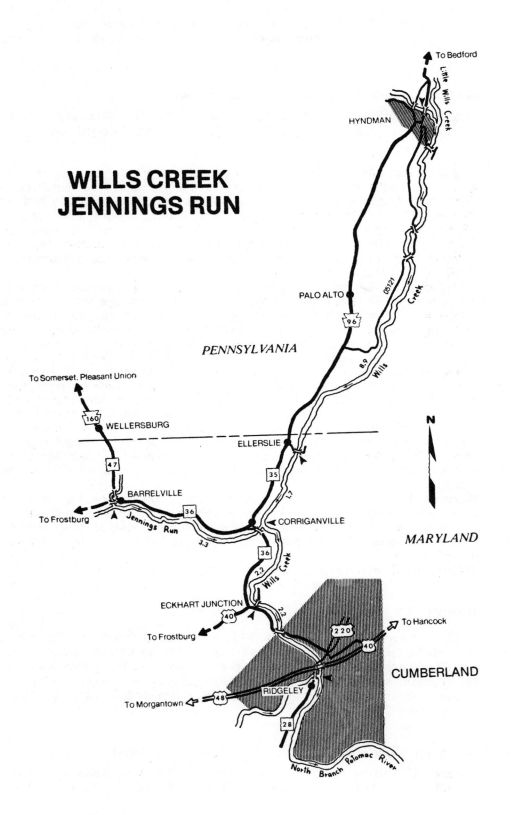

WILLS CREEK
JENNINGS RUN

To Bedford

Little Wills Creek

HYNDMAN

PENNSYLVANIA

PALO ALTO

05121

96

8.9

Wills   Creek

To Somerset, Pleasant Union

160   WELLERSBURG

ELLERSLIE

N

47

35

1.7

BARRELVILLE

36

CORRIGANVILLE

To Frostburg

Jennings Run

3.3

MARYLAND

36

2.2

Wills Creek

ECKHART JUNCTION

2.2

40

220

To Hancock

To Frostburg

40

CUMBERLAND

48   RIDGELEY

To Morgantown

28

North Branch Potomac River

⑬

Trip Description: Wills Creek has now broken out of the Allegheny Plateau and settles into a more gentle pace through a trough nestled between the Allegheny Front and Wills Mountain. The run is initially busy, dropping over cobble bars in a bouncy, uncomplicated manner. One particularly steep rapid, about a mile below the start, throws up waves big enough to swamp an open boat. The rapids gradually get shorter and the pools longer with one long straight unusually dead one below Ellerslie. While the scenery in the valley is pretty, the view of it from the river is poor, obscured by high banks and dense vegetation. The last two miles are also scarred by large scale quarrying on the side of Wills Mountain.

Hazards: Low bridge about a mile below Corriganville might not be passable at high water.

Water Conditions: Winter or spring within week of rain or thaw.

Gauge

Minimum level would be about 1.5 feet on painted gauge at Hyndman and 3.0 feet on USGS gauge at Eckhart Junction (right bank).

Section 4. Eckhart Junction to North Branch Potomac River

Gradient	Difficulty	Distance	Time	Width	Scenery	Map
20	2 or 6	2.0	.25	40-60	Unusual	13

Trip Description: Did you ever stand on a city street during a rain, watching a piece of flotsam float down the gutter and wonder what it would be like if that flotsam was your boat and the gutter was a river? Here is your big chance. The last 1.4 miles of Wills Creek through Cumberland is now, courtesy of the magical hand of the Corps of Engineers, a giant trapezoidal concrete storm drain, i.e. a real live paved river.

Your entry is made via The Narrows, a massive gap cut by Wills Creek through Wills Mountain, and is bounded by cliffs that are among the most spectacular in the Potomac Basin. Although the river shares the gap with U.S. Rte. 40 and the Chessie System, it is beautiful. Then comes the U.S. 40 bridge and "The Channel". Once into "The Channel" the paddler is committed. It is indeed a strange sensation to travel down a high velocity river of uniform width, uniform depth and with no eddys or nothing to even grab onto. Even if one could stop, the sloping concrete walls are capped by vertical concrete walls which are capped with chainlink fences, meaning no escape. Luckily the gradient is expended over gentle inclined planes which usually have incredibly uniform channelwide surfing waves at the bottom. One exception is a hydraulic beneath the first railroad bridge which can be punched through with speed or snuck on the extreme left. Take out directly across the North Branch where a car can be driven up to the backside of the levee.

Hazards: The whole channel is a hazard if you flip. While it is an easy uncomplicated run (as long as you do not broach on a bridge pier), a swimmer or inverted boater would be severely beaten and abraided and since there is no way out except the end, it would be a long swim.

Water Conditions: Winter or spring during any wet spell or after locally intense summer showers.

Gauge

Same as Section 3.

Brush Creek

Introduction

Brush Creek drains an isolated piece of plateau northwest of Fairhope, Pa. This seldom run torrent makes an ideal introduction to a Wills Creek run when the water is up and, if water is really high, a reasonable alternative to an overly pushy Fairhope to Hyndman flush.

Section 1. Covered Bridge to Wills Creek

Gradient	Difficulty	Distance	Time	Width	Scenery	Map
75	4	3.0	1.0	20-30	Excellent	12

Trip Description: Brush Creek is a beautiful mini-wilderness run that enters Wills Creek just above the Railroad Cut Falls at Hyndman. It flows through a wild wooded gorge decorated by falls, rock cliffs, hemlock and rhododendron and only civilized by one roadbridge and a cluster of rustic log structures. Rapids, formed by boulders, gravel and ledges are almost continuous, separated only by short pools. There is an unrunable ten-foot falls under the covered bridge at the put-in and about a mile downstream there is a steep tier of ledges that form a chute dropping about ten feet. Take out above Railroad Cut Falls on Wills Creek about a half mile below the confluence.

The purist can add about three miles to this run, if water is very high by starting at a roadbridge about a half mile northwest of Johnsburg. Although the aesthetics are fine, one alder jungle and numerous dangerously placed fallen trees will make this an expedition.

Hazards: Steep ledge rapid about a mile below start. Scout and if desired, carry along old lumber railroad grade on left.

Water Conditions: Canoeable only in winter and spring after a good rain or thaw.

Gauge

Painted gauge at Hyndman should read at least 2.5 feet. Also one can eyeball conditions at Fairhope-Glencoe Road Bridge.

Little Wills Creek

Introduction

Little Wills Creek flows down a narrow valley between the Allegheny Front and Wills Mountain to enter Wills Creek just below Hyndman. It draws most of its flow off of the well-watered Allegheny Plateau and generally is up if upper Wills Creek is up. The stream is paralleled by and never more than a half mile away from Pa. Rte. 96.

Section 1. Madley (Rte. 96) to Wills Creek

Gradient	Difficulty	Distance	Time	Width	Scenery	Map
39	1-3	7.0	2.0	15-25	Good	12

Trip Description: Fans of small shallow busy streams will delight in Little Wills. It is a descent down almost continuous easy rapids over gravel bars and rock gardens with some swift flatwater in between. The proximity of the highway means some trash and other eyesores but most of the time the view is only of farmlands and mountainsides. Put in on Wolf Camp Run at the Village of Madley. The take-out at the junction with Wills Creek is poor so continue downstream on Wills for a half mile to a roadbridge accessible from Hyndman.
Hazards: Fallen trees where the stream occasionally braids (not visible from the highway).
Water Conditions: Canoeable in winter or spring after a hard rain or big snow melt.

Gauge

If Wolf Camp Run looks passable at the Rte. 96 bridge then there is plenty of water on Little Wills.

Jennings Run

Introduction

Jennings Run drops off the Allegheny Front to join Wills Creek at Corriganville, two miles above The Narrows. Md. Rte. 36 follows closely on the left, greatly facilitating rescue and escape.

Section 1. Barrelville (Rte. 36) to Wills Creek

Gradient	Difficulty	Distance	Time	Width	Scenery	Map
75	4	3.5	1.0	15-20	Poor	13

Trip Description: Jennings Run is 3.5 miles of nonstop terror. It has only one rapid, also 3.5 miles long formed by ledges, boulders, gravel, tree trunks and one demolished bridge. Eddys are rare and you can bet that they will not be where the fallen trees are. The water is muddy, reeks of sewage and the bank scenery, if you notice it, ranges from drab to miserable. This is a good one for cheap thrills when everything else is in flood.

Hazards: Ruins of a concrete bridge about halfway down requires a tricky cross current maneuver that could result in a serious broach if not executed properly. Also fallen trees in bad spots.

Water Conditions: During winter or spring immediately after a heavy rain.

Gauge

None. Judge condition from road.

Evitts Creek

Introduction

Evitts Creek occupies the narrow trough between Wills Mountain and Evitts Mountain north and east of Cumberland, Md. With its limited watershed and two water supply reservoirs that intercept a substantial piece of its flow, this is a good stream to take advantage of when everything else is in flood. Do not be discouraged by its proximity to an urban area for it is still quite attractive and a lively run.

Section 1. Lake Gordon Dam to Md. Rte. 51

Gradient	Difficulty	Distance	Time	Width	Scenery	Map
21*	1-3	13.5	4.0	15-40	Good	14

*reaches 100fpm in Pa.

Trip Description: To reach the put-in drive north on U.S. Rte. 220 three and a half miles past the Cumberland city limits where Pine Ridge Road (no sign) forks to the right. Follow Pine Ridge Road about two miles, turn right at the fork onto Dam Road and follow to bridge over Evitts Creek immediately below Lake Gordon Dam. Between Dam Road and Hazen Road (Md. line) the creek rushes busily and with a surprising amount of pushiness over rapids formed by gravel and small ledges and a three-foot dam best run to right of center. The route is through wooded ravines, past shale cliffs and little meadows. To U.S. Rte. 40 the gradient very gradually decreases but the stream flows over a continuous series of riffles and easy rapids over a rocky and gravelly bottom, complicated now and then by a barbed wire fence or downed tree. The scenery here is more open with more roads and houses. Below Rte. 40 the creek slows to fast flat water with occasional riffles. There are more houses and civilization now but it still winds against enough wooded hillsides and cliffs and through enough open fields to maintain attractiveness. It also passes through an amusement park where there is a three-foot dam that can be bumped over on the far right and through a golf course with a three-foot dam that is run down an exciting but easy chute in the center. Take out just above Md. Rte. 51 on the left at the site of the old weir. The creek joins the North Branch Potomac about a quarter mile downstream after passing under the Chessie System yards (through a most impressive tunnel) and the C&O Canal aqueduct.

Hazards: Fallen trees and barbed wire above Rte. 40 and the three dams described above.

Water Conditions: Runable within two days of hard rain preceded by substantial wet weather. This is because before water can gush down Evitts Creek, Lake Koon and Gordon must be full and overflowing.

Gauge

None. Rapid at foot of Lake Gordon Dam should be passable to do upper creek.

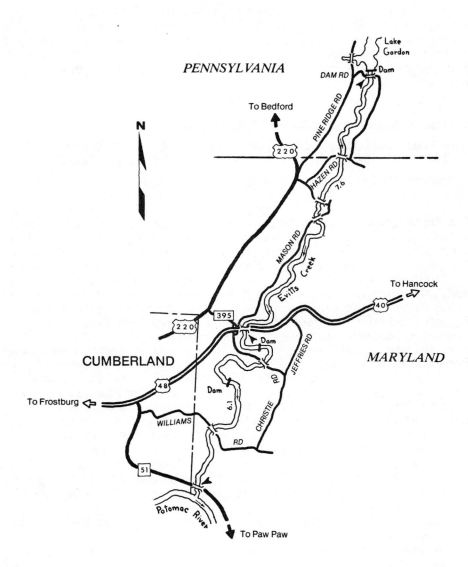

EVITTS CREEK

Town Creek

Introduction

Town Creek flows out of the heart of Bedford County, Pennsylvania to wind across the center of Allegany County and enter the Potomac below Oldtown, Md. This is rugged mountain country where numerous level-topped ridges fringe valleys filled with steeply rolling hills. These hills are all underlain with limestone so that besides some very scenic canoeing there is a lot of interesting caving to be found in this neighborhood.

Section 1. Chaneysville, Pa. to U.S. Rte. 40

Gradient	Difficulty	Distance	Time	Width	Scenery	Map
15	1-2	15.0	5.0	10-30	Very Good	15

Trip Description: Town Creek is formed by the confluence of Sweet Root Creek, Elklick Creek and Wilson Run. Put in one half mile southeast of Chaneysville on Elklick (watch out for fences) or a half mile south of Chaneysville where Pa. Rte. 326 comes close to Town Creek. This part of Town Creek meanders through a sparsely inhabited valley. The stream bumps against countless little shale cliffs while winding through woodlands and by attractive farms. There is one lovely white covered bridge near Hewitt. The fairly clear water rushes over numerous, short, easy riffles formed by gravel and some broken ledges and the only complications may be a fallen tree or new fence. Take out at the Old Rte. 40 bridge just downstream of the main highway.
Hazards: Trees or fences.
Water Conditions: Paddleable in winter or spring after wet spell or heavy rain.

Gauge

None.

Section 2. U.S. Rte. 40 to Md. Rte. 51

Gradient	Difficulty	Distance	Time	Width	Scenery	Map
9	A,1	24.5	8.0	20-35	Good	15

Trip Description: This section is neither as interesting nor as pretty as the upper but is a little easier to catch at a runable level. The valley is still either woodlands or small farms and there are some very pretty cliffs. But there are also many summer homes although fortunately they are fairly spread out as opposed to the congested slums that are found along the Potomac. The water is fairly clear and mostly flat but has a good current and occasional riffles. The trip can be shortened by entering or leaving at Pumpkin Center which is nine miles below Rte. 40.
Hazards: None
Water Conditions: After any wet weather in winter or spring.

Gauge

None

TOWN CREEK
FLINTSTONE CREEK

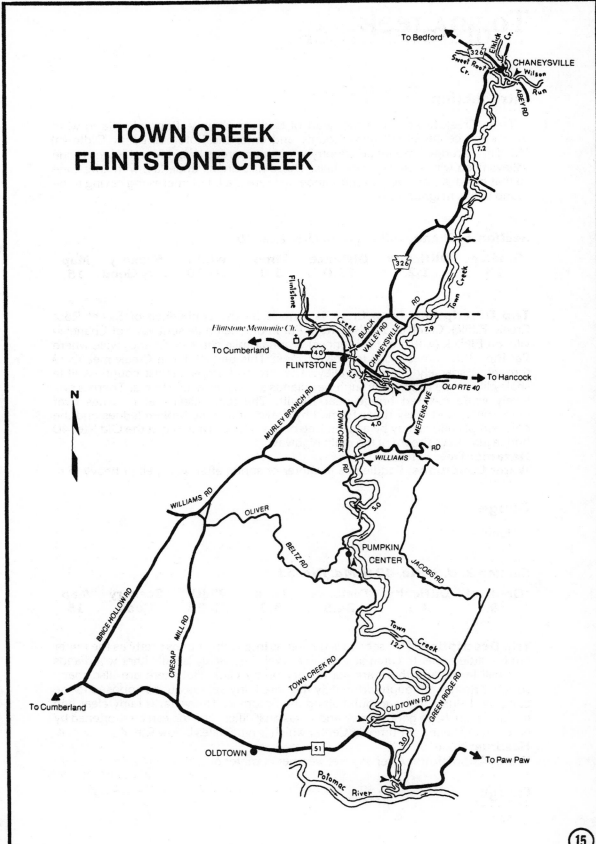

Flintstone Creek

Introduction

Flintstone Creek drains a tiny valley between Evitts Mountain and Tussey Mountain in Franklin County, Pa. Its exit from that valley around Tussey Mountain and through Warrior Ridge into Town Creek affords a short exhilarating run for microstream enthusiasts.

Section 1. Flintstone Creek Road to Town Creek

Gradient	Difficulty	Distance	Time	Width	Scenery	Map
46	1-3	3.5	1.0	10-20	Fair	15

Trip Description: This is a very tiny, busy run from start to finish, dropping over ledges, boulders and gravel. There are ledges up to three feet high at the start but they offer no problems. Trees in fast spots are a problem so be alert. The scenery unfortunately is cluttered with houses, roads and trash but the river will usually manage to distract your attention. Take out on east bank of Town Creek at old Rte. 40 bridge.
Hazards: Trees, logs and, if you put in farther upstream, barbed wire fences.
Water Conditions: Canoeable only within 24 hours of a hard rain.

Gauge

None but you can assess the situation by driving up the riverside road from Rte. 40.

Other Information

Probably the most notable feature while passing down Sideling Hill Creek and many other streams in the Valley and Ridge area, besides the strikingly beautiful rock formations, are the cliffs and slopes of crumbling shale. Shale is a sedimentary rock formed by the consolidation of mud that was deposited in shallow seas millions of years ago. This is a soft rock that weathers by breaking away, piece by piece, as thin smooth-faced and sharp-edged fragments. Pick up a piece and you will find it easy to break. Piles of these fragments form the slopes that you keep seeing. As with sand, any rain that falls upon this surface quickly drains away and in the process also leaches away any nutrients. As a result, a rather desert-like and barren environment is created that is only suitable for habitation by the heartiest of plant types. Notice that most of the trees that you see living (or dying) there are pines and eastern red cedar both rather scrubby looking species adapted for hardship. A more interesting resident is the prickly pear cactus. Possessing pads that are only about four inches long they blend easily into the shale background except for one glorious week, usually in mid or late June, when they show off their beautiful roselike yellow blossoms. One other tenacious plant that you may be likely to notice here and also on the rocky cliffsides is the columbine. This plant is most prominent in early May when it displays its intricate red drooping flowers that contrast so brilliantly with the grays and browns of the bare rock.

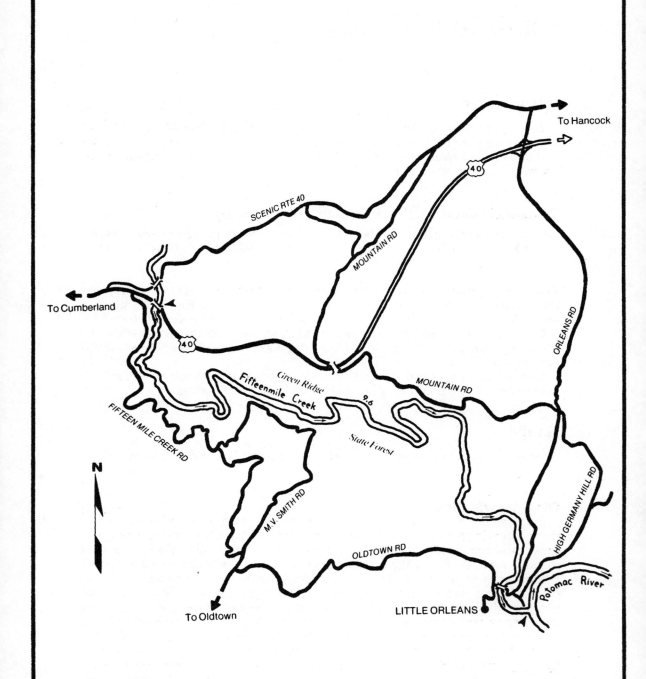

FIFTEENMILE CREEK

Fifteenmile Creek

Introduction

Fifteenmile Creek drains the dry shaley ridges of Buchanan State Forest in Pennsylvania and Green Ridge State Forest in Maryland. Consider it quite a prize as it is really tiny and really hard to catch up. Its unorthodox direction of flow across the grain of Town Hill and the surrounding hills takes it through some rugged uncivilized country and assures it a lively gradient.

Section 1. U.S. Rte. 40 to Potomac River, Little Orleans

Gradient	Difficulty	Distance	Time	Width	Scenery	Map
29	1-3	9.5	3.5	10-40	Excellent	16

Trip Description: An easy put-in is found just downstream of the forestry camp below Rte. 40. Most of the run is through a beautiful isolated wooded gorge decorated by numerous shale cliffs and rock formations. There are lots of riffles and rapids, formed by gravel bars and small broken ledges. At a few spots watch out for hard tight right-angle turns where rapids pile up against cliffs (these spots drive home the value of leaning downstream like nothing else can). Also there are quite a few fallen trees to tangle with, especially where the stream splits around islands. Take out at the low-water bridge at Little Orleans, which is usually not runable or better yet proceed another half mile down to and under the C&O Canal aqueduct to a launching ramp at the confluence with the Potomac.
Hazards: Trees and a low-water bridge at Little Orleans.
Water Conditions: Winter and spring after a hard rain.

Gauge

If riffle below Pratt Hollow (stream running down along Rte. 40 from west) is passable, then level is adequate.

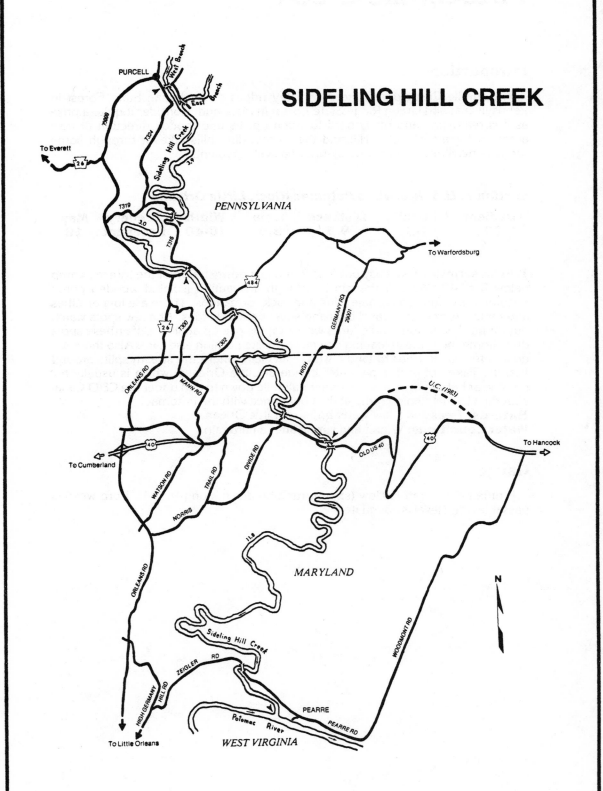

SIDELING HILL CREEK

PURCELL

West Branch

East Branch

7000

To Everett — 26

T324

Sideling Hill Creek

3.9

PENNSYLVANIA

T319

3.0

T316

To Warfordsburg

484

GERMANY RD

26

T300

2900

T302

6.8

HIGH

U.C. (1983)

ORLEANS RD

MANN RD

40

Old US 40

40

To Cumberland

DIVIDE RD

To Hancock

WATSON RD

TRAIL RD

NORRIS

11.8

MARYLAND

N

ORLEANS RD

Sideling Hill Creek

WOODMONT RD

ZEIGLER RD

HIGH GERMANY HILL RD

PEARRE

PEARRE RD

Potomac River

To Little Orleans

WEST VIRGINIA

17

Sideling Hill Creek

Introduction

Sideling Hill Creek drains the eastern edge of Bedford County, Pa. and after crossing a corner of Franklin County enters Maryland to form the boundary between Washington and Allegany counties. To westbound travelers on U.S. Rte. 40 it is the creek that you whiz over at 65 mph after nearly killing yourself on the hairpin curve atop its namesake mountain.

Section 1. Purcell, Pa. to U.S. Rte. 40

Gradient	Difficulty	Distance	Time	Width	Scenery	Map
16	1	14.0	4.5	10-30	Very Good	17

Trip Description: All of the small Potomac tributaries in the ridge and valley province from Evitts Creek to Licking Creek are rather similar and all pleasant canoe streams but Sideling Hill Creek just puts all their finest qualities together and comes out with something better than all the rest. The put-in is at a secondary roadbridge on the West Branch about a half mile above the East Branch junction. If there appears to be enough water here then there is plenty below. The following miles are past a few farms and a few summer cottages but mostly through woods filled with hemlock and rhododendron. There are shale cliffs covered with ferns, moss and lichen and in mid-winter, with intricate ice decorations. The creek is graced by plenty of easy riffles separated by deep pools of hazy green water. Take out at the old Rte. 40 bridge, just downstream of the main highway.
Hazards: Possible trees.
Water Conditions: Paddleable in winter and spring after a good rain.

Gauge

Need about six inches of runable water at Rte. 40.

Section 2. U.S. Rte. 40 to Potomac River

Gradient	Difficulty	Distance	Time	Width	Scenery	Map
16	1-2	12.0	4.0	15-30	Excellent	17

Trip Description: Lower Sideling Hill Creek is an almost wild river. The first half of this section passes through undisturbed woodlands partly within the bounds of a state wildlife management area. The stream twists and turns at the base of Sideling Hill, bouncing into beautiful cliffs and crumbly shale slopes. It rushes over numerous rapids of gravel and broken ledges that can be quite tricky where they pile up against cliffs to form ninety degree turns. The gradient gradually slows down and woods yield to some farmland but the farms are abandoned and going to seed. The creek makes a grand exit from its wilderness-like valley as it passes beneath the 110-foot arch of the old C&O Canal aqueduct and on to the Potomac, where a half mile downstream, opposite Lock 56 at Pearre is an easy take-out.

Hazards: None

Water Conditions: After wet spell or hard rain.

Gauge

Primitive; there is a large U-shaped root growing in the old stone bridge abutment at the put-in, river right. The bottom of the root is about nine inches above zero.

Another Point of View

Nothing so rounds out a river tour as a good birdseye view of that river. The more aggressive and prosperous paddler can go out and charter an airplane but for the more down to earth majority knowing where to drive or hike for a good view should suffice. Here are a few recommended scenic overlooks in the Potomac Basin.

North Branch Potomac at Luke: It is possible to gain a panoramic if not scenic view of this industrial valley from old W. Va. Rte. 46. Cross the North Branch into Piedmont, W. Va. and find some local who can give you directions to old Rte. 46 as there are no longer any signs. This precariously perched road may be closed (it should have been condemned years ago) but is well worth hiking up.

Wills Creek Narrows: It is possible to drive up, from the Cumberland side, to Lovers Leap, on the northeast rim of this spectacular gap.

Potomac River near Paw Paw: Land at the mouth of the second tiny creek on the right about a mile below where the Little Cacapon River joins the Potomac. Climb onto the railroad grade and from there follow a primitive path that ascends the knife-edge ridge that lies between the creek and the river. This affords grand views both upstream and down.

Potomac River near Doe Gully: About three miles west of Little Orleans on the Oldtown Road is a sign pointing the way to an overlook of a stretch of one of the huge loops of the river.

Potomac River, Prospect Peak: Ascend W. Va. Rte. 9 east out of Great Cacapon to spectacular view of river and Sideling Hill.

Potomac River, Harpers Ferry: A short climb to Jeffersons Rock in Harpers Ferry yields a view that Thomas Jefferson though worthy of a trip across the ocean for. Another fine view, peering straight down on the town, can be found on the Maryland side of the Potomac by ascending a trail starting at the east end of the railroad tunnel to the top of the black cliffs of Maryland Heights.

Potomac River, Mather Gorge: Foot trails run along both sides of this shallow gorge offering a glut of fine scenery.

Tonoloway Creek

Introduction

Tonoloway Creek drains an area of rolling hills and low ridges east of Sideling Hill to join the Potomac at Hancock. This is apple country and many a hillside is decorated by the orderly patterns of orchards. Yet little of this activity is apparent to the paddler who sees and enjoys mainly a sparsely inhabited landscape.

Section 1. Needmore, Pa. (U.S. Rte. 522) to Little Tonoloway Creek

Gradient	Difficulty	Distance	Time	Width	Scenery	Map
10	1	14.0	4.5	15-25	Excellent	18

Trip Description: Put in at U.S. Rte. 522 or at a tiny concrete arch bridge about one mile downstream, east of Needmore. The following miles describe an incredibly serpentine course that advances you about one mile down the valley for every two paddled. While there are occasional farms and fields, most of the way is through woodlands of which there are good views thanks to the generally low banks. Almost every bend exposes pretty shale cliffs and almost every northern exposure has a cool green hemlock grove clinging to it. Most of the surrounding hills are close by and steep and the combined effect is one of intimacy and remoteness. There are many easy riffles but this still is not really a whitewater run. However since the stream is narrow, look for trees to be an occasional problem. Take out just above Little Tonoloway Creek at bridge east of Johnsons Mill.
Hazards: Occasional fallen tress.
Water Conditions: Catch within day or two of hard rain during winter or spring.

Gauge

If riffle at concrete arch bridge east of Needmore is just cleanly runable then level is just adequate.

Section 2. Little Tonoloway Creek to Md. Rte. 144, Hancock, Md.

Gradient	Difficulty	Distance	Time	Width	Scenery	Map
10	1	6.0	2.0	20-30	Good	18

Trip Description: Put in at Johnsons Mill either on Little Tonoloway Creek or on Tonoloway Creek. This section is slightly larger than above, slower, more settled and more open. Nevertheless it is still pretty.
Hazards: None
Water Conditions: Can catch up maybe a day longer than the upper section.

Gauge

None.

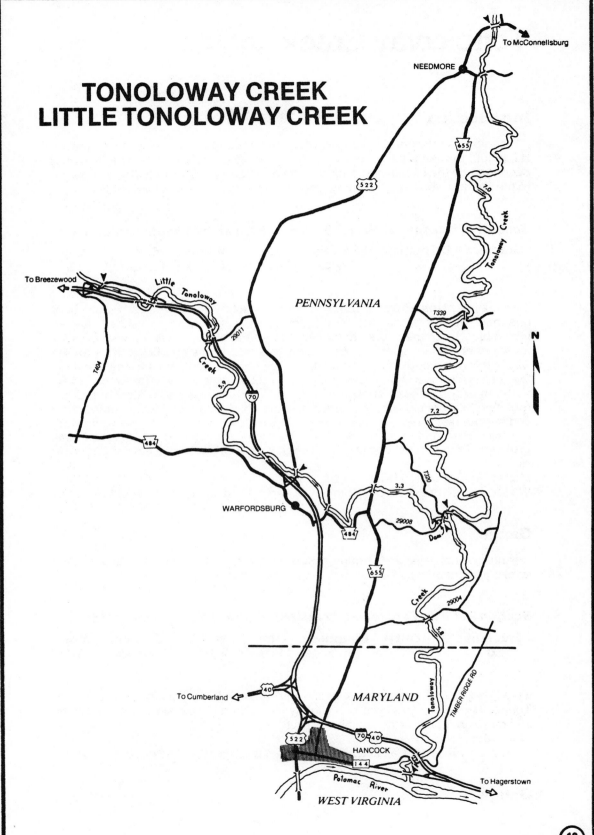

TONOLOWAY CREEK
LITTLE TONOLOWAY CREEK

Little Tonoloway Creek

Introduction

Considering that Interstate 70 follows over half of this course it is amazing what a pleasant run Little Tonoloway is. It accomplishes this seemingly impossible feat by twisting behind little hills and cliffs which not only block the view but screen out the sound of the busy highway. Little Tonoloway does not have much of a watershed so you have to rush to catch it up and that is where the Interstate can be very useful.

Section 1. Deneen Gap to Johnsons Mill

Gradient	Difficulty	Distance	Time	Width	Scenery	Map
21	1-2	10.0	3.5	10-25	Good	18

Trip Description: To reach the put-in, get off I-70 (heading north) at Exit 32, turn right, then left and park. The stream is about a hundred feet across the grassy field, down a steep bank. The stream gets off to a lively start as it tumbles out of a gap in Sideling Hill and heads eastward cutting across the geological grain of the land. Whitewater is almost continuous over rapids formed by small ledges and gravel bars and there are many tricky spots caused by bends with swift water sweeping under trees or roots. The scenery alternates between rural and woodsy while shale cliffs abound all the way. Around Warfordsburg things slow down and scenery turns rather drab with sumptious views of the Interstate and a large gravel quarry. There is a two-foot high rock dam at the quarry best run on the left. Below here the good scenery returns but the water is mostly slow. However one gets a final splash at a crumbling dam above Johnsons Mill. If not clogged with debris, there is a runable breach on the far left that drops three and a half feet into a juicy hole. The take-out is a tenth mile above Tonoloway Creek.
Hazards: Trees and roots on bends on upper river. Old mill dam near end of trip where road hits river; run on far left.
Water Conditions: Winter or spring within day of hard rain.

Gauge

If little ledges at the put-in are clearly runable or rock dam at Mellott Quarry near Warfordsburg has a clean chute on the left, level is adequate.

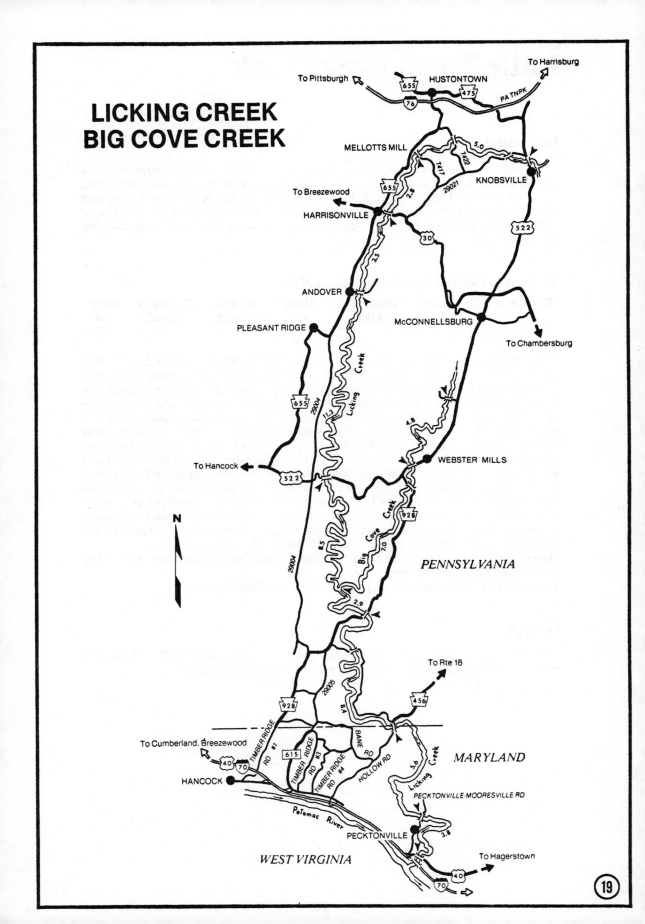

Licking Creek

Introduction

Licking Creek starts on the west slope of Tuscarora Mountain near Cowans Gap State Park, twists and turns through eastern Fulton County, Pa., a corner of Franklin County and finally through Washington County, Md. to empty into the Potomac above Fort Frederick. It cuts through a beautiful landscape of low parallel ridges covered with orchards, forests and pastures. Many of the roads in the area follow the ridgetops which afford enough good views to make shuttling for this stream almost as pleasant as the paddling.

Section 1. Knobsville, Pa. (U.S. Rte. 522) to U.S. Rte. 30

Gradient	Difficulty	Distance	Time	Width	Scenery	Map
20	1-2	8.0	3.0	10-20	Good	19

Trip Description: Only the real hardcore purist will want to put in at Rte. 522. Here the stream is no more than 10 feet wide, shallow even at high water and bristles with obstacles. After leaving Rte. 522, it immediately rushes through a long tunnel of arching alder bushes best negotiated on your belly. This can be avoided by putting in at a bridge three quarters of a mile downstream leaving you with only fallen trees, barbed wire, footbridges and sharp turns for interest. Actually the reason for putting up with all of this nonsense is that it is the only way to gain access to the full length of the beautiful three mile long wooded gorge above Mellotts Mill. Here you will find the going easy, riffles frequent and the solitude almost complete.

Hazards: The usual small stream obstacles; trees, logs, overhanging shrubbery and both above and below the gorge, barbed wire.

Water Conditions: Only up within 24 hours of hard rain during winter and spring.

Gauge

None. Judge conditions at put-in.

Section 2. U.S. Rte. 30 to Pa. Rte. 456

Gradient	Difficulty	Distance	Time	Width	Scenery	Map
10	1	35.0	10.0	20-30	Very Good	19

Trip Description: The creek now settles into a course suitable for nonmasochistic novices in search of beauty and solitude. Like other rivers in these parts it twists unbelievably, bumps up against a lot of pretty shale cliffs and flows through mostly woods and past occasional farms. Below Andover there are few roads or structures. The water is mostly flat but there are enough riffles and strong current to make you feel that the river is doing the work. This section can be broken into three leisurely paced runs: Rte. 30 to Rte. 522, distance 15 miles; Rte. 522 to Rte. 928, 11.5 miles; and Rte. 928 to Rte. 456, 8.5 miles. If the water is up you will find that 15 to 20 miles is a reasonable, easy day's run.

Hazards: Some fallen trees and fences in the first ten miles.
Water Conditions: This is usually a winter or spring run. Above Rte. 928 catch within three days of a hard rain. Below Rte. 928 it is usually passable within a week of hard rain.

Gauge

Use gauge described in section 3. Need about a foot of water for upper reaches.

Section 3. Pa. Rte. 456 to U.S. Rte. 40

Gradient	Difficulty	Distance	Time	Width	Scenery	Map
5	A-1	9.5	3.0	20-35	Good	19

Trip Description: Rte. 456 marks the transition to a slower and less meandering stream flowing through an open pastoral valley. The valley is still sparsely settled and surrounding scenery is still quite pretty. The take-out at U.S. Rte. 40 involves a steep climb up to a side road on the west (right) bank.
Hazards: Possibly a barbed wire fence.
Water Conditions: Usually passable within week or two of rain during winter or spring.

Gauge

Concrete footing on west pier of Rte. 40 bridge. Three inches below top of upstream corner is a minimal but passable level. Riffle above bridge should be passable.

Big Cove Creek

Introduction

Big Cove Creek starts up by McConnellsburg, Pa. and drains the eastern edge of Fulton County, Pa. Like Licking Creek it twists a lot and possesses copious quantities of peace, solitude and beauty. Unlike Licking Creek it has some real live whitewater.

Section 1. Secondary road north of Webster Mill to Licking Creek

Gradient	Difficulty	Distance	Time	Width	Scenery	Map
21*	1-3	12.0	3.5	10-20	Very Good	19

*reaches 80fpm

Trip Description: To reach put-in drive 2.3 miles north of Webster Mill on U.S. Rte. 522 and turn left onto paved side road making sure not to blink or you may miss the creek. Big Cove Creek is extremely tiny at the put-in, flows across obviously private property (open cow pastures) and access is across someone's front lawn. Accordingly please ask permission to put in and do not invade with a large party. For at least the first mile count on lots of fences, some trees and log jams and herds of curious cattle on the banks trotting downstream with you. The stream then leaves the cowpastures and burrows into a beautiful wooded gorge. The gradient increases and soon the creek is rushing over continuous gravel bars and some broken ledges. The pace does not slow down until Big Cove Tannery, about five miles below the start. The novice might consider putting in here where Pa. Rte. 928 parallels the creek as the water is much slower from here on. One can take out at a ford just below the mouth or continue about three miles down Licking Creek to Rte. 928.

Hazards: Fences at the start and trees all along. There is a two-foot high wooden weir at Big Cove Tannery visible from Rte. 928 with a strong roller but runable with caution.

Water Conditions: Within a day of hard rain during winter or spring.

Gauge

None. If everything that you cross on the way looks really high then this might be up.

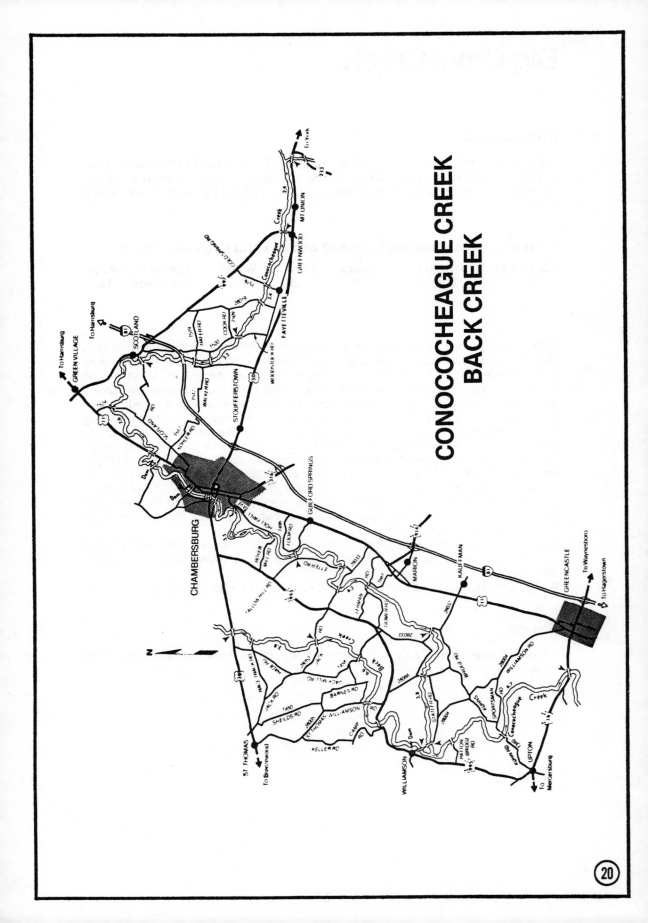

CONOCOCHEAGUE CREEK
BACK CREEK

20

Conococheague Creek

Introduction

Conococheague Creek drains the prosperous Cumberland Valley of Franklin County, Pa. and Washington County, Md. The valley which is the northern extension of the Shenandoah Valley is devoted to agriculture; corn, cattle and orchards from South Mountain on the east to Tuscarora Mountain on the west. Since this is obviously civilized territory, the stream's best attractions are its cultural features, such as well-built barns, farm houses, covered and stone arch bridges, old mills, and the beautiful old towns nearby such as Williamsport, Mercersburg and Greencastle. The creek is fed by two navigable tributaries, the West Branch and Back Creek, also described.

Section 1. Caledonia State Park (U.S. Rte. 30) to Chambersburg (U.S. Rte. 30)

Gradient	Difficulty	Distance	Time	Width	Scenery	Map
22	1-3	17.0	5.5	15-40	Fair	20

Trip Description: The main stem of Conococheague Creek starts on South Mountain and becomes canoeable at the confluence with Carbaugh Run and Rocky Mountain Creek. Put in at the Rte. 30 bridge over Rocky Mountain Creek in Caledonia State Park. The stream drops steeply and continuously over gravel bars and rock gardens and quickly rushes off into a beautiful grove of giant hemlocks. Unfortunately after a short, pleasant interlude the channel braids and you will find yourself intimately involved with many of these fallen giants. The going gets easier below Caledonia but fallen trees and split channels still present occasional problems as far down as Scotland. The creek remains fast and riffly to Chambersburg. There are three dams on this section; a two-foot dam at Scotland run on right, a seven-footer about four miles below Scotland (Siloam Dam) that should be carried on left and a seven-footer in Chambersburg carried on right. Although the route passes through some thick woods and past some pretty rural areas the scenery also includes too many stretches of dredged river bed, mobile homes and gravel pits. So if whitewater is not your priority, better to start your tour below Chambersburg.
Hazards: Fallen trees, especially congested in Caledonia Park. A runable two-foot dam at Scotland, unrunable seven-foot dam four miles below Scotland and unrunable seven-foot dam in Chambersburg.
Water Conditions: Runable winter and spring within day of hard rain.

Gauge

If rapids at put-in look runable then level is fine the whole way.

Section 2. Chambersburg (U.S. Rte. 30) to West Branch Conococheague

Gradient	Difficulty	Distance	Time	Width	Scenery	Map
6	1	26.5	8.0	30-60	Very Good	20, 21

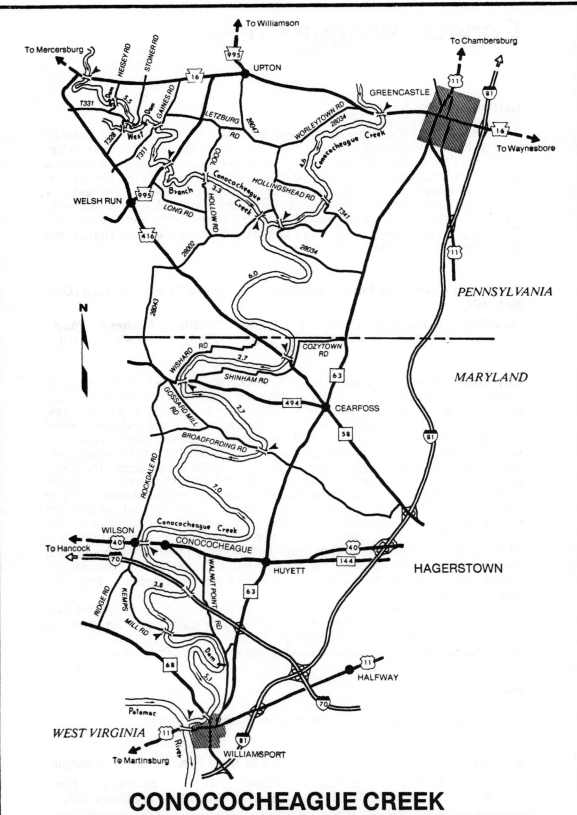

CONOCOCHEAGUE CREEK
WEST BRANCH CONOCOCHEAGUE CREEK

Trip Description: Below Chambersburg the Conococheague winds through a remarkably beautiful predominately rural setting. Banks are usually low and afford a wonderful view of what appears from the boat to be very sparsely settled territory. This section also includes two graceful stone arch bridges and an exceptionally long covered bridge. There is a sharp-crested two-foot dam located below the Chambersburg sewage treatment plant that paddlers with delicate boats might choose to carry and there are a few fences to watch out for (electric fences are very popular around here). Otherwise there is no more excitement than an occasional riffle. This trip can be shortened by five miles by putting in on Loop Rte. T486 or further rearranged using any one of eleven other bridges that cross this section (see map). Take out at bridge a quarter of a mile above West Branch.
Hazards: Two-foot dam below sewage treatment plant and electric and barbed wire fences.
Water Conditions: Winter and spring within three days of hard rain.

Gauge

None

Section 3. West Branch to Williamsport, Md.

Gradient	Difficulty	Distance	Time	Width	Scenery	Map
3	A-1	27.5	8.5	60-100	Good	21

Trip Description: Put in at roadbridge over main stem or West Branch just above their confluence. With the addition of the West Branch the stream gets noticeably wider and slower. There are very few riffles and the gradient is expended in a mostly swift current. The only excitement on this segment is a sloping five-foot dam at Kemps Mill above Williamsport which can be run at center or carried on left. The scenery alternates between wooded bluffs and views of farmland. This section is well endowed with beautiful stone arch bridges including the C&O Canal aqueduct at Williamsport. Take out at the Williamsport Town Park at the junction with the Potomac River. Intermediate access points can be found at Md. Rte. 58, mile 6.0, Fairview Road, mile 8.5, Broadfording Road, mile 11.5 and U.S. Rte. 40, mile 18.5.
Hazards: Five-foot dam at Kemps Mill.
Water Conditions: Runable winter and spring within week of rainfall.

Gauge

USGS gauge located half mile above Fairview Road on Wishard Road (right bank) should read at least 2.0 feet. Also can judge conditions from riffle above the old abandoned stone arch bridge just upstream of Rte. 58 bridge. It is not desirable to run Sections 2 or 3 at levels approaching zero because the very uniform configuration of the riverbed would result in long stretches of very tedious shallow water paddling.

Back Creek

Introduction

Back Creek feeds into the Conococheague at Williamson, Pa. It is a rather mediocre run through uninspiring scenery via mostly slow flat water. The best part of your day may be running shuttle which is much more scenic, and is as at least an exciting way to enjoy this beautiful countryside.

Section 1. U.S. Rte. 30 to Williamson

Gradient	Difficulty	Distance	Time	Width	Scenery	Map
3	A-1	9.5	3.0	20-30	Fair	20

Trip Description: After a rather dismal start as a channelized ditch through a suburban housing development, the stream winds through fields and woods. Although there are only occasional riffles keep an eye ahead for there are many electric fences blocking your way. There is also a four-foot mill dam at Williamson that is carried on right. The Conococheague is about a third of a mile below town.
Hazards: Electric fences and four-foot dam at Williamson.
Water Conditions: Winter or spring within two days of hard rain.

Gauge

None. Judge shallows at put-in.

Something Else to Think About

Since the scenery along Back Creek is rather closed in, it gives the paddler a lot of time to contemplate trees. A handful of species dominate the streambank scenery here and on most other rivers and creeks from the fall line west to the Allegheny Front. Most prominent is the sycamore, which is recognized by its often impressive dimensions, its fuzzy brown seed balls and its gray and pure white mottled bark that contrasts so brilliantly against a blue winter sky. Also if one of your childhood pleasures was crunching through leaves in late fall, the big brown curled sycamore leaf should be remembered as the prize crunchable. Probably just as common as the sycamore is the silver maple identified by its smooth gray bark (not as smooth as beech) and thin-lobed leaves. Willows, especially black willows display long thin branches bristling with long thin leaves. The box elder has toothed oval leaves in clusters of three, looking awfully similar to poison ivy. But this tree is most noticeable after the leaves have fallen, exposing curtins of winged seeds that at a distance add a pastel hue, reminiscent of spring buds, to the streambank scenery. Finally you may see the river birch which is recognized by the curls of paperlike bark peeling from its trunk.

These trees live along the banks because they love water, lots of it. With the water table only a few feet below the surface they require only a shallow root system to meet their needs. Unfortunately shallow root systems make poor anchors and that is why water and wind topple so many of these giants across your favorite creeks. These species have little commercial value so about the only other threats to their longevity are hungry beavers and the occasional foolish farmer who chops them down to gain a few more square feet of pasture.

West Branch
Conococheague Creek

Introduction

The West Branch Conococheague Creek flows for almost the entire length of western Franklin County, Pa. before finally joining the main stem near Greencastle, Pa. It is a mountain stream in its early stages and a rural open valley stream for the rest of the way, resembling very much the main Conococheague. All the way it is a suitable run for beginners.

Section 1. Pennsylvania Turnpike to Fort Loudon (U.S. Rte. 30)

Gradient	Difficulty	Distance	Time	Width	Scenery	Map
9	1-2	23.0	8.0	25-40	Fair	22

Trip Description: To reach the put-in drive north on Pa. Rte. 75 past the Pa. Turnpike and a quarter mile past Fannett-Metal High School, turn right and follow to concrete arch bridge over West Branch. Most of this run down to Richmond Furnace is rather bland. The water is mostly flat, shallow and fairly slow while the scenery of fields, farms and scrubby woods is not particularly striking. There is a small lake to paddle across at Fannettsburg formed by an old twelve-foot dam easily carried left of spillway. The lakewater powered a small hydroelectric plant, now crumbling away, that is very unusual in that the generators were driven by a water wheel rather than a turbine. Below Richmond Furnace the scenery turns woodsy with pretty views of nearby mountains. The gradient and volume pick up and pleasant riffles abound. Really the best way to handle this section would be to run from Fannettsburg to Fort Loudon, a distance of sixteen miles. Take out in Fort Loudon at the old Rte. 30 bridge.
Hazards: Trees and fences on the upper river, a twelve-foot dam at Fannettsburg and an unusual doubledecker low-water bridge below Fannettsburg.
Water Conditions: Winter and spring within two days of hard rain.

Gauge

Riffle at put-in must be passable for at least minimal but sometimes scrapey level. The stream flows through a narrow valley with many small tributaries so enough water at start will be plenty by Richmond Furnace.

Section 2. Fort Loudon (U.S. Rte. 30) to Conococheague Creek

Gradient	Difficulty	Distance	Time	Width	Scenery	Map
7	A-2	22.0	7.0	30-60	Good	21, 22

Trip Description: The West Branch leaves the mountains behind at Fort Loudon and spends its last miles winding about a wide valley. The scenery is predominately agricultural with high banks partially obscuring things above Pa. Rte. 16 and with low banks offering good views across the countryside below Rte.

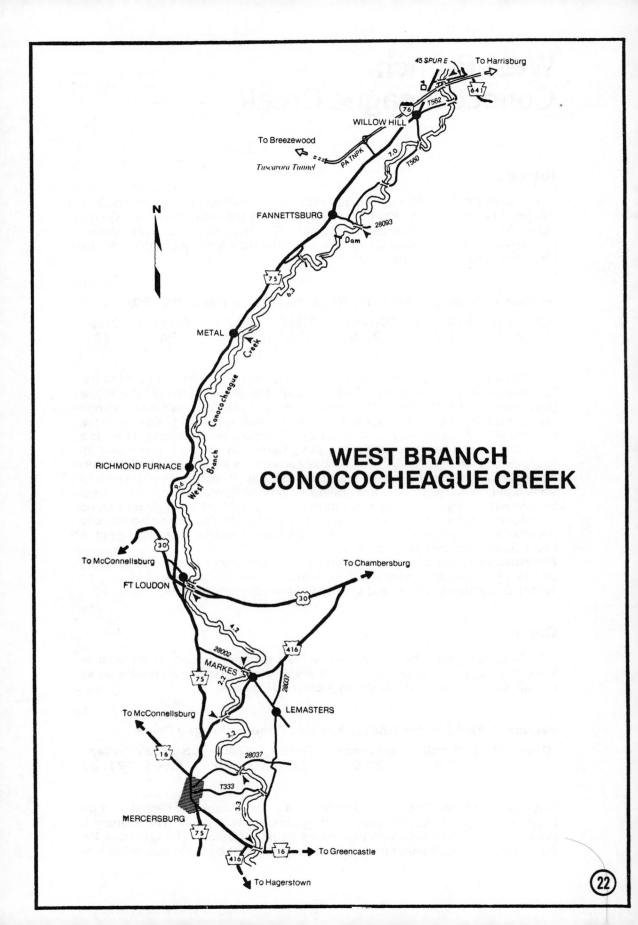

**WEST BRANCH
CONOCOCHEAGUE CREEK**

45 SPUR E

To Harrisburg

641

T562

76

WILLOW HILL

To Breezewood

PA TNPK

Tuscarora Tunnel

7.0

T560

FANNETTSBURG

28093

Dam

75

6.3

METAL

Conococheague Creek

RICHMOND FURNACE

West Branch

9.6

30

To McConnellsburg

To Chambersburg

FT LOUDON

30

4.2

416

28002

MARKES

75

2.2

28037

LEMASTERS

To McConnellsburg

3.2

16

28037

T333

3.3

MERCERSBURG

75

416

16

To Greencastle

To Hagerstown

22

16. The stream hurries over plenty of riffles in its first few miles but then slows down to fast flat water and only occasional riffles for the rest of the way. There is a runable two-foot dam at the fish hatchery below Fort Loudon, a five-foot mill dam at the first bridge below Rte. 16 that is carried on the left across private property and another five-foot mill dam a half mile below Licking Creek (below single span stone arch bridge) also carried on left. Take out at bridge a quarter mile above the Conococheague. A recommended run is from Rte. 16 to Rte. 58 on the Conococheague, a distance of fifteen miles (nine on West Branch).

Hazards: Dams; runable two-footer at fish hatchery, unrunable five-footer at first bridge below Rte. 16 and unrunable five-footer below Licking Creek.

Water Conditions: Winter or spring within week of hard rain.

Gauge

None. Judge riffles at put-in. A rough winter correlation with Frederick gauge on the Monocacy would be to look for at least 3.5 feet.

If You Are Not Afraid of the Dark

Many paddlers have found caving or spelunking to be an ideal compliment to their sport. After all, look at how similar these two masochistic pastimes are. Both are enjoyed in a cold, wet, damp and often muddy environment. Both satisfy the urge to explore and to travel under one's own muscle and wit. Cavers, like decked boaters, often spend hours in cramped quarters and like canoeists use their knees a lot. Furthermore paddler's helmets can be easily converted to lamp bearing caver's helmets and a wet suit can suffice for caver's coveralls, hence saving equipment costs.

Most of Washington and Allegany counties and to a lesser extent Garrett and Frederick counties are underlain by limestone and this continues on north into Pennsylvania. Caves are formed when rainwater, which is slightly acidic, slowly dissolves away the limestone as it seeps into cracks and fissures in the rock. Similarly some limestone drops out of solution to form deposits that become the lovely flowstone formations that decorate some caves. Driving through cave country one will often notice a telltale sign of caves, sinkholes, which are crater-like depressions in the landscape formed when the roofs of caves collapse. If you do not get the hint driving, the alert paddler cannot help but notice intriguing holes in the cliffs and rock outcrops along streams of this region. Crabtree Cave (for experienced cavers only) lies in the canyonside just above Savage River Dam, River (Indian) Cave is prominent on a Potomac River cliff just below the mouth of Opequon Creek and Revells Cave forms a fascinating subterranean maze behind an outcrop along Licking Creek. These are just a few. If you are seriously interested in expanding your horizons below ground, two excellent guides are available: *Caves of Maryland*, 1971, by the Md. Geological Survey (available from Md. Geological Survey, 214 Latrobe Hall, The Johns Hopkins Univ., Baltimore, Md. 21218 for $2.00) and *State of West Virginia Geological and Economic Survey, Volume XIXA, Caverns of West Virginia.*

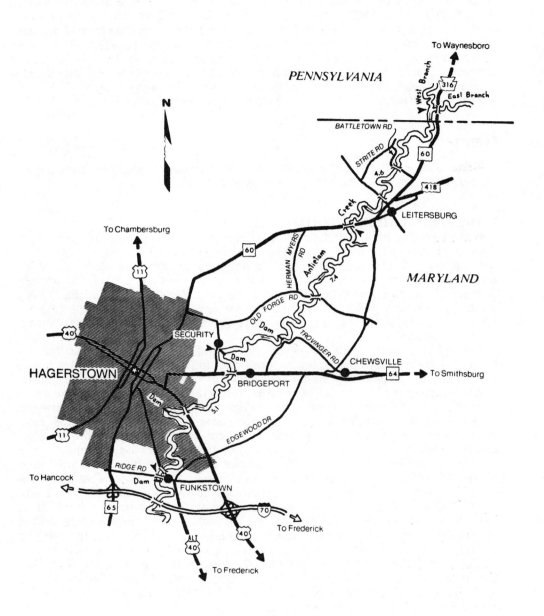

ANTIETAM CREEK

Antietam Creek

Introduction

Antietam Creek drains the eastern edge of Maryland's Cumberland Valley beneath the western slope of South Mountain. It forms at the confluence of the West and East branches just north of the Mason-Dixon Line and winds and twists for almost forty-one miles to the Potomac River below Shepherdstown, W. Va. This has long been a favorite for novice whitewater paddlers.

Section 1. Confluence E. and W. branches to Security, Md.

Gradient	Difficulty	Distance	Time	Width	Scenery	Map
6	A-1	12.0	3.5	30-50	Good	23

Trip Description: This trip begins on the East Branch at Pa. Rte. 316, a few feet above the point where the West Branch joins. This section of Antietam twists and turns through attractive farm country complimented by the normal array of big decorated barns and sturdy old farmhouses. The narrow stream is always fairly swift and there are plenty of riffles. There is a scrapey three and a half-foot dam to carry about two miles below Old Forge Road and a four-foot dam with a nasty roller located at the take-out, which is where Antietam Drive touches the creek at Security.
Hazards: Two dams mentioned above and possible fallen trees and fences.
Water Conditions: Runable winter and spring within week of moderate rain.

Gauge

No convenient gauge. The USGS gauge at Burnside Bridge should read over 4.0 feet and for a rough correlation the Frederick gauge on the Monocacy (call 301-899-3210 after 11:30 A.M.) should also read around 4.0 feet.

Section 2. Security to Funkstown (Ridge Road)

Gradient	Difficulty	Distance	Time	Width	Scenery	Map
4	A-1	5.0	1.5	50-60	Poor	23

Trip Description: Most paddlers will choose to bypass this section as it is rather ugly. The attractive rural landscape of the upper section is now replaced by houses, unsightly commercial buildings, an old power plant, and an obnoxious quantity of stream-bank trash. The water is mostly flat, partly the backwater of a three-foot dam at the power plant below U.S. Rte. 40 and a sloping four-foot dam under the Ridge Road Bridge at Funkstown. All will chose to carry the power dam and most will choose to carry the latter.
Hazards: Dams described above.
Water Conditions: Runable most of normal winter or spring.

Gauge

None

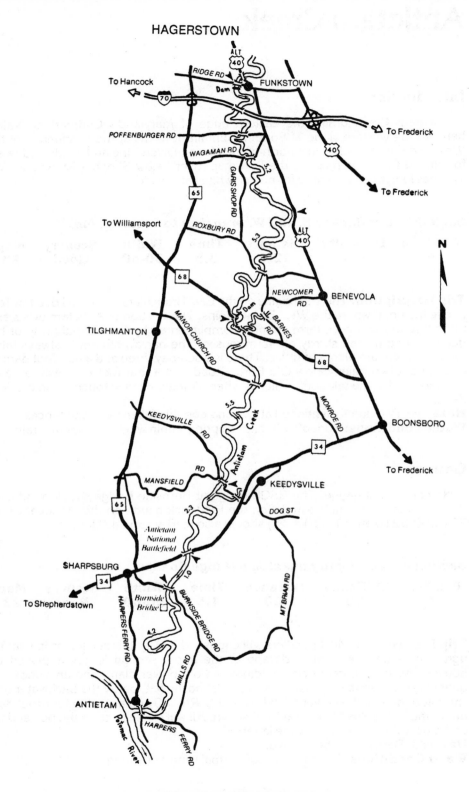

ANTIETAM CREEK

Section 3. Funkstown (Ridge Road) to Antietam (Harpers Ferry Road)

Gradient	Difficulty	Distance	Time	Width	Scenery	Map
7	A-2	23.5	7.0	50-100	Good	24

Trip Description: Except for some lingering odors from the local sewage treatment plant, Antietam Creek quickly recovers from its bad urban trip and, once past I-70, the scenery and atmosphere are once again delightfully rural. Actually on this section the human influence has enhanced its beauty and interest. Several graceful stone arch bridges, crumbling mills, and old farmhouses, also constructed from the plentiful native limestone, lend an Old World charm to the journey. The mills have also served to spice up the run as their crumbling or crumbled dams form some interesting and sometimes relatively heavy rapids at Poffenberger Road, Wagaman Road, Roxbury Road, Md. Rte. 34 and just above the take-out at the village of Antietam. Still intact are the six-foot dam at Devils Backbone Park (Md. Rte. 68) that requires a carry and a sharp three-foot dam about a mile downstream from Backbone Park that is usually carried. In between all of this artificial whitewater are numerous riffles formed by low ledges and gravel. The lower portion of this section winds through Antietam Battlefield, Maryland's only major Civil War engagement. Harpers Ferry Road, located about a quarter mile above the mouth is the most convenient take-out but if you are a purist you can continue and then paddle up the Potomac a few hundred yards to a C&O Canal campground.

Hazards: Dams at Devils Backbone Park and a mile below.

Water Conditions: Runable most of normal winter and spring except after prolonged rainless period.

Gauge

USGS gauge at old Burnside Bridge at Antietam Battlefield should read at least 3.4 feet to run down to Rte. 68 and at least 3.1 feet for the rest of the river. For a rough correlation the Frederick gauge on the Monocacy (call 301-899-3210 after 11:30 A.M.) should read at least 2.8 feet.

Roots and Origins

The Antietam Valley and the nearby Conococheague, Catoctin and Monocacy valleys were settled in the mid 18th century by Pennsylvanians of German extraction (Pennsylvania Dutch). Most of these people had originally migrated from the fertile farmlands of the Palatinate section of Germany and the rich farming tradition that they carried with them shows today in the neat well-tended farms of southeast Pennsylvania and central Maryland. In the mid 18th century the proprietorship of Maryland, anxious to settle and stabilize its frontier and recognizing this group's skills and potential permanence, offered families 200 acres apiece of free land to lure them across the border. It worked, as told by geographical names like Funkstown, Myersville, Zullinger, Altenwald and Poffenberger Rd. which dot the countryside.

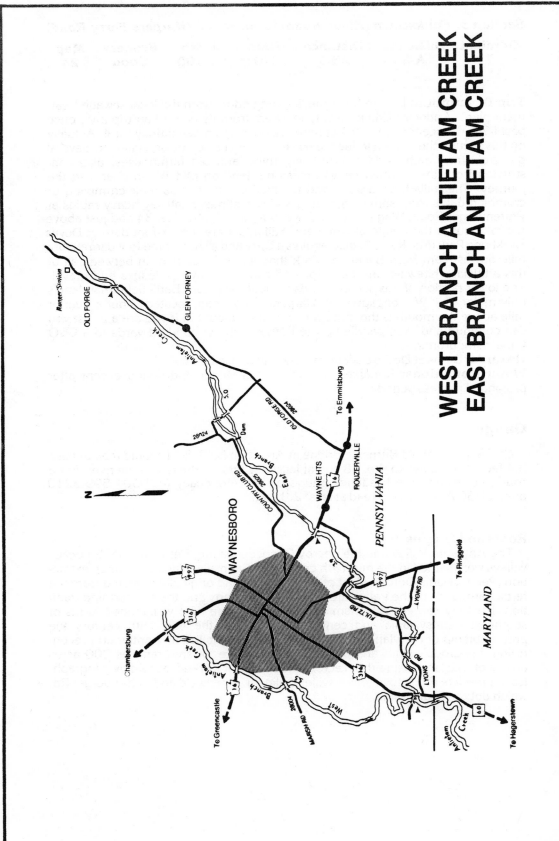

WEST BRANCH ANTIETAM CREEK
EAST BRANCH ANTIETAM CREEK

25

West and East Branches
of Antietam Creek

Introduction

The West and East branches of Antietam gather their waters from the farmlands and mountainsides surrounding Waynesboro, Pennsylvania. Considering the interest, charm and pleasure of Antietam Creek the West and East branches seem to be very improbable headwaters. One meanders its way through mediocrity and the other has stretches tailored for ex-Kamikaze pilots only. Nevertheless, for the curious this is what you can expect to find just north of the Mason-Dixon Line.

Section 1. West Branch, Pa. Rte. 316 to confluence East Branch

Gradient	Difficulty	Distance	Time	Width	Scenery	Map
16	A-1	5.5	2.0	25-35	Fair	25

Trip Description: The West Branch meanders about the open farmlands west of Waynesboro. The put-in is in a cow pasture and that is the story much of the way. While the valley is quite attractive, eroded mud banks detract from and sometimes block the scenery. The water is fast, but gentle gravel riffles are the only whitewater. Fences and trees repeatedly block the way and will plague the novice paddler who otherwise might enjoy this run.
Hazards: Trees and fences.
Water Conditions: Passable winter and spring within two days of rain.

Gauge

None. For rough correlation, the Frederick gauge on the Monocacy (call 301-899-3210 after 11:30 A.M.) should read over 4.5 feet.

Section 2. East Branch. Old Forge to Pa. Rte. 316

Gradient	Difficulty	Distance	Time	Width	Scenery	Map
34	1-4	9.0	3.0	20-40	Fair	25

Trip Description: The East Branch starts out as a tiny terror dropping off the west slope of South Mountain at a gradient in excess of a hundred feet per mile. Put in at the Mont Alto Forest roadbridge below Old Forge or you can even start three quarters of a heart-stopping mile upstream opposite the ranger station. Do not put in unless you have superb ability at stopping on a narrow eddyless torrent or at abandoning ship in a flash, for fallen trees repeatedly block your way. The gradient gradually lessens but trees and later fences persist. The scenery, which you will not see while paddling, consists initially of pretty woodlands but downstream summer homes dot the valley. By the time the stream reaches the Waynesboro Country Club (Sec. Rte. 20824) the whitewater has mellowed substantially but the creek is still mean. Passing through the golf course, the creek braids into several channels that would be canoeable if it where not for the frequent low foot-bridges. At the lower end of the golf course, the channels rejoin and the stream drops over a five-foot dam, carried on the right. Below here, trees and fences still are an occasional annoyance. The final four miles below Pa. Rte. 16 are not complicated by trees and fences (as of this writing) and the segment is quite suit-able for novices. The current is swift and there are still plenty of riffles. The scenery is the typical rural landscape of the Antietam.

Hazards: The upper river is a high-speed obstacle course. The obstacles, trees, and fences appear as far down as Rte. 16 but with each mile downstream from the put-in, negotiating them becomes more reasonable. The footbridges and dam at the golf course must be carried.

Water Conditions: Canoeable winter and spring from one to three days after a hard rain.

Gauge

None. For a rough correlation, the Frederick gauge on the Monocacy (call 301-899-3210 after 11:30 A.M.) should read at least 5.5 feet for the far upper creek and at least 4.0 feet for the lower creek.

The Plague of Fences

Certainly fences must be the most sinister trap found on the river. This bain of small stream enthusiasts is generally placed there by farmers for the purpose of keeping their livestock in, for while the cold swollen torrent you are paddling may seem an effective enough barrier, remember that in a few months or even a few days all that may remain are a few inches of easily fordable water. The most com-mon variety of fences are barbed wire, electric, large-mesh woven wire and board fences. Barbed wire is most frightening due to its potential to maim and its diffi-culty to spot before it is too late. Accordingly, one who travels a barbed wire infested stream pushing darkness, into the blinding glare of early morning or late afternoon sun or in a fog is really playing floating Russian roulette. It is often pos-sible to negotiate barbed wire with marginal clearance by having one member of the party wade out (from below) and raise or lower the strand, as there is usually some slack. Electric fences are recognized as (usually) single strands suspended from white ceramic insulators. Contact with electric fences will not fry you but it is certainly uncomfortable. These barriers work on the principle that after the average cattle bumps into a strand and is shocked by it, the beast will painstaking-ly avoid that strand ever after. This is so effective that after all of the cattle in a herd are "educated" it is seldom necessary to run current through the wire. Only people, especially dumb paddlers, seem to never learn. There is little to elaborate about woven wire fences. Just stay away from them as they are the ultimate strainers. Board fences consist of one or two stout cables from which are hung vertical wooden boards or sections of board fence. When composed of sections it is often possible to swing a section open enough to squeeze a boat through.

As vile as these contraptions are please do not damage them as they are vital to the farmer-landowner. Finally if you really fear and detest fences, the best time to run a small potentially fence infested stream is early spring after heavy ice has been broken out by high water. Such an event will almost always rip out every lousy fence on the river.

Catoctin Creek

Introduction

Running down the western edge of Frederick County, Catoctin Creek drains the beautiful rolling farmland of the Middletown Valley between South Mountain and Catoctin Mountain. It is a popular and delightful springtime novice run for those competent enough to handle sharp turns and occasional surprise strainers.

Section 1. Myersville (Harmony Road) to Md. Rte. 17

Gradient	Difficulty	Distance	Time	Width	Scenery	Map
28	1	9.5	3.0	25-40	Good	26

Trip Description: The recommended put-in is just below U.S. Rte. 40 but it is possible for more experienced paddlers to start about three miles upstream at Ellerton and enjoy a more challenging run over a steep and rocky bed complicated by fences, trees and low-water bridges. The section below Harmony Road abounds with gravel type riffles, but sharp bends and occasional fences or trees add a bit of challenge to this section. The surrounding countryside is mainly pastoral but the noise from I-70 tends to disrupt the rural serenity that should fit with the scenery.
Hazards: Trees and fences.
Water Conditions: Runable winter and spring within two days of hard rain.

Gauge

USGS gauge downstream of Rte. 17 bridge. Reading of 2.5 is minimal.

Section 2. Md. Rte. 17 to Potomac River

Gradient	Difficulty	Distance	Time	Width	Scenery	Map
11	1	15.0	4.5	30-50	Good	26

Trip Description: This section of Catoctin Creek is deeply cut into the bottom of this rugged valley. The scenery is of pastoral and wooded hillsides, the whitewater is of numerous easy riffles, and the fence/tree problems are only occasional. Many paddlers, preferring a convenient take-out, finish the run at Md. Rte. 464, three miles above the Potomac. Those preferring to go the whole way can take out at Lander, a half mile down the Potomac or continue another two and a half miles to Point of Rocks Bridge (state landing on both sides of the river).
Hazards: Possible trees or fences.
Water Conditions: Runable winter and spring within three or four days of hard rain.

Gauge

USGS gauge at Rte. 17 should read at least 2.3 feet.

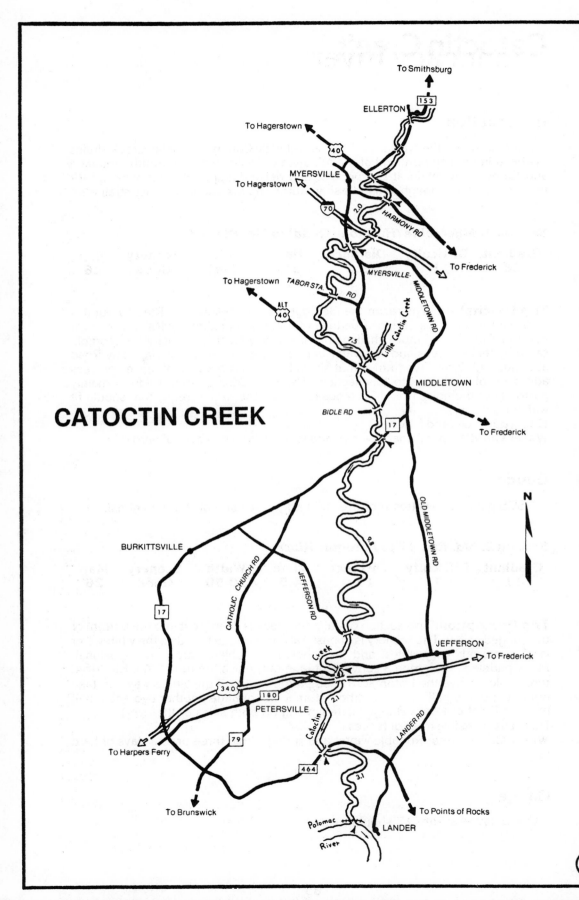

CATOCTIN CREEK

Monocacy River

Introduction

The Monocacy is the second largest tributary to the Potomac in Maryland, draining almost a thousand square miles of prime agricultural land in Adams County, Pa. and Frederick, Carroll, and Montgomery counties in Maryland. Only the North and South Branch of the Potomac and the Shenandoah, the latter two in Virginia and West Virginia, drain greater areas. Its size makes it one of the more reliably floatable streams in the state.

The river is officially born at the confluence of Marsh Creek and Rock Creek right on the Mason-Dixon Line. In its passage to the Potomac it collects several small tributaries that if caught in wet weather offer attractive and sometimes even exciting cruising. The scenery on this river is remarkably consistent, typified by a wooded bluff on one side, fields and farms on the other and a million gawking cattle. The river is also consistent, typified by a generally strong current broken by an occasional approximation of a riffle. Unfortunately the scenery suffers from too many over-the-bank trash dumps, the remains of which are usually strewn for miles downstream and the water suffers from agricultural pollution, mostly a lot of mud and gawking cattle by-products. All in all though it is a good place to fall back on for a quiet day in the outdoors not far from the population centers of the state.

Section 1. Harney Road to Potomac River

Gradient	Difficulty	Distance	Time	Width	Scenery	Map
3	A-1	58.0	17.0	70-250	Fair	27, 28

Trip Description: This river can be easily covered in four moderately lengthed sections: Harney Road to Md. Rte. 77, a distance of sixteen miles; Md. Rte. 77 to Devilbiss Bridge Road, twelve miles; Devilbiss Bridge Road to U.S. Rte. 40 (Jug Bridge), thirteen miles; and Jug Bridge to the Potomac River, seventeen miles. Or you can select your own length using any pair of at least twenty bridge crossings. The stream to Rte. 77 is relatively narrow and though mostly flat is quite swift. A group can easily cover it in three and a half hours of easy paddling at moderate levels. There is a three-foot dam (Starners Dam) to carry about two miles below the start and two low runable weirs. Except for some summer camps around Starners Dam, the scenery is typical Monocacyscape; wooded bluffs and pretty farms with occasional views of distant Catoctin Mountain. Rte. 77 is a rotten access point with steep slopes and poor parking but it is conveniently located. At Rte. 77 Double Pipe Creek joins and doubles the flow. The river responds by widening, slowing down and becoming even flatter than before, with the exception of one lively riffle at LeGore Bridge. From here on down to the Potomac the scenery and water change little. There is a three-foot rubble dam at Buckeystown that if no debris is clogging it can be run down a millrace on the right or with enough water (over 4.0 feet) can be run anywhere. The trip ends at the beautiful white arches of the old C&O Canal aqueduct. The take-out is reached from Md. Rte. 28 east of the river, turning off onto Mouth of Monocacy Road.

Hazards: There is a three-foot dam to carry two miles below Harney Road and a runable three-foot dam at Buckeystown.

Water Conditions: Runable throughout any normal late fall, winter, spring and up to mid-July. Summer shower activity often raises the river below Rte. 77 to passable levels even in late summer and fall.

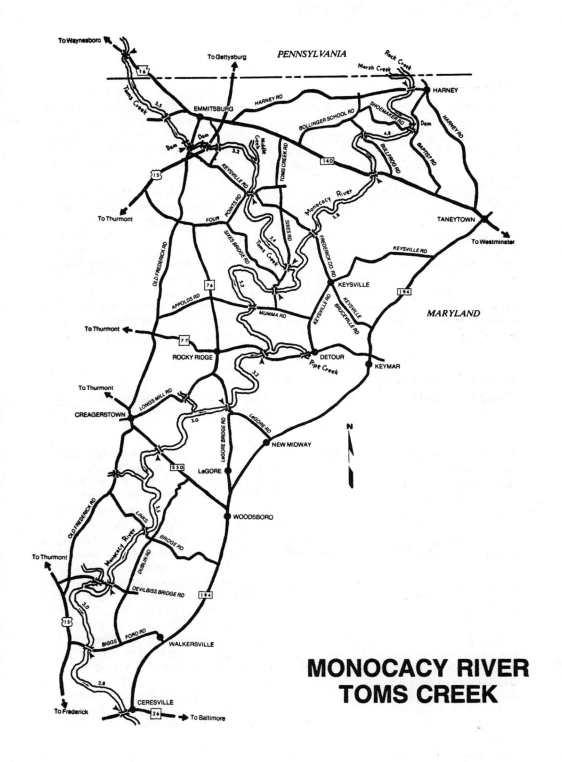

**MONOCACY RIVER
TOMS CREEK**

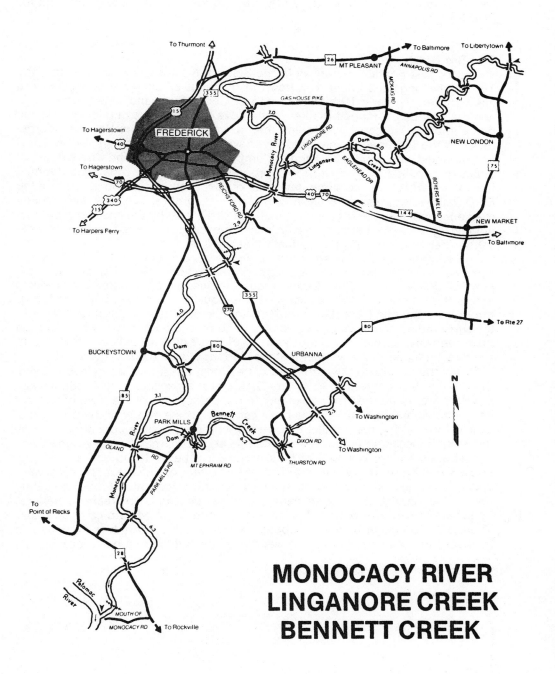

To Thurmont

To Baltimore   To Libertytown

26 MT PLEASANT   ANNAPOLIS RD

355   GAS HOUSE PIKE   MCKAIG RD   4.1

15   7.0   Monocacy River   LINGANORE RD   Dam 8.0   NEW LONDON

FREDERICK   Linganore   Linganore   Creek

To Hagerstown   40   EAGLEHEAD DR   BOYERS MILL RD   75

To Hagerstown   70   REICHS FORD RD   40 70   NEW MARKET

340   2.0   144   To Baltimore

15

To Harpers Ferry

355

270   80   To Rte 27

4.0

Dam   80   URBANNA

BUCKEYSTOWN

85   3.1   2.5   To Washington

River   PARK MILLS   Bennett   Creek   DIXON RD   To Washington

OLAND   Dam   6.2   THURSTON RD

RD   PARK MILLS RD   MT EPHRAIM RD

Monocacy

To
Point of Rocks   6.3

28

Potomac

River

MOUTH OF
MONOCACY RD   To Rockville

N

MONOCACY RIVER
LINGANORE CREEK
BENNETT CREEK

Gauge

USGS gauging station on right bank above Jug Bridge. Read outside staff or call 301-899-3210 after 11:30 A.M. (referred to as Frederick gauge). Gauge should read at least 2.9 feet to run river above Rte. 77 and at least 2.1 feet for river below Rte. 77.

The Big Ditch

The longest nontidal waterway in the State of Maryland was at one time the 184.5 mile long C&O Canal. This now mostly tree-filled ditch was conceived as a link between the early 19th century port of Georgetown and Washington, D.C. and the vast barely tapped market of the developing American midwest. As the name implies, the canal was to link the tidewater Chesapeake Bay via George-town on the Potomac to the Ohio River system. Construction started in 1828 and muddled along until 1850 and to Cumberland, Md. when and where financial difficulties spelled an end to further progress. Actually the canal was doomed from the start for on the same day of its official groundbreaking ceremony the B&O Railroad was also officially launched from Baltimore. The canal and the railroad engaged in a race for the west that was easily won by the cheaper and technologically superior railroad. Nevertheless the canal managed to survive until 1924 when one too many floods finally finished it off.

The engineering and construction of such a canal was no small feat in a day when earth moving was performed with only pick, shovel, wheelbarrow and black powder. Just to get to Cumberland required constructing 7 water supply dams across the Potomac, 74 lift locks, 11 stone aqueducts and a 3100-foot tunnel through a mountain (as a shortcut). Manning the project was a problem because the surrounding countryside was labor poor so most workers had to be imported from overseas, especially Ireland. With all of these difficulties coupled with constantly tight money it is a wonder that the glorious old ditch got as far as it did.

Today the canal and towpath are a recreational treasure. Twenty-two miles of the canal from Georgetown to Violets Lock and short sections near Oldtown and Big Pool are rewatered. Those desiring to paddle sections of the rewatered canal between Georgetown and Violets Lock can gain access at any of the points suggested for entering the parallel Potomac. If you plan to do a continuous trip on this stretch please note that at times certain segments may be drawn down and almost always there is a mile of interruptions just below I-495 and a short gap below Great Falls. These rewatered segments offer not only beautiful calmwater canoeing but also in a cold winter they convert into excellent outdoor ice skating rinks. The towpath is ideal for hiking, backpacking and, upstream of Seneca, horseback riding. Are you tired of overcrowded trailer-filled auto campgrounds? There are hiker-biker campsites about every five miles with tables, latrines and fireplaces, but no cars. For an old weed-filled ditch it is not a bad place to visit.

Marsh Creek

Introduction

Marsh Creek is the main headwaters of the Monocacy River, draining the Blue Ridge foothills west of Gettysburg, Pennsylvania. It passes through an attractive valley filled with prosperous looking dairy farms and a lot of history. While most of the stream is suitable for novices, a short gorge below U.S. Rte. 15 offers whitewater that will interest intermediate and advanced paddlers.

Section 1. Seven Stars (U.S. Rte. 30) to Business Rte. 15

Gradient	Difficulty	Distance	Time	Width	Scenery	Map
9	A-1,2	10.0	3.5	25-75	Very Good	29

Trip Description: What a fine way to tour beautiful, rural Adams County, Pa. When not winding through deep woods Marsh Creek glides past lovely well-kept dairy farms with their big brightly painted barns decorated with hex signs, sturdy old farm houses, and herds of sleek cattle. Banks are generally low allowing liberal views of all that is worth seeing. There are a few downed trees early in the trip and one rocky rapid at the ruins of an old mill dam but otherwise there is nothing more challenging than straightforward riffles. About two and a half miles below Pa. Rte. 116 is a covered bridge below which is a low sharp dam worth carrying.
Hazards: Fallen trees and a two-foot dam at Gettysburg Water Works.
Water Conditions: Winter and spring within two or three days of a good rain.

Gauge

None. USGS gauge at Jug Bridge near Frederick (call 301-899-3210 after 11:30 A.M.) should be at least 4.0 feet.

Section 2. Business Rte. 15 to Harney Road

Gradient	Difficulty	Distance	Time	Width	Scenery	Map
12*	1-3	6.0	2.0	50-100	Fair	29

*1 mile at 40 fpm

Trip Description: This section starts off fairly flat with another small dam to carry (runable with a clunk) and flows through fair scenery marred by summer homes. Below U.S. Rte. 15 the creek cuts a short wooded gorge through Harpers Hill creating some interesting whitewater that climaxes with three exciting, complex, boulder-choked rapids. Looking more like the Yough than Marsh Creek, this is by far the best piece of whitewater in the Monocacy Basin, short as it may be. The action concludes about a half mile below these rapids with a nasty plunge over a masonry-capped four-foot ledge. This is runable via a tight slot right of center or easily carried. Below here the stream quickly reverts to its original tranquil pace and, excepting an easy rapid through a washed out dam below Rock Creek, stays that way to the take-out at Harney Road, a half mile down the Monocacy.
Hazards: A thinly watered three-foot dam a half mile below Bus. Rte. 15 preferably carried, possible debris lodged in rapids and a sharp four-foot ledge below

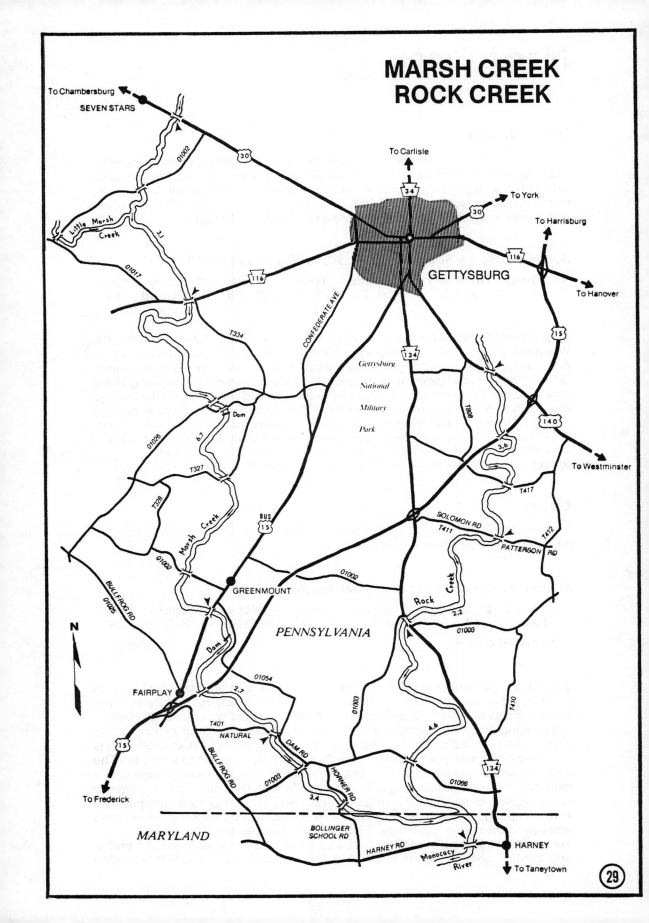

Harpers Hill Gorge.
Water Conditions: Same as Section 1.

Gauge

Same as Section 1.

Making Iron

In the late 18th and early 19th centuries an iron industry operated on a small and localized scale throughout the Middle Atlantic states. Remains of the old blast furnaces stand scattered about the countryside and include among them the well preserved structure at Stafford Bridge on Deer Creek, Catoctin Furnace south of Thurmont and one located between Metal and Richmond Furnace along the West Branch Conococheague Creek in Pennsylvania. The furnaces were supplied with raw materials from local sources. Various forms of iron ore are found throughout the region, even on the coastal plain of the Eastern Shore where it was called bog iron. Fuel was usually charcoal made from the wood of surrounding forests. The final ingredient, limestone, could be mined in much of central and western Maryland and adjacent Pennsylvania and on the coastal plain seashells were used. The furnaces were usually located near running water which was used to power the bellows that provided the essential blasts of hot air. Pig iron from these mills supplied most local needs, were a major source of cannon and cannonballs during the Revolution and War of 1812 and Rogers Mill on Deer Creek even supplied part of the iron that covered the Civil War iron-clad "Monitor".

Finally did you ever wonder why they call it pig iron? It seems that to receive the molten iron that was tapped from the base of the furnace a narrow channel was dug in the dirt floor in front of the furnace and branching off of this channel were identically shaped molds also dug in the ground. This configuration reminded somebody of a litter of piglets nursing on a sow, hence the term pigs for the molded iron forms.

Rock Creek

Introduction

Rock Creek is a rather mediocre stream winding through mostly farmland southeast of Gettysburg, Pa. The water is flat and the scenery contains nothing particularly memorable. It is really not worth driving a long way to paddle.

Section 1. Gettysburg (U.S. Rte. 140) to Harney Road

Gradient	Difficulty	Distance	Time	Width	Scenery	Map
7	1	10.5	3.5	20-50	Fair	29

Trip Description: One can start at Rte. 140 on the southeast side of Gettysburg or if the water level is marginal, at the roadbridge below Littles Run about three and a half miles downstream. These first three and a half miles flow past a rock quarry and busy Rte. 15 and is very drab and noisy. Below here are some pretty shale outcrops and some attractive farm structures; but high mud banks tend to block any real views across the countryside. The only thing resembling white-water on this trip is a curving rapid through the ruins of an old dam above the take-out. The take-out is on the Monocacy about a half mile below Marsh Creek. There is limited parking space at the east end of the Harney Road bridge.
Hazards: None
Water Conditions: Runable winter and spring after a hard rain.

Gauge

Need at least 4.5 feet at Frederick USGS gauge (call 301-899-3210 after 11:30 A.M.).

Toms Creek

Introduction

Toms Creek drains off the east slope of Catoctin Mountain around the Pennsylvania line west of Emmitsburg, Md. It offers the paddler a lot of easy whitewater while passing through a variety of attractive scenery which includes mountains, farms and one college campus.

Section 1. Carroll Valley (Pa. Rte. 16) to Sixes Bridge Road

Gradient	Difficulty	Distance	Time	Width	Scenery	Map
12	1-2	10.5	4.0	15-40	Good	27

Trip Description: The put-in is about a mile northwest of the Pennsylvania line. Here the stream is clear, shallow and rushes over a gravel bottom at the foot of Catoctin Mountain. Riffles may be complicated by fallen trees or barbed wire. There is a four-foot high dam about a hundred yards upstream of Business Rte. 15 that should be carried and another four-foot dam on the St. Josephs College Campus that can be run with a clunk. At moderate levels there is a safe playing keeper at the bottom. Below Emmitsburg the gradient slows but there are still plenty of riffles and a swift current to carry you through a pleasant pastoral landscape. The take-out road is narrow and offers poor parking so one might consider continuing a mile and a half downstream to Sixes Bridge on the Monocacy where conditions are slightly better.
Hazards: Trees and fences on the upper river. Two dams described above around Emmitsburg.
Water Conditions: Winter and spring within a few days of a hard rain.

Gauge

None. Judge riffles at put-in. Frederick gauge on the Monocacy (301-899-3210) should be reading at least 4.0 feet.

Head For the Hills

The western edge of the Monocacy Valley is dominated by the gentle bulk of Catoctin Mountain. Over ten thousand acres of this spur of the Blue Ridge, west of Thurmont, are protected and available for the public's enjoyment as they lie within the bounds of Catoctin Mountain Park and Cunningham Falls State Park. The parks feature over twenty-five miles of hiking trails (which in winter make dandy cross-country skiing trails), nature trails and interpretive exhibits, campgrounds, swimming, lake and trout stream fishing and points of interest such as Catoctin Furnace, Wolf Rock and Cunningham Falls. It is a fine place to retreat to when your knees can not take another hour in the canoe.

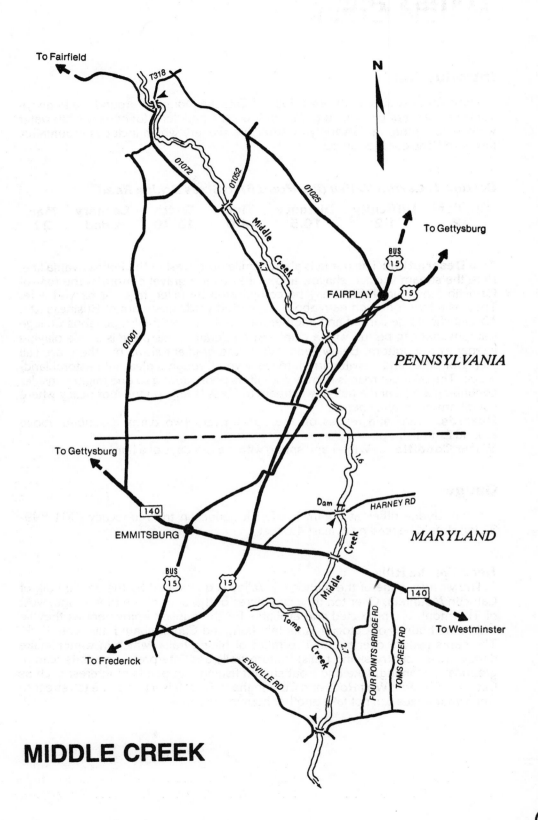

MIDDLE CREEK

30

Middle Creek

Introduction

Middle Creek is born on the eastern slope of the Blue Ridge Mountains and from there flows through a lightly populated valley in Adams Co., Pa. and Frederick Co., Md. to join Toms Creek near Emmitsburg. Neither the creek nor its watershed are very large but its forested mountain headwater drainage seems to sustain navigable water levels long enough for the lucky paddler to exploit them. The finest quality of Middle Creek is the presence of a delightful mile and a half stretch of white-water in a little gorge above Harney Road. It is well worth a visit when all the streams in the neighborhood are running high.

Section 1. Township Road T318 to Toms Creek

Gradient	Difficulty	Distance	Time	Width	Scenery	Map
18	A-3	8.0	2.5	15-25	Good	30

1 @ 40 fpm

Trip Description: The stream that you find at the put-in is not for the claustrophobic paddler for it is only about fifteen feet wide and squeezes even tighter downstream. The creek starts off flowing across a bed peppered with fairly large rounded boulders but since the gradient is rather modest there is no great danger or difficulty here, just some interesting natural slaloming in a woodland setting. An occasional fallen tree and three very stout cattle fences will require carries. The following miles to old Rte. 15 wind in and out of fields and woods with low banks allowing good views of what appears to be very thinly settled countryside. The current here is relatively sluggish with only occasional riffles and easy rapids. Below old Rte. 15 Middle Creek begins an enjoyable descent of low intermediate difficulty over a rocky bed through a gently sloped wooded gorge that cuts through what appears to be the same rock mass that forms the exciting Harpers Hill Gorge on nearby Marsh Creek. Rapids are formed by small boulders and ledges. Although not as exciting and as intense as the rapids on Marsh Creek, the unusually sharp streambed rocks should encourage one to paddle with their best form and finesse. The rapids end in the short pool of an eight-foot dam upstream of Harney Road. Just below Harney Road is a sharp two-foot weir that can be clunked over anywhere. Below here the creek slows its pace, displaying at best some gentle riffles. Meanwhile mudbanks begin to rise and block out a large portion of the view of the pretty farm country beyond. There is no access to the mouth of Middle Creek so continue another mile down Toms Creek to Keysville Road.

Hazards: Trees and fences will block the way on the upper stretches and an old mill dam above Harney Road is easily carried on the left.

Water Conditions: Runable within two days of hard rain in winter and spring. Snow melt conditions on Catoctin Mountain can sustain water even longer.

Gauge

None. Judge conditions along the road near the put-in or at Harney Road where the riffle below the mill dam should be clearly passable. Frederick gauge on the Monocacy (call 301-899-3210 after 11:30 A.M.) should probably read over five feet.

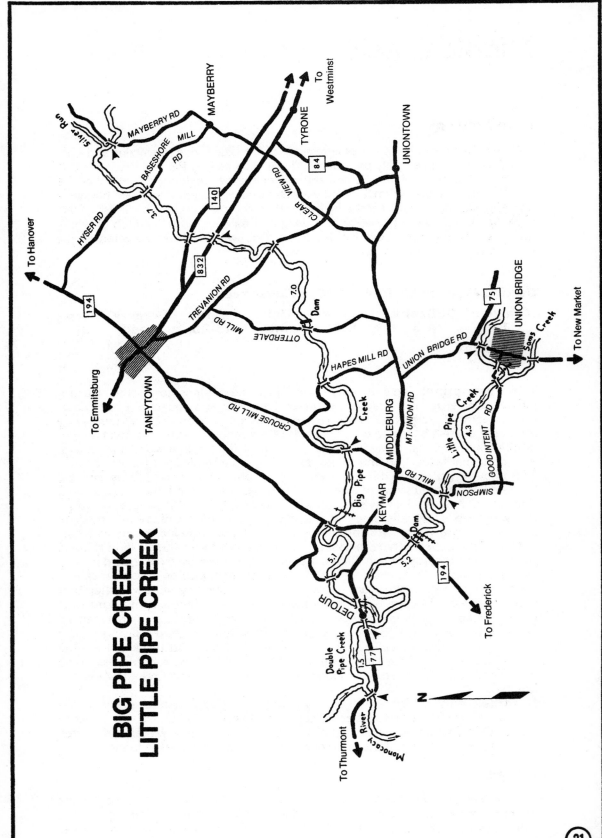

BIG PIPE CREEK,
LITTLE PIPE CREEK

31

Big Pipe Creek

Introduction

Big Pipe Creek is the Monocacy's largest tributary. Together with its tributary, Little Pipe Creek, it drains much of the western half of Carroll County, Maryland, flowing peacefully through a markedly rolling countryside of woodlands and well-kept dairy farms. In spite of its mild gradient Pipe Creek, like other streams of the Piedmont, was once extensively exploited for its water power. Today five old mills still stand along the miles described below as reminders of the importance of even these two-bit cow pasture brooks to the development of this country.

Section 1. Mayberry Road to Detour (Md. Rte. 77)

Gradient	Difficulty	Distance	Time	Width	Scenery	Map
9	A-1	16.0	5.0	25-80	Good	31

Trip Description: A navigable Pipe Creek is born with the addition of Silver Run at Mayberry Road. The initial few miles are rather small and a few trees, and maybe a fence, could impede your progress. But with the addition of Bear Branch and Meadow Branch below Md. Rte. 832 the volume swells and the going gets easy. Just below Rte. 832 is a low-water bridge that at most levels must be carried. There is a six-foot dam at Otterdale Mills with a short tight carry on the left. A two-foot dam at Crouses Mill is run through a lively chute on the left and there is a small breached dam at the Penn-Central R.R. bridge at Bruceville that presents no problems at moderate levels. Outside of the dams, the closest thing to whitewater are well-spaced gravel bar riffles. The scenery ranges from well-kept farms to overgrown fields to cool hemlock-covered bluffs to low red sandstone and shale cliffs. Little Pipe Creek joins just above the town of Detour and the stream now officially is called Double Pipe Creek. Incidentally, Detour was once also called Double Pipe Creek but the Western Maryland R.R. needed a shorter name to fit on their timetable so for some unknown reason the name Detour was adopted. Detour is an easy and convenient place to take out; but if you are a purist, continue another one and a half miles to Md. Rte. 77 bridge below the confluence with the Monocacy.

Hazards: Low-water bridge below Rte. 832 and six-foot dam at Otterdale Mill carried on left.

Water Conditions: Runable within three days of a hard rain during winter or spring. Water runs off faster in streams draining into the Monocacy from the agricultural lands to the east than from the forested slopes of Catoctin Mountain.

Gauge

USGS gauge at Bruceville, downstream left of Rte. 194 bridge, should read at least 1.75 feet and Frederick gauge on the Monocacy (call 301-899-3210 after 11:30 A.M.) should read approximately 4.0 feet to negotiate entire run.

Little Pipe Creek

Introduction

Little Pipe Creek starts on the west side of Westminster, Maryland, seat of beautiful rural Carroll County. It gathers enough water to float a canoe by the time it reaches the town of Union Bridge and from there twists and turns along the Frederick County line to join the Big Pipe at Detour.

Section 1. Union Bridge (Md. Rte. 75) to Detour (Md. Rte. 77)

Gradient	Difficulty	Distance	Time	Width	Scenery	Map
8	A-1	9.5	3.0	20-40	Fair	31

Trip Description: The suggested trip starts at Union Bridge, so named as the original bridge here over Pipe Creek united several Quaker settlements in the area. The start is not too inspiring as the scenery which includes houses, trash, and scrubby vegetation is rather drab and the stream may be blocked by a log jam or two and at least one fence. Below Sams Creek the volume increases enough to flush out most obstacles and the scenery improves progressively with the appearance of pretty farms and small red cliffs. Most of the water is flat with one sharp three-foot dam located under the Penn-Central Railroad trestle, above Md. Rte. 194, requiring a short brushy carry. The take-out is on Big Pipe Creek.
Hazards: Trees, log jams and fences come and go, mostly in the first few miles and an unrunable three-foot dam above Rte. 194.
Water Conditions: Runable winter and spring within two days of hard rain.

Gauge

None. Frederick gauge on the Monocacy should read at least 4.5 feet.

News From the Underground

The Little Pipe Creek Valley gives the impression of being wall to wall farmland but underlying this area are extensive mineral deposits and there has been considerable activity about this region to exploit this wealth. During colonial times copper was mined southeast of Johnsburg and Maryland's only lead mine operated near Union Bridge around 1880. The most valuable mineral mined here today is limestone. The huge Lehigh-Portland Cement plant at Union Bridge consumes massive quantities of limestone pulled from its quarry along Sams Creek and other quarries in the neighborhood mine the stone for use as aggregate for construction. Even the shale around here has worth as Lehigh-Portland mines the material from a deposit southwest of here near Woodsboro where it roasts the rock to produce a special form of lightweight aggregate.

Linganore Creek

Introduction

Linganore Creek once offered a pleasant uncomplicated cruise through the rolling farmlands of eastern Frederick County. Then in the early '70s private interests dammed the prettiest gorge on the creek creating a four mile long lake to be fringed by a housing development. Today you get to run the leftovers.

Section 1. Md. Rte. 75 to Linganore Road

Gradient	Difficulty	Distance	Time	Width	Scenery	Map
11	A-1	12.0	4.0	20-45	Fair	28

Trip Description: The run starts out nicely enough, passing through attractive woods and pastureland and past some pretty rock formations. The water is swift, muddy and spotted with many easy riffles. This all ends below Gas House Pike with the backwater of Lake Linganore. The lake entails about four miles of dead-water paddling with scenery that is not particularly interesting unless you are shopping for a homesite. The only reward for this lousy paddle is to get to behold what has to be the world's most imaginative (which is synonomous with hideous) dam design. After seeing the dam, the rest of the day will be anticlimatic. The scenery continues fair as the stream passes in and out of short, wooded gorges and the current remains swift. The suggested take-out is about a quarter mile above the Monocacy River. Those desiring to float the whole way can take out on the Monocacy at Jug Bridge about a half mile below the confluence.
Hazards: Lake Linganore Dam, carry on left.
Water Conditions: Winter and spring within day of hard rain.

Gauge

Painted canoe gauge on Old Annapolis Road bridge, must read above zero; USGS gauge below Lake Linganore should read at least 2.8 feet and Frederick gauge on the Monocacy should roughly be at least five feet.

Bennett Creek

Introduction

Bennett Creek starts near Clarksburg in western Montgomery County, flows into Frederick County, around the base of Sugarloaf Mountain, and empties into the Monocacy six miles above the mouth. It is a pleasant run through thinly populated rolling farm country and it is ideal for novices who are skilled enough to stop for trees, fences, and other strainers in a fast current.

Section 1. Md. Rte. 355 to Monocacy River

Gradient	Difficulty	Distance	Time	Width	Scenery	Map
11	A-1	8.5	3.0	15-40	Good	28

Trip Description: It is possible to drive right past the put-in for the stream, as it is only a fifteen foot wide brook meandering about a pastoral bottomland. Except for the rather persistent presence of a high voltage powerline, this is a scenic cruise; first through farmland, then below I-270 through woodlands. The stream passes striking rock formations, well-preserved old houses, and the nearby bulk of lonely Sugarloaf Mountain. There are hundreds of little riffles over gravel bars and a few broken ledges. Fallen trees and log jams are common but most have a passage around them. There is a low-water bridge about a mile below Little Bennett Creek that must be carried, and just below Park Mills Bridge, there is a three and a half-foot dam that should be scouted. Take out at Lilypons Bridge over the Monocacy about a quarter mile below the confluence.

As you cruise down past the pretty hemlock shaded slopes approaching Park Mills, try to picture yourself paddling through a major colonial industrial center. Almost two hundred years ago, a bustling self-contained company town peopled by over 300 mostly German immigrants and structured around the manufacture of glass, was carved out of the wilderness near this spot; big time industry by the standards of the time. Like many such ventures, it thrived for a while, then declined; now, trees, birds, and solitude give little hint of the area's former glory.

Hazards: Trees and log jams, a low-water bridge below Little Bennett Creek, and a small dam below Park Mills that is runable in dead center but has a powerful reversal at the bottom that should be considered before attempting.

Water Conditions: Canoeable within two days of hard rain.

Gauge

USGS gauge on Mt. Ephraim Road just upstream from Park Mills should read at least 2.0 feet..To judge at put-in, there should be at least six inches of water in the little gravel riffle immediately below Rte. 355.

Seneca Creek

Introduction

Seneca Creek drains the heart of Montgomery County. Although the suburbs creep closer every year it still affords a chance to paddle a small stream through fields and woods close to Washington, D.C.

Section 1. Brink Road to Md. Rte. 28

Gradient	Difficulty	Distance	Time	Width	Scenery	Map
10	1	13.5	4.5	15-25	Fair	32

Trip Description: This section is officially called Great Seneca Creek but it is really quite small. The stream winds about between often high mud banks through scrubby woods. There are a lot of fallen trees and some huge log jams blocking the way. Also there is a low-water bridge early in the trip and just below the B&O Railroad bridge is a four-foot high dam (sewer crossing) of jagged rubble with protruding sharp strands of wire that should be carried. The best part of this section is located below Md. Rte. 118, where the creek rushes through a pretty wooded gorge, over some lively riffles, and past the old Blackrock Mill.
Hazards: Logs and log jams, a culvert-type low-water bridge and the jagged sewer dam below the B&O Railroad.
Water Conditions: Winter and spring within day of hard rain.

Gauge

USGS gauging station on right bank below Md. Rte. 28 bridge should read at least 3.25 feet to put in as high as Brink Road.

Section 2. Md. Rte. 28 to Potomac River

Gradient	Difficulty	Distance	Time	Width	Scenery	Map
7	A-1	6.0	2.0	25-40	Fair	32

Trip Description: The stream, now joined by Little Seneca Creek is a little larger but still blocked occasionally by big log jams. It contains nothing more challenging than easy riffles, flowing over fine gravel, and the crumbling ruins of an old dam. The view, when there is one, is still of fields and woods with a few pretty rock outcrops thrown in. The last half mile below River Road is a backwater of the Potomac filled with motorboats and lined with shabby summer dwellings. Take out at the old C&O Canal aqueduct.
Hazards: Log jams.
Water Conditions: Winter and spring within week of rain.

Gauge

USGS gauging station at Rte. 28 should read at least 2.1 feet.

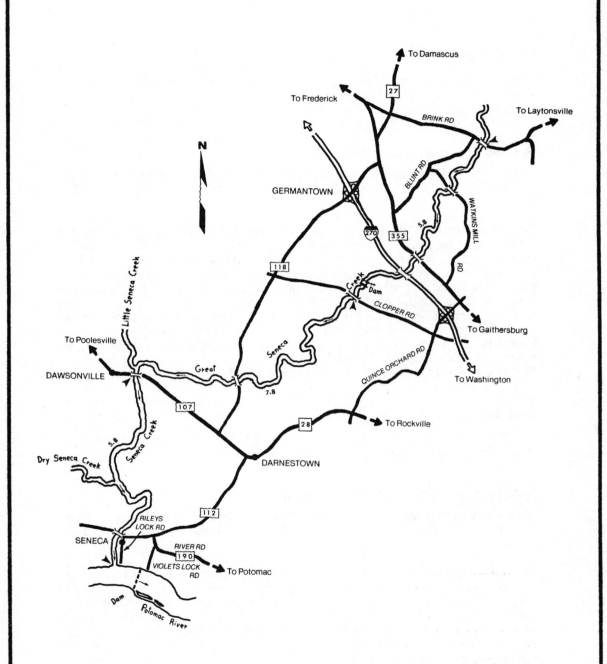

SENECA CREEK

Rock Creek

Introduction

Rock Creek slices down the middle of Montgomery County and Washington, D.C., to join the Potomac at Georgetown. Because it flows through a basin that has been almost completely and comprehensively urbanized, the creek has been reduced to a storm drain function with flows fluctuating radically between flash floods and trickles. Nevertheless, a spacious floodplain park in Montgomery County and one of the finest city parks in the nation in Washington has screened off the stream from most of the surrounding sprawl and created an ideal backyard refuge for local paddlers who can get there on time.

Section 1. Rockville (Md. Rte. 28, Baltimore Road) to Potomac River

Gradient	Difficulty	Distance	Time	Width	Scenery	Map
12*	1,4	21.0	6.0	20-50	Good	33

*.5 at 80 fpm

Trip Description: Most of the Montgomery County portion is characterized by fast flat water broken by easy gravel bar riffles. There are a lot of trees, log jams, and snags in the upper part, but most can be paddled around or under at medium levels. At a few spots, oxbow channels offer fine bypasses around the tree-blocked main channel. A long curving box culvert under the Chessie tracks and Knowles Avenue offers a cheap thrill, flushing through total darkness at high velocity. As of this writing, the left channel is unobstructed. The scenery behind the usually steep mud banks is mostly woods or open park land; some highway noise and a few miles of Beltway are the only really obnoxious civilized intrusions. This section is at its best during summer when the dense foliage screens off much of the outside world.

Before paddling into D.C. the canoeist must first secure a permit from the National Park Service to boat on Rock Creek. To obtain this permit, which is good for a year, write the Park Superintendent, Rock Creek Park, 5000 Glover Road, N.W., Washington, D.C. 20015, being sure to describe your craft, level of skill, experience, and what section you want to run. A final word of caution; the authorities frown on paddling the creek at rush hour because gawking motorists on nearby Beach Drive would quickly cause a mammoth traffic jam. This is a very real problem, so stay off during rush hours.

As Rock Creek enters D.C., the surrounding slopes close in and form a lovely shallow gorge that extends to the Potomac. At Military Road, the creek undergoes a total change in personality as the bottom suddenly drops out. This section plunges over the Fall Line at an initially violent rate of 80 feet per mile. There, the bed is filled with sharp boulders, current increases in velocity, and the visibility of underwater obstacles is extremely poor due to the thick muddy water. The gradient eases off after a half mile and by Pierce Mill Dam, two miles below Military Road, the water is mostly flat again. Pierce Mill Dam is a picturesque seven foot high structure with a churning, hungry-looking reversal at the bottom that makes a portage the best of decisions. Below here, Rock Creek is a smooth coast with only a few fords (scrapey) and pipe crossings to add excitement. The exit into the Potomac is dramatic with views of the Kennedy Center, Rosslyn, and the broad Potomac. Take out a few yards upstream at the docks of the Harry Thompson Boat Center (good parking just opposite Virginia Avenue).

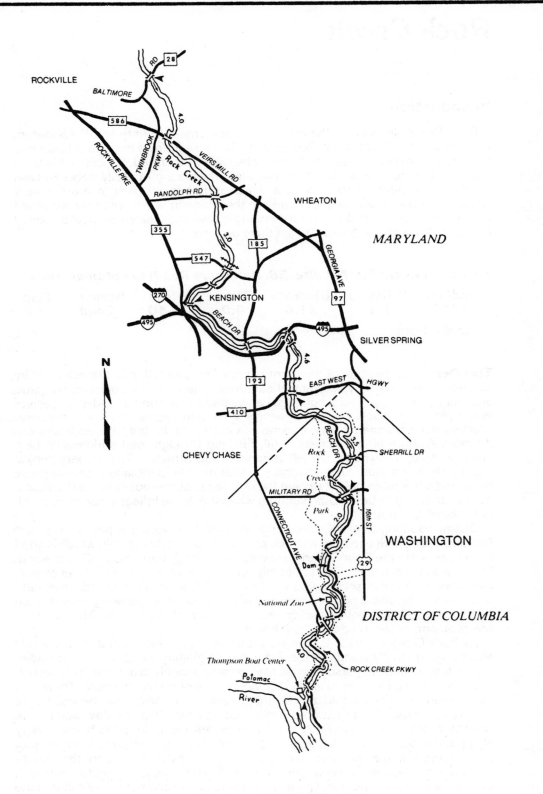

ROCKVILLE

BALTIMORE

RD 28

586

TWINBROOK PKWY

ROCKVILLE PIKE

Rock Creek

VEIRS MILL RD

4.0

RANDOLPH RD

WHEATON

MARYLAND

355

547

3.0

185

GEORGIA AVE

270

495

KENSINGTON

BEACH DR

495

97

SILVER SPRING

N

193

410

4.6

EAST WEST HGWY

CHEVY CHASE

BEACH DR

Rock

3.5

SHERRILL DR

Creek

MILITARY RD

CONNECTICUT AVE

Park

2.0

16th ST

WASHINGTON

29

Dam

National Zoo

DISTRICT OF COLUMBIA

4.0

Thompson Boat Center

Potomac

River

ROCK CREEK PKWY

ROCK CREEK

33

This trip is easily subdivided at East-West Highway, mile 11.5. Above East-West Highway, the trip has Class I and obstacles; below, it has the fall line and the major rapids. Below Pierce Mill dam, the right bank is the National Zoo. Good scouting and easy access is afforded by Beach Drive which parallels the stream throughout D.C. and part of Montgomery County.

Hazards: Fallen trees, log jams and even floating picnic tables at high water. Pierce Mill Dam two miles below Military Road should be carried on right.

Water Conditions: Runable within 24 hours of hard rain, but ideal water levels last only for a few hours after the rain stops.

Gauge

USGS gauge at Sherrill Drive. For the steep section about 2.5 feet is minimal and 5.0 feet is ideal plus the highest level that the Park Police will let you run it at. For the rest of the creek any riffle on a wide spot is an adequate indicator.

Paddlers Unite

The growing popularity of paddling has resulted in the appearance of paddling communities and clubs in about every sizable town. A membership in a canoe club will be the best buy for your boating dollar that you will ever find. Besides offering you the chance to meet other people of similar interests many clubs conduct excellent educational programs. Here is a chance to pick up techniques that might take you years to learn on your own, and it is free. Clubs serve as a marketplace to buy and sell the highly specialized boating equipment that regular newspaper ads could never serve. This is the place to keep up with the latest techniques, materials and other consumer information. If a new safety hazard appears on a nearby stream, this will be your first opportunity to learn about it other than the hard way. If a property owner along a stream likes to use canoeists for target practice, this is the most attractive way to learn about it. Essentially a club is your contact with the world of paddling and no matter if you go boating once a year or every week or if you are a rugged loner or love to immerse yourself in crowds, you will unquestionably get the most out of the sport if you keep in touch.

The following are some clubs that frequent the area described in this guidebook. Since most club contacts change from year to year an inquiry at your local outing store should produce an address.

Washington, D.C.: Canoe Cruisers Association (P.O. Box 572, Arlington, Va. 22216)
Blue Ridge Voyageurs
Baltimore: Greater Baltimore Canoe Club (P.O. Box 591, Ellicott City, Md. 21043)
Wilmington: Wilmington Trail Club (P.O. Box 1184, Wilmington, Del. 19899)
Buck Ridge Ski Club
Frederick: Monocacy Canoe Club (P.O. Box 1083, Frederick, Md. 21701)
Hagerstown: Mason Dixon Canoe Cruisers
York: Conewago Canoe Club
Pittsburgh: Three Rivers Paddling Club
Philadelphia: Philadelphia Canoe Club (4900 Ridge Ave., Philadelphia, Pa. 19128)
West Virginia: West Virginia Wildwater Association (P.O. Box 8361, S. Charleston, W.Va. 25303)
Virginia: Coastal Canoeists (P.O. Box 566, Richmond, Va. 23204)

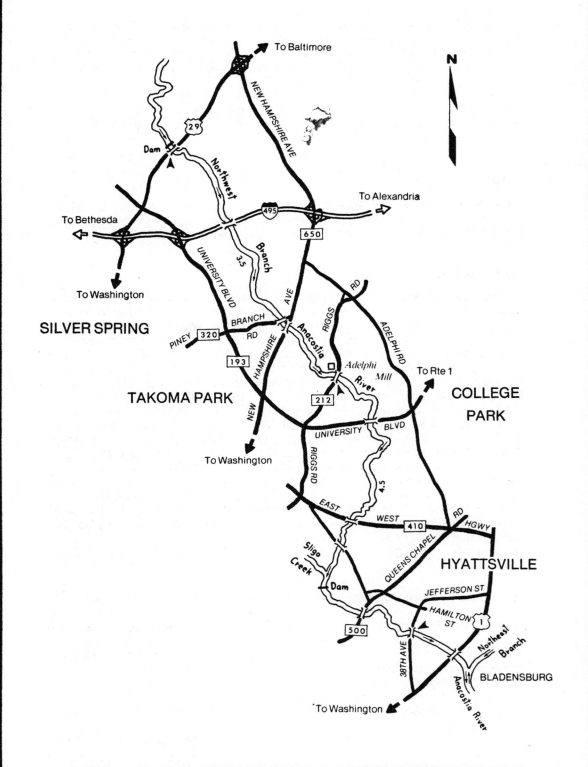

NORTHWEST BRANCH ANACOSTIA RIVER

Northwest Branch Anacostia River

Introduction

The Northwest Branch is the aesthetically redeeming silver lining in the dismal cloud of the Anacostia Basin. This is a basin that provides countless textbook examples of the ill effects of totally urbanized watersheds, water pollution, erosion and sedimentation problems, surface mining abuse (sand and gravel), flash flooding and suburban blight. Amazingly however, this list does not include a relatively bad record of ravaging floods; thanks to the wise foresight of the local bicounty planning agency, most of the local floodplains were long ago purchased and converted to parkland. In one such park lies a narrow fall line gorge and in this gorge runs the Northwest Branch, hidden for three and a half pleasant miles from the surrounding drab development. This and maybe even the section downstream is a worthwhile choice for the Washington or Baltimore area paddler waking up from an all night rain and wondering what to paddle.

Section 1. U.S. Rte. 29 to Hyattsville (38th Avenue)

Gradient	Difficulty	Distance	Time	Width	Scenery	Map
25	1-3	8.0	2.5	25-50	Good to Poor	34

Trip Description: Most paddlers will be only interested in cruising the first three and a half miles to Riggs Road (Adelphi Mill). The purist will want to put in right at the U.S. Rte. 29 bridge at the head of an enticing rapid but before doing so be sure to hike downstream (left bank) about 150 yards and decide if you care to risk a possible swim through the cataract below. Either way, the non-death wish paddler will want to portage about a hundred yards along a narrow path high on the left bank and put back in at a small grassy area below. The final four-foot ledge of this steep stretch has a narrow, clean slot on the right (if not clogged by logs) and at high levels can be run dead center. Following the bouldery runout below, the stream calms to just straightforward riffles and fast current through a lovely gorge with few views of houses and apartments that lie just beyond the rim. Directly under the high I-495 bridge rushes a narrow, twisting, and with more than a foot of canoeable water, a rather pushy rapid. Poor visibility and chance of a surprise log make this one worth scouting. The stream slowly calms down again but all the way to Riggs Road it maintains the ability to throw up some bouncy waves, rocky passages, and playable holes. A paved bicycle path and sewer right-of-way detract some from the wild atmosphere of the gorge but nevertheless it is still very pretty, especially in the summertime when the surrounding foliage is thick and steaming. At Riggs Road the surrounding slopes diverge and the stream enters the coastal plain. Now it winds about open parkland backed by houses, shopping centers, and apartments. The water now runs flat but at a very high velocity. Paddlers must still be alert for trees, low bridges and most importantly, just below Sligo Creek (right) within sight of two large gas storage tanks, a very sharp four-foot dam with a terminal roller at the bottom. Do not get swept into this trap. The take-out at 38th Avenue offers a final bouncy manmade rapid before the stream is channelized and levee-bound to tidewater at Bladensburg.

It is worth noting that two hundred years ago Bladensburg was an active seaport serving the thriving local tobacco industry. However, tobacco cultivation resulted in rampant soil erosion that eventually turned the harbor to a swamp. The river in recent times has been dredged and channelized but siltation still continues and Bladensburg's future as even a motorboat harbor seems insecure.

Hazards: Series of large, vicious drops starting about a hundred yards below Rte. 29 should be carried; easiest on left. A four-foot dam, just below Sligo Creek, forms a dangerous roller; carry right. If water is really high there will be some bridge clearance problems.

Water Conditions: Runable only within 24 hours of a hard rainfall. This is unfortunately a flash flooding type stream and gets more so each year as the watershed becomes increasingly developed.

Gauge

There is a USGS gauge on the right end of the Queens Chapel Road bridge (Md. Rte. 500) but this tends to be meaningless when the height there reflects a crest that probably left the put-in two hours ago. Accordingly, the only reliable way to judge the stream's fast changing levels, is to go to the put-in and if water looks passable there, then exploit it immediately. If putting in at Rte. 29, check out the rock garden at the foot of the cataract section which will represent the scrapiest spot that you will find.

Other Information

As stated earlier the Anacostia River and its tributaries are not distinguished for their beauty. Oddly enough, the State of Maryland has passed a bill designating this a State Wild and Scenic River, a move that no doubt can be attributed to some far out political chicanery that you or I will never understand. The Anacostia is fed by six major tributaries; Sligo Creek, Northwest Branch, Paint Branch, Little Paint Branch, Indian Creek and Northeast Branch. Sligo has some excellent whitewater and flows through a pretty park but is difficult to catch up and you may be harrassed by park police if you try it. Paint Branch has an interesting and attractive fall line gorge but most of it is off limits, flowing through the Naval Ordnance Laboratory grounds (blocked by solid chain-link fence). Little Paint Branch is little and ugly. Indian Creek has too many trees. And the Northeast Branch, while possessing one exciting bouncy rapid at Riverdale Road formed by the rubble dam at the head of the leveed flood channel, is pure drabness.

The mainstream Anacostia is all tidal. It was once a broad marsh fringed estuary but over the years dredging spoils from the river have been used to fill the marshes to form the present shape of the river and its adjacent parklands. Besides the normal collection of tennis courts, baseball diamonds and other recreational facilities these parklands include such attractions as the Kenilworth Aquatic Gardens, National Arboretum and Washington Navy Yard Museum. Actually a rather pleasant urban excursion of nine miles can be had here, starting at Bladensburg Marina and finishing at the Roaches Run boat ramp located off of the Potomac just north of National Airport (accessible via George Washington Memorial Parkway). Besides being conveniently near for D.C. area paddlers, exploring the woodsy backwaters around the Aquatic Gardens can turn up a lot of waterfowl while the outdoor riverside display of missiles, submarines and other armaments at the Navy Museum will be quite unlike any riparian environment you will see elsewhere.

Mattawoman Creek

Introduction

Mattawoman Creek starts in Cedarville State Forest, forms part of the Prince Georges-Charles County border and then finally joins the Potomac at Indian Head. It is small, winding, tangled and choked; a classic coastal plain obstacle course. The paddler, who makes it down this one, will have done a real day's work.

Section 1. Bealle Hill Road to Md. Rte. 225

Gradient	Difficulty	Distance	Time	Width	Scenery	Map
8	A-1	11.0	10.0	10-20	Fair	35

Trip Description: One can and probably will want to shorten this trip with access at Billingsley Road, Md. Rte. 227 or Bumpy Oak Road. There is no preferable section to attempt as the fallen trees are rather evenly distributed with maddening frequency throughout the length. Understand that negotiating fallen logs is no safe endeavor. One risks breaking one's neck getting out on one of the many slippery, black rotting ones and terminal dermatitis getting out on one of the high and dry ones which often support lush growths of poison ivy (in winter recognized by hairy vines with pretty white clusters of berries). Those trees that are best portaged around have invariably fallen in dense patches of greenbriars, poison ivy, etc., which you will almost invariably have to wade through. Since this stream has some gradient, a misjudgment in water level could add dragging over gravel bars to your troubles. Finally because the scenery includes power lines, some houses, and a wide, grassy right-of-way (purpose unknown) paralleling the left bank the whole way, the aesthetic compensation just does not justify the effort. If you want to paddle a swamp, try Zekiah or the Patuxent.
Hazards: Fallen trees, briars, poison ivy and beaver dams.
Water Conditions: Passable in late fall, winter, and spring within few days of rain.

Gauge

There is an old staff gauge in the left bank about a hundred feet below the Rte. 227 bridge. A level of 2.0 feet is zero.

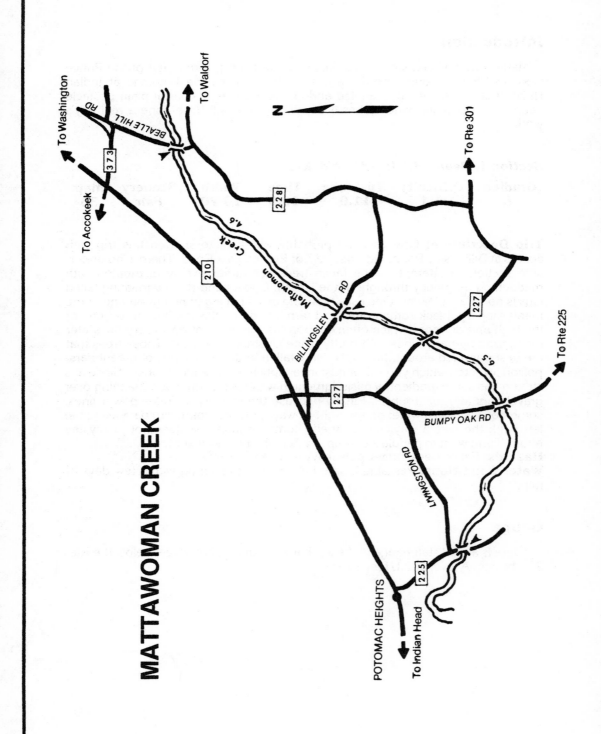

MATTAWOMAN CREEK

Nanjemoy Creek and
Hill Top Fork

Introduction

Nanjemoy Creek is a tidal tributary to the Potomac River in Charles County, Maryland, located only forty miles south of Washington, D.C. Despite its proximity to the big city, it and its little tributary, the Hill Top Fork, remain still relatively undeveloped: a fine place for leisurely paddling, good birdwatching and for soaking up peace and quiet.

Section 1. Md. Rte. 6 to Friendship Landing

Gradient	Difficulty	Distance	Time	Width	Scenery	Map
0	A	6.0	3.5	20-500	Very Good	36

Trip Description: The suggested route is on the upper reaches of this creek as its lower four miles swell to a monstrous lakelike estuary with relatively little intimacy or character and lots of wind, waves and developed shoreline. The put-in at Rte. 6 is at the absolute head of tidewater. The first few yards are narrow and shallow and may be complicated by a log or two. But then for the rest of the way it is all easy going. The banks are initially swampy but that quickly gives way to broad marshes backed by graceful wooded bluffs. A few houses and duck blinds are all the development that you will find until approaching Friendship Landing and it is easy to imagine this as typical Chesapeake Bay country scenery that one might have enjoyed three hundred years ago. Tempting camping opportunities abound here but since this is all private land, permission should be secured first. A public launching ramp at Friendship Landing provides easy egress.

An additional bit of pleasant exploring is to be had by striking eastward from Friendship Landing and ascending Hill Top Fork. This is initially a wide shallow estuary with a channel found on its east side. The creek rapidly narrows though and then twists for about a mile up through the marshes until you can proceed no further. The surrounding wooded bluffs are undeveloped and the remote atmosphere is even more complete than back on Nanjemoy.

Hazards: None
Water Conditions: Tidal. Runable year round except when frozen.

Gauge

None.

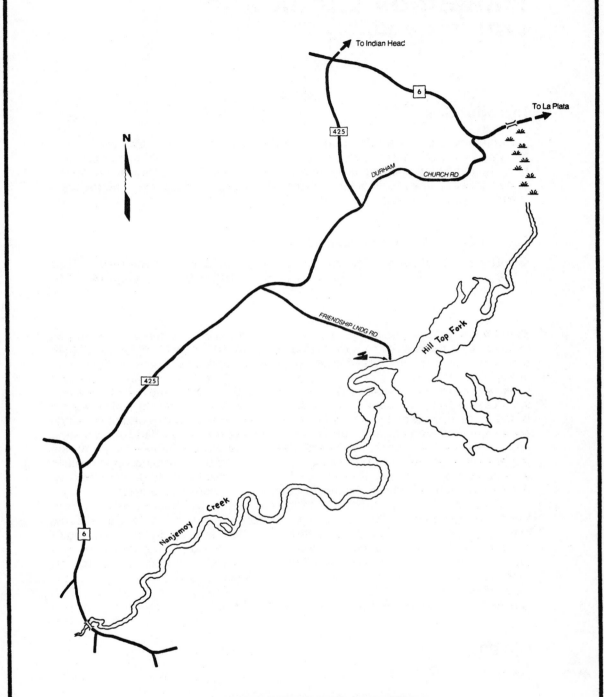

To Indian Head

6

425

DURHAM CHURCH RD

To La Plata

N

FRIENDSHIP LNDG RD

Hill Top Fork

425

Nanjemoy Creek

6

NANJEMOY CREEK
HILL TOP FORK

36

Zekiah Swamp Run

Introduction

Zekiah Swamp cuts a north-south swath across Charles County from Cedarville State Forest to tidewater at the head of the Wicomico River. Zekiah Swamp Run is a meandering, often braiding, sometimes rushing, and sometimes oozing ribbon draining the heart of this sodden woodland. The Swamp envelopes a sizeable wilderness, less than an hour from the center of Washington, D.C., while the Run is the best path to explore it. And here is where the problem lies, for Zekiah Swamp Run is probably the most uncanoeable stream for its size in the state. If you are just a casual paddler, skip this description; but, if you feel that something worth seeing is worth fighting for, then read on.

Section 1. Md. Rte. 5 to Allens Fresh (Md. Rte. 234)

Gradient	Difficulty	Distance	Time	Width	Scenery	Map
8	A-1	11.0	14.0	3-30	Good	37

Trip Description: Zekiah is the ultimate challenge to navigability. Like other troublesome small coastal plain streams, progress is repeatedly blocked by scores of fallen trees. But that is not all. The run periodically braids, not just into two or three channels but dozens, all of which degenerate into trickles too small to float a boat. But that is not all. Cute cuddly little beavers have dammed and flooded portions of the swamp, creating shallow ponds filled to the surface with dense growths of water weeds (even in winter). This forms a media that is too thick to paddle through but too thin to walk on or pole through. But that is not all. A lot of the dead, flooded still-standing trees in the beaver ponds have been cemented together by thick mats of airborne vines that almost require the services of a machete to penetrate. Nevertheless, people have beaten their canoes through this jungle and so can you. The described run is divided almost in half by Md. Rte. 6. Use this access. With progress, sometimes measured inch by inch, consider five to six miles of Zekiah a full day's work.

Having been forewarned of its faults, let us not overlook the charms of Zekiah. First and foremost, it is wild. The swamp is about a mile wide and surrounded by farms and more woodlands. Hence it is quiet down there. You will not see another soul except maybe during hunting season; the water is clear and clean, there is no trash and litter, and except for an occasional deer stand, there is no development. The trees of the swamp are lovely but particularly memorable are the dense groves of holly trees in the last few miles. Finally the last few miles are an exception to the above mentioned hardships. Here the stream gushes its healthy volume down only a few channels, at least one of which is usually unobstructed, and even rushes over little riffles formed by bars of fine gravel. The last few hundred yards are tidal and if you go there in early spring when the perch and shad are running, this stretch will be elbow to elbow with fishermen. Take out on the left at Rte. 234 bridge.

Hazards: Trees during high water and even at normal levels in the last three miles can be dangerous due to the strong current.

Water Conditions: Runable late fall, winter and spring except after prolonged dry period.

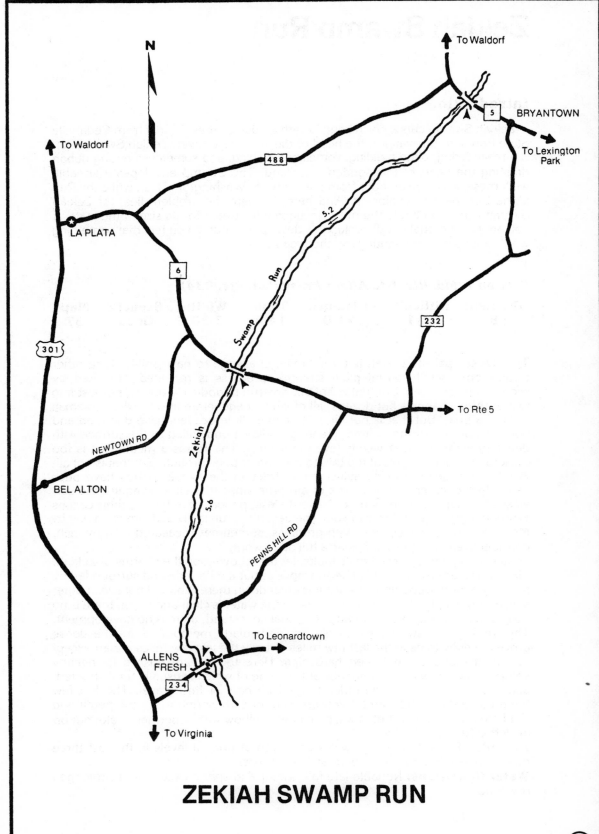

ZEKIAH SWAMP RUN

Gauge

None.

Inside Swamps

Swamps and low floodplains are the closest you will get in Maryland or Delaware to canoeing through a jungle. Since the rich botanical diversity of this environment is one of its finest features the paddler should at least be able to recognize some of the more common tree types in this forest. The most unusual tree found in the swamp is the bald cypress and Maryland marks the northern limit of its range. Cypress has needles and cones like an evergreen but sheds its leaves (needles) in the fall like a hardwood. The tree can grow to immense size and live to an incredible age and even after it is dead its wood is extremely rot resistant. The most unusual feature of the cypress though are its knees. The knees are conical projections of the root system that rise from the water at the base of the tree to provide air for the roots. Most of the local cypress grows on the Eastern Shore but the Western Shore has one small beautiful stand, owned by the Nature Conservancy, found along Battle Creek in Calvert County and this can be partly explored on foot. One of the most common swamp trees is the red maple. This usually modest-sized tree with small three-lobed leaves distinguishes itself in autumn with a flaming display of red foliage. Another fall standout is the black tupelo, recognized by small oval leaves that turn scarlet in autumn and pairs of tiny blue-black fruit. While Christmas comes only once a year, the coastal plain swamps are bountifully decked with holly year round. The red fruit of the American holly is best appreciated after October when they stand in such bold contrast to the gray and black of the winter swamp. An even better display is put on by the possumhaw with its large clusters of red fruit. Another common tree, the sweet gum, is identified by its five-lobed starlike leaves that also turn brilliant colors in fall and its burlike round seedpods. The pods, about an inch and a half in diameter, are also popular as Christmas decorations. When high ground appears in coastal plain swamps, beech trees also appear. Possessing paper smooth gray bark, toothed oval leaves and often reaching great size, these trees bear small chestnut-like burs which yield two tetrahedral nuts per bur which in turn contain a very edible and delicious meat. Finally there is poison ivy. True, this is not a tree but it grows all over so many of them that it should be discussed here. Most people know poison ivy by its three shiny leaves but since much swamp paddling is done in colder months, winter identification is important. At this time it is recognized by its black hairy vines and clusters of small white berries. The author learned this lesson the hard way. It seems that upon first sighting the shrub he misidentified it as mistletoe and being a few weeks before Christmas he decided to participate in tradition by picking a sprig, taking it back to his office and hanging it over the doorway in hopes of coercing a kiss from the cute blond secretary down the hall. The days came and went, so did the secretary and so did mysterious rashes and chronic itching. After a few months he tossed the sprig away in disgust and without ever so much as a lousy peck on the cheek.

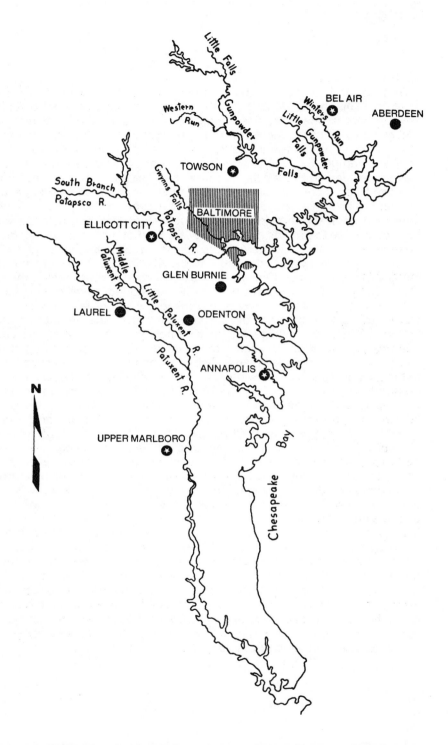

WEST CHESAPEAKE BAY TRIBUTARIES

Chapter 4

West Chesapeake Drainage

The West Chesapeake Drainage encompasses all streams flowing into the Chesapeake between the Potomac and the Susquehanna. All of these streams are small and relatively short and those described herein all start on the rolling agricultural lands of the Piedmont and from there tumble over the fall line to the coastal plain and sooner or later, tidewater. The fall line descent, with its miles of whitewater, has proven a bonanza to the droves of whitewater paddlers that inhabit the nearby metropolitan areas. Most streams in this region flow within the confines of wooded gorges excepting the Patuxent system where in addition many miles course through secluded swamplands. Either way the rivers are usually remarkably screened from their often urbanized and suburbanized surroundings and hence provide some fine paddling environments close to home.

The following streams are described in this chapter:

Patuxent River
    Little Patuxent River
       Middle Patuxent River
Patapsco River
    South Branch Patapsco River
    Gwynns Falls
Gunpowder Falls
    Little Falls
    Western Run
    Little Gunpowder Falls
Winters Run

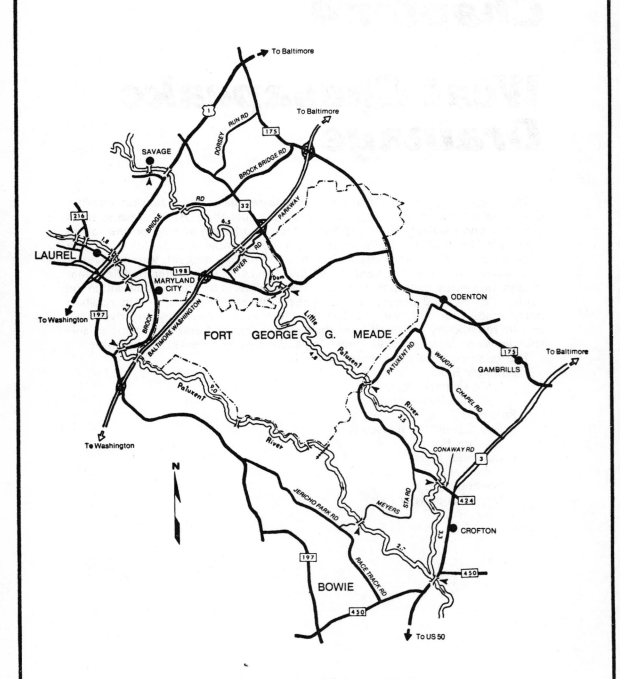

PATUXENT RIVER
LITTLE PATUXENT RIVER

Patuxent River

Introduction

The Patuxent is a river that has suffered at the hands of man in the name of progress. Most of its whitewater has been buried under two water supply reservoirs for suburban Washington. The reservoirs have intercepted most of its flow allowing only a trickle to flow past Laurel, Md. The river always runs muddy from serious soil erosion problems in the basin, and it smells of sewage from too many sewage treatment plants that discharge poorly treated effluents. Nevertheless, much of it possesses a semi-wilderness character that makes for some attractive cruising right in the heart of the Washington-Baltimore megalopolis.

Section 1. Laurel, Md. (9th Street) to Md. Rte. 3

Gradient	Difficulty	Distance	Time	Width	Scenery	Map
7	A	16.0	10.0	30-40	Good	38

Trip Description: The first few miles are not much to write home about. The stream winds about dense tangled woods, part of which have fallen across the stream. The trees and log jams in turn trap an incredible load of trash, including flood debris, milk jugs, plastic, tennis balls, and anything else you could imagine. Much of this unpleasantness can be avoided by putting in at Brock Bridge Road located four and a half miles downstream and just above the Baltimore-Washington Parkway. Just below the river enters the Patuxent Wildlife Refuge and later on Fort Meade and an amazing transformation occurs. The surrounding woods change to a healthy looking bottomland and swamp forest decorated here and there by big graceful (and uncarved) silvery beech trees. The trash suddenly disappears seemingly filtered out by upstream log jams. Unfortunately navigation through here is a challenge as the river periodically braids into numerous tiny channels, all liberally blocked by fallen trees. The channels reunite, the going is easy and then they split again and so on and on and on. By the end of the long day you will feel that you have fought your way down this river.
Hazards: Numerous fallen trees.
Water Conditions: Up only when Rocky Gorge Reservoir is overflowing (extended wet weather) or after locally heavy rains fall downstream of the reservoir.

Gauge

None.

Section 2. Md. Rte. 3 to Md. Rte. 4

Gradient	Difficulty	Distance	Time	Width	Scenery	Map
3	A	15.0	5.0	50-150	Good	39

Trip Description: The Little Patuxent joins just above the put-in and adds enough flow and width to now allow easy passage around most trees. There is a strong current to Rte. 214 shortly below which tidewater is reached. The river continues as on Section 1 to wind about a wide forested floodplain and bumping

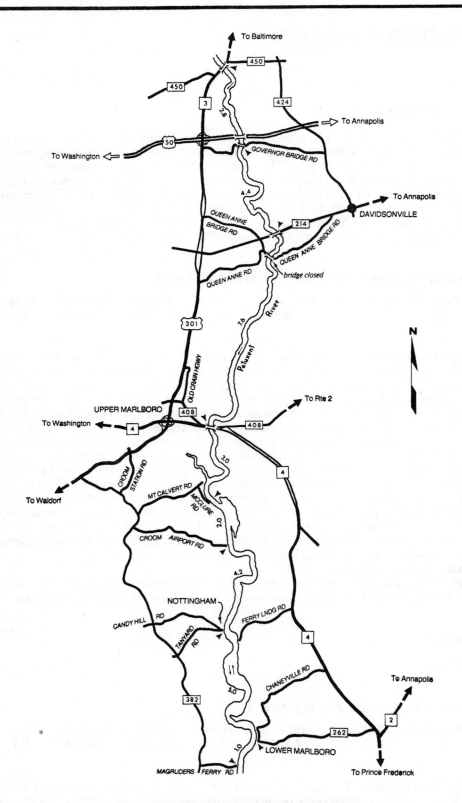

PATUXENT RIVER

up against pretty beech-covered hillsides. Below Rte. 214, the scenery degenerates with the appearance of several sand and gravel pits and trash dumps.
Hazards: None.
Water Conditions: Runable most of the year except after prolonged dry spell.

Gauge

None.

Patuxent Below Rte. 4
The Patuxent from Rte. 4 to Magruder Ferry has pleased many paddlers who have found this the closest piece of fairly natural tidewater riverscape to the Washington area. This relatively wide, placid river describes great bends past marshes, wooded bluffs and farms. You can put in from Calvert County at the public dock at Lower Marlboro or in Prince Georges County at Rte. 4, Jug Bay boat ramp, Selby Landing or Magruder Ferry Road. The latter three are in Patuxent River Park which requires that you first obtain a permit ($5.00 annual fee) for their use. Call the park at 301-627-6074 for current requirements. Below this section the Patuxent balloons into a miniature Chesapeake Bay.

Other Information
A substantial portion of the upper Patuxent drainage is occupied by the new city of Columbia. A project of a private developer, Columbia was started in the early 1960's with the goal of creating a complete city; a place touted by its architects as where one could work, live and play, as an alternative to living in just another bedroom community. The project unfortunately did not work completely as planned but must be at least credited as a good faith effort to manage the wanton suburban sprawl that has been devouring the countryside.

While Columbia attempts to cure our urban ills, there are facilities further downstream devoted to solving some of our environmental problems. Patuxent National Wildlife Refuge conducts programs in protection and reestablishment of endangered wildlife, its most glamorous project being one to protect the whooping crane. Further downriver at Benedict the Academy of Natural Sciences of Philadelphia Lab conducts water quality research while at Solomons Island near the river's mouth, The University of Maryland Chesapeake Bay Lab conducts estuarine research.

The coastal plain segment of the Patuxent flows through Maryland's tobacco belt. Tobacco has been cultivated here from the first days of colonial settlement. Back then the economy revolved around the weed and it was even an acceptable substitute for cash. The best means of transportation in those days was by boat, using the intricate network of tidal creeks, so most Maryland plantations clustered along tidewater for this reason. Many of the old plantation houses still stand, and though usually in private hands, many are opened for public inspection for a week or two each spring as part of various garden tours. Probably the most beautiful of these houses remaining along the Patuxent is Sotterly, a rambling structure located near the town of Hollywood. To serve those plantations that were landlocked, the colony authorized the construction of rolling roads. The roads received their names because tobacco was loaded into huge wooden casks called hogsheads and rolled (pulled by oxen, horses, etc.) over them to the nearest wharf. The name still lives today as in Rolling Road in Catonsville. Tobacco is no longer king in this state but in southern Maryland it still occupies an important niche in the economy and the large gray curing barns with their louvered walls stand as monuments to its persistant presence.

Little Patuxent River

Introduction

The Little Patuxent starts on the Piedmont, north of Columbia, Md., drops over the fall line at Savage, Md. and finally meanders the rest of its miles away across the coastal plain through Fort Meade to the Patuxent River at Rte. 3, north of Bowie. Unlike most of Maryland's coastal plain rivers, the Little Patuxent is sufficiently large to flow fairly tree-free and hence is a good run for non-masochistic novices.

Section 1. Savage, Md. (Foundry Street) to Md. Rte. 3

Gradient	Difficulty	Distance	Time	Width	Scenery	Map
6	A-1	19.0	6.5	35-50	Fair	38

Trip Description: The trip starts off for the first three miles with many easy rapids and riffles over mostly gravel to Brocks Bridge Road but from there on down to the Patuxent, the river is flat with a strong current. There is a six-foot dam, recognized by a pumphouse on the right, located above Md. Rte. 198. Carry this as there is an ugly churning roller waiting for you at the bottom. It is six and a half miles from Savage to Rte. 198 where the paddler must presently take out because the following five miles flow through Fort George Meade. The Army does not allow passage down this section due to periodic shooting practice in the neighborhood. Future policy may allow passage on safe days so contact the Wild-life Office at the fort for current regulations. Legal and lead-free paddling may resume at Patuxent Road. Most of the scenery along the Little Patuxent is of rather unimpressive woodlands occasionally upgraded by some beautiful patches of well-developed floodplain forest or beech covered hillsides. As on the Patuxent, the water quality suffers from soil erosion and discharges from over-loaded sewage treatment plants. If these problems are ever cleaned up, this section could turn into a very popular run.

Hazards: Six-foot dam at Fort Meade's water intake; carry. Flying bullets through Fort Meade and fallen trees throughout.

Water Conditions: Canoeable above Brocks Bridge within three days of hard rain and below Brocks Bridge Road most of a normal late fall, winter and spring.

Gauge

Staff gauge nailed to piling on east abutment of Md. Rte. 424 bridge should read at least 1.0 feet for river below Brocks Bridge Road. Judge upper river at

Boating on Triadelphia and Rocky Gorge Reservoirs

For those who enjoy lake paddling, limited boating is allowed on these two Washington Suburban Sanitary Commission reservoirs. A boating permit is required, costing ten dollars for the season, or one dollar for a day, and can be secured at the reservoir office at Brighton Dam (Triadelphia Reservoir).

Middle Patuxent River

Introduction

The Middle Patuxent drains the middle of Howard County, entering the Little Patuxent at Savage, Md. It flows past the doorstep of the burgeoning new city of Columbia and then through a major industrial and transportation corridor but hidden away in its gorge, the paddler would hardly know it. It is one of a half dozen fall line streams that if given a good rain can save the Washington or Baltimore area paddler a long drive to the mountains to find good scenery and whitewater.

Section 1. Md. Rte. 108 to Savage (Foundry Street)

Gradient	Difficulty	Distance	Time	Width	Scenery	Map
15*	A-2,4	11.0	3.5	25-35	Good	40

*1 mile @ 60 fpm

Trip Description: This entire run is set in a shallow, wooded gorge with the only significant civilized intrusions being occasional road crossings, some sewer construction scars and one rock quarry (at I-95). Fallen trees make some slow going in the first two miles and due to the steep mud banks and dense undergrowth, these trees are more troublesome than on most streams. But a sizeable tributary then joins on the right and below that point downed trees seldom block the whole channel. There is initially nothing more challenging than gentle gravel bar riffles until just above Simpsonville where some interesting rock gardens break the monotony followed by a two-foot ledge below Rte. 32. A few miles below U.S. Rte. 29, the stream begins its descent of the fall line, marked by numerous small rapids of rock gardens and little ledges. The fall line scenery is beautifully decorated with big rock outcrops often clothed in hemlock and ferns (norther exposure) and mountain laurel (southern exposure). The Middle Patuxent joins the Little Patuxent a half mile above the first convenient take-out at Savage. It is this last half mile that holds the whitewater climax of this cruise, The Falls. Located just around the bend from the confluence The Falls consist of a short steep staircase of sharp ledges dropping a total of about ten feet. Scout this. Although there is a feasible route down the left of center, the boater runs a serious risk of vertically pinning in the biggest ledge. A short carry on the left is recommended. A few hundred yards downstream, the swift river flows under an old abandoned factory. A log jam has developed here creating a serious strainer situation so approach with caution. Take out at the old steel truss bridge.
Hazards: Trees on upper river. Falls of Little Patuxent; scout and if in doubt, carry. Log jam at factory in Savage will probably require a carry on right.
Water Conditions: Runable only within a day of a hard rain during winter and spring.

Gauge

Rock weir at put-in should be at least scrapeably runable. For a rough correlation, Frederick gauge on the Monocacy (call 301-899-3210 after 11:30 A.M.) will be reading over 4.0 feet.

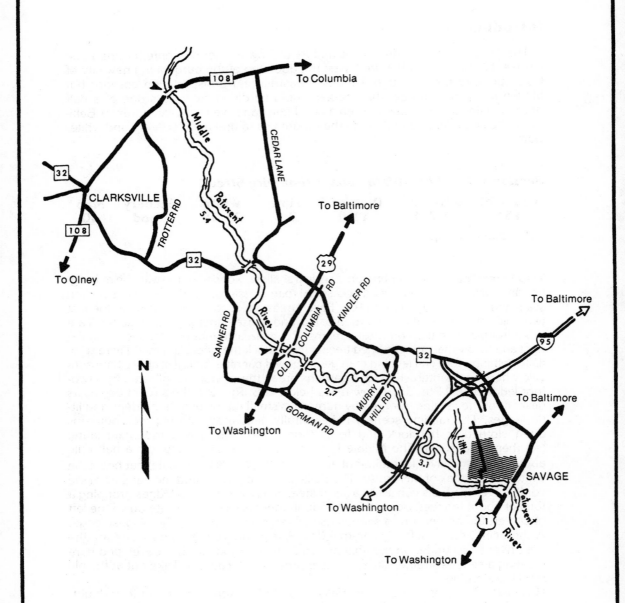

MIDDLE PATUXENT RIVER

Patapsco River

Introduction

The Patapsco flows through the geographical heart of Maryland and down the state's most important valley to join the Chesapeake Bay near Baltimore, Maryland's largest city, transportation center, and industrial powerhouse. A major estuary of the Patapsco is Baltimore's harbor, one of the country's busiest ports. The free flowing portion of this river remains a paddler's retreat and is surprisingly isolated, considering it is located only ten miles from the center of a metropolitan area. The Patapsco Gorge was once also a major industrial area, comprised of factories powered by the river's falling waters; however, floods, time, and obsolesence have silenced most of these mills and the valley, now mostly within the bounds of a state park, is slowly reverting to a more primitive state.

Section 1. Woodstock to Glen Artney

Gradient	Difficulty	Distance	Time	Width	Scenery	Map
14	1-3	16.0	5.0	50-100	Fair	41

Trip Description: Woodstock, located one and a half miles below the confluence of the North and South branches, is the first available access point. Initially, the river winds through an attractive wooded gorge in a rather peaceful fashion. At Daniels, there is a fifteen-foot dam that requires a carry (right). A few more riffles and rocks begin to appear but otherwise all is calm until the river passes under the high U.S. Rte. 40 bridge. Immediately below this bridge, there is the hulk of the old Union Dam now breached on the far right. The twisting chute through here can be nasty in high water, so scout first. The next two miles are almost continuous whitewater; complex and sometimes tedious rock gardens at low levels and an uncomplicated bouncy chain of waves at high water. This section climaxes in a steep bouldery rapid at the old Dickey Mills at Oella. The rapids continue on past Ellicott City until reaching a short backwater formed by a twelve-foot dam at Thistle (steep carry on right). After a few riffles comes another pool ending about a half mile downstream at a twenty-five foot dam also carried on right. Below here, there are plenty of easy rapids and riffles until the take-out at Glen Artney Area of Patapsco State Park located below the old dam ruins. The scenery along much of the river below Daniels was severely butchered in 1972 when Hurricane Agnes' floodwaters roared through and much healing still remains to be done. Paddlers only interested in the best of the whitewater can put in at Hollofield and take out a half mile below Md. Rte. 144 bridge, Ellicott City, along River Road, a distance of five miles.

Hazards: Dams at Daniels, Thistle, and a half mile below Thistle; all require carries. The crumbling Union Dam below Rte. 40 should be approached with care.

Water Conditions: Canoeable winter and spring within three days of hard rain.

Gauge

None. A check of the rapids below Rte. 144 bridge in Ellicott City provides an adequate indication of water conditions upstream.

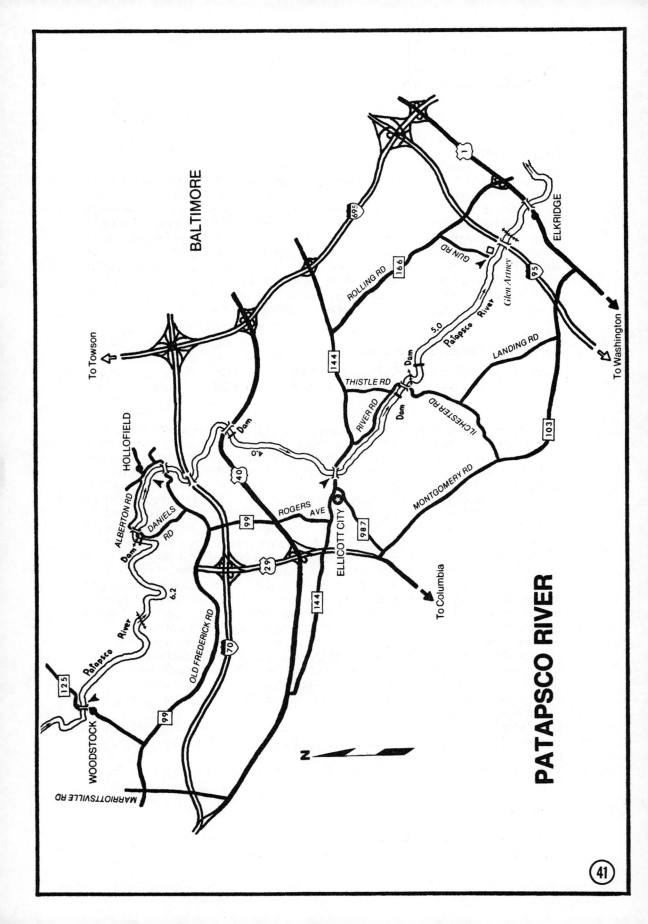

PATAPSCO RIVER

BALTIMORE

To Towson

To Washington

To Columbia

ELKRIDGE

Glen Artney

Patapsco River

5.0

GUN RD

LANDING RD

ILCHESTER RD

MONTGOMERY RD

ROLLING RD

THISTLE RD

RIVER RD

Dam

Dam

Dam

4.0

HOLLOFIELD

ALBERTON RD

DANIELS RD

Dam

6.2

Patapsco River

WOODSTOCK

MARRIOTTSVILLE RD

OLD FREDERICK RD

ROGERS AVE

ELLICOTT CITY

N

695

1

95

166

103

144

40

99

29

144

987

70

99

125

41

South Branch Patapsco River

Introduction

The South Branch of the Patapsco River bubbles out of Parrs Spring on the Frederick County line to flow eastward forming the boundary between Howard and Carroll counties and finally joining the North Branch Patapsco near Woodstock. As it rolls across the Piedmont Plateau (land of flat rivers), this little creek pulls a pleasant surprise by rushing over miles of moderate but interesting whitewater. If you like your streams tiny and your whitewater rocky and twisting, then head for this stream after the next hard rain.

Section 1. Woodbine (Md. Rte. 94) to Woodstock

Gradient	Difficulty	Distance	Time	Width	Scenery	Map
17	A-3	14.0	4.5	20-80	Good	42

Trip Description: The first four miles flow through fields and woods, but the scenery is cluttered by too many houses, too much trash, and an obtrusive railroad. However, there are the easy riffles over gravel bars and through rock gardens, the bouldery ruins of an old mill dam at Rte. 97, and a mess of fallen trees between Morgan and Rte. 97 to distract you. Below Gaither, the valley narrows into a wooded gorge that confines the river all the way to Elkridge and tidewater on the Patapsco. In this gorge, the stream begins tumbling over complex little boulder patch rapids that continue through Sykesville and on a few more miles below. When the whitewater starts letting up, there is a short stretch of fallen trees and log jams to add interest and/or aggravation to the trip. Most of the remaining few miles are flatwater, with the notable exception of the Falls of the Patapsco about a half mile below Marriottsville. Here the river, suddenly, with no warning, plunges over a high sloping ledge which, while probably runable, should be carried on the left by most paddlers. There is no convenient access to the mouth of the South Branch, so continue down the Patapsco a mile and a half to Woodstock.

Hazards: Fallen trees and log jams below Morgan and below Sykesville. Small falls a half mile below Marriottsville after stream makes short bend away from railroad tracks; get out well above and scout before approaching.

Water Conditions: Runable winter and spring within a day of hard rain.

Gauge

USGS gauge at Henryton. Level of 2.5 feet is about minimal passable level. Also if riffles at Md. Rte. 94 bridge in Woodbine are cleanly runable, then there is adequate water.

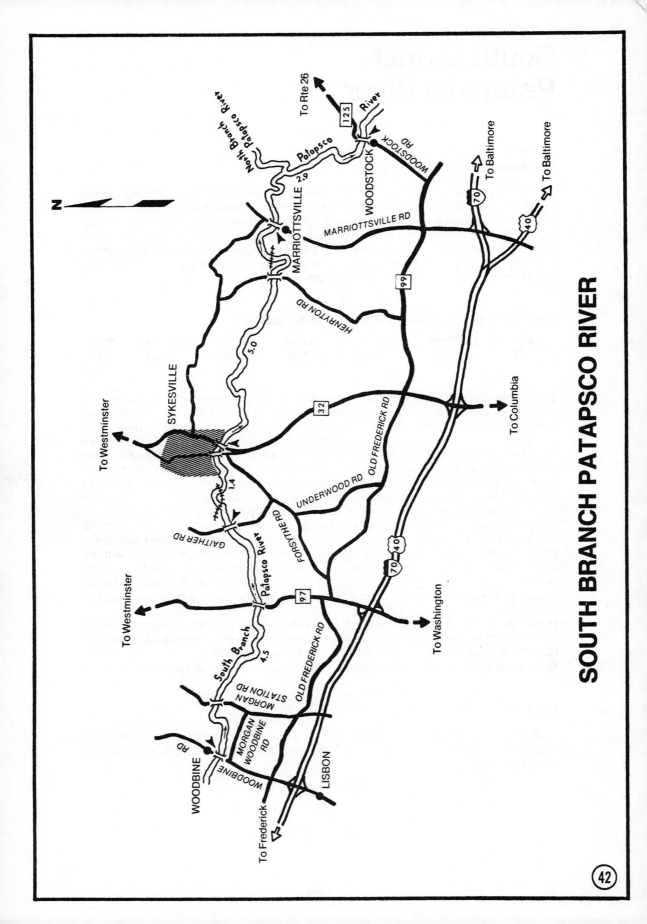

SOUTH BRANCH PATAPSCO RIVER

42

Gwynns Falls

Introduction

Baltimoreans will be pleased to know that when the big rains hit they can break the whitewater gypsy routine and save some gas by looking inward from the Beltway to little and forgotten Gwynns Falls. Although over 200 years of habitation, civilization and industrialization have exacted a heavy toll from this once clear wild torrent, all the abusers did not destroy the rapids which remain in quantity and quality found on few other fall line streams.

Section 1. Liberty Heights Ave. to Washington Blvd.

Gradient	Difficulty	Distance	Time	Width	Scenery	Map
38	A-3	9.0	3.0	25-200	Poor	43

Description: While not the head of navigation, the put-in at Liberty Heights Ave. marks the transition from mellow headwaters to fall line whitewater. The creek soon starts dropping over gentle rock gardens as it passes first through woods and then through Woodlawn Cemetery. Following a short interlude on a pool ending with a carry around a three-foot dam, the riffles resume and the gradient increases. The creek rushes through an attractive residential neighborhood climaxing in the charming restored mill town of Dickeyville. Allow some time to explore its narrow streets lined by white stone and frame houses and notice the white mill factory across the creek. Also notice the five-foot dam which you should portage. The rapids, formed by sharp black rocks, become quite interesting now and some are notably steep. While the woodland setting of Gwynns Falls Park is pleasant, the increasingly common odor of raw sewage bubbling forth from Gwynns Falls' infamous leaky sewers begins to offend the nostrils and make one wary about unscheduled immersions. Next the creek eases off into a stretch of long gentle gravel formed rapids until Edmondson Ave. Know what this bridge looks like because just downstream on a blind swift bend is a double iron pipe which at minimal levels crosses at canoeist chest height and in addition often supports a frightening strainer of jammed debris. The short carry is least rotten on the right. Not far below is surprise number two, a five-foot ledge runable by a nasty tortuous chute on the left or a shear drop on the right. A few more ledges shortly below maintain the excitement. This is a good place for rough rapids as they might distract you from the surrounding grotesque canyon of natural rock outcrops, glaciers of poured waste concrete and assorted trash. Below Baltimore St. the scenery gets really revolting while the whitewater mellows to well spaced riffles and easy rapids. The most exciting activity here is watching the crane at the junkyard feed cars to the compactor machine. Take out at a small park on the right at Wilkens Ave. or at Carroll Park Golf Course at Washington Blvd.
Hazards: Two dams, the double iron pipe, the big ledge which has serious pin potential and the filthy water.
Water Conditions: Runable only within twelve hours of a hard and intense rain.

Gauge

None.

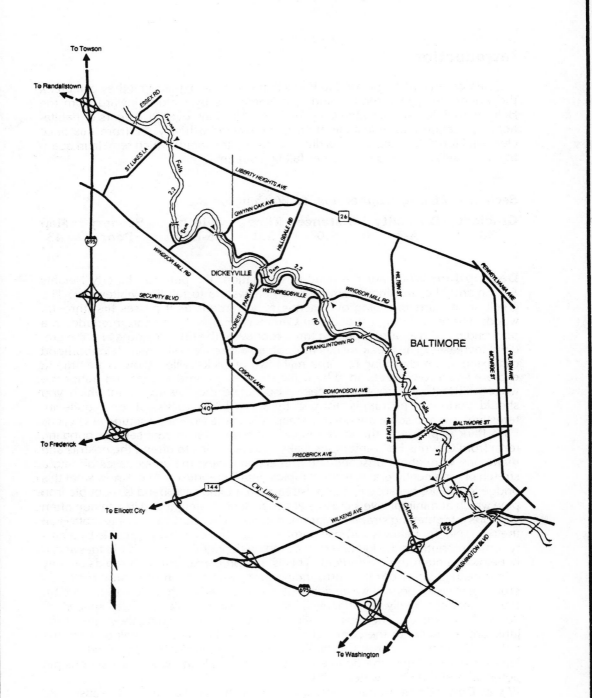

GWYNNS FALLS

Gunpowder Falls

Introduction

Gunpowder Falls rises in the low hills along the Pennsylvania Line, zig-zags a southeastward course through beautiful upper Baltimore County and over the fall line to the tidal Gunpowder River east of Baltimore. The stream provides most of the Baltimore metropolitan area's water supply so it is the sections remaining between the two large municipal reservoirs that are of most interest to the paddler. Its proximity to Baltimore and relatively reliable flows in wet years has made this a favorite of Maryland paddlers.

Section 1. Prettyboy Dam to Md. Rte. 45

Gradient	Difficulty	Distance	Time	Width	Scenery	Map
18*	1-3	4.0	1.5	25-35	Very Good	44

*1 @ 40 fpm

Trip Description: This short section is a tantalizing appetizer to the exploration of the Gunpowder System. The price of admission is a slippery scramble down a breakneck path of about a hundred verticle feet to the foot of the south end of Prettyboy Dam. The reward for that effort is the pleasure of a beautiful wild, steep, wooded gorge. The small stream starts off by tumbling down continuous boulder gardens and broken ledges but soon eases off to easy riffles and fast flat water down to Rte. 45.

Hazards: The carry into the put-in and possibly fallen trees.

Water Conditions: Canoeable winter and spring within three or four days of a good rain providing that Prettyboy Reservoir is full. If the reservoir is not full, a condition most common in summer or fall or after a prolonged dry spell, only a trickle will flow down the bed. However, because the city water supply people must maintain a certain minimal level in Loch Raven Reservoir where their water intakes are situated, they do so during dry spells by releasing moderate volumes of water from Prettyboy Reservoir. In a really prolonged drought these releases, which are canoeable-size flows, become increasingly prolonged and frequent. The city so far has been unable or unwilling to announce these releases to boaters.

Gauge

None.

Section 2. Md. Rte. 45 to Phoenix Road

Gradient	Difficulty	Distance	Time	Width	Scenery	Map
7	A-1	12.5	4.0	30-50	Good	44

Trip Description: This portion of the Gunpowder is quite popular among novices. The water is generally flat but swift but with enough interesting riffles along the way to make beginners feel that they have run some real whitewater.

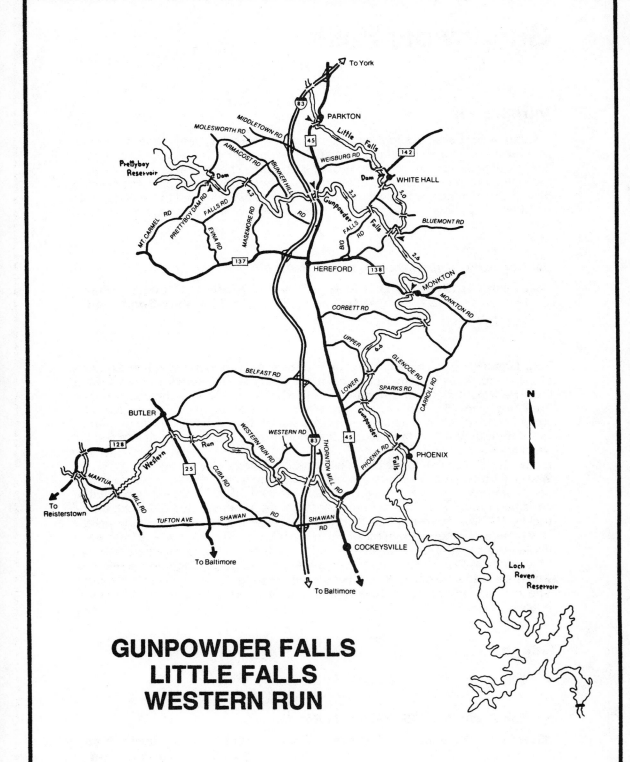

GUNPOWDER FALLS
LITTLE FALLS
WESTERN RUN

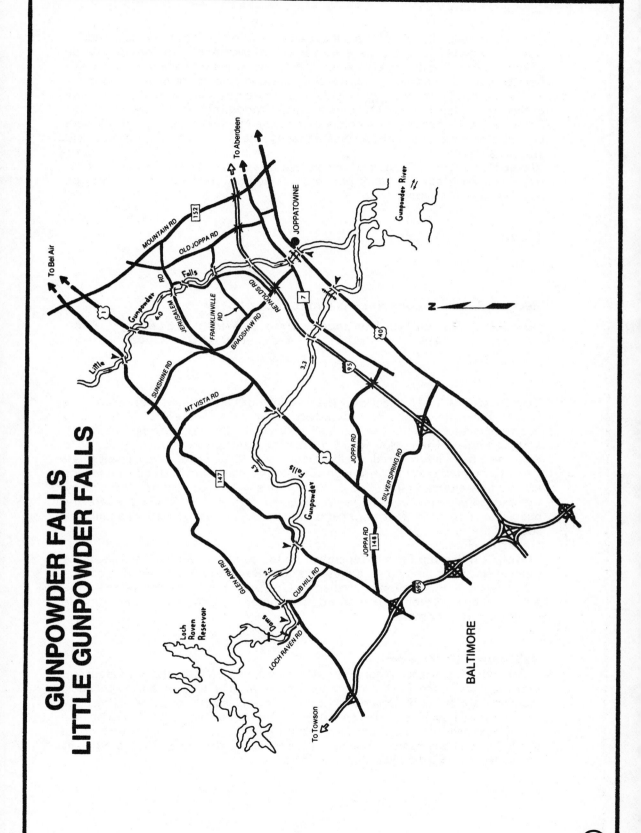

GUNPOWDER FALLS
LITTLE GUNPOWDER FALLS

The river is generally shut off from the rest of the world by the pretty rock-studded walls of a wooded gorge but there are also views into the surrounding countryside of horse farms, fields gone to seed, more woodlands and scattered attractive homes, both old and new. Unfortunately the combination of high-priced desirability of the adjacent lands and incidents of abuse stemming from the popularity of this stream has brought on some inevitable landowner-paddler bad relations. Some very convenient access points such as the Monkton Road now bristle with posted and no-parking signs. So please practice the utmost courtesy on your visit.

Hazards: None.

Water Conditions: Runable winter and spring within week of hard rain if Prettyboy Reservoir is already full or during prolonged dry spells when there may be releases from Prettyboy.

Gauge

None.

Section 3. Lower Loch Raven Dam to U.S. Rte. 40

Gradient	Difficulty	Distance	Time	Width	Scenery	Map
15*	1-4	10.5	4.0	100-150	Good	45

*2 @ 30 fpm

Trip Description: This section of the river includes the exciting descent over the fall line. Put in along Loch Raven Road above Cromwell Bridge Road. As on many good whitewater runs this one starts off slow with nothing more complicated than scattered riffles. Then below Rte. 1 the fall line is reached and the river begins to earn its name as it tumbles down its bouldery and ledgey bed. At low levels this is a rocky complex passage while high conditions create a big flush down one long roaring hole-studded rapid. The entire trip runs within the confines of a shallow wooded gorge. Take out at Rte. 7 for convenience or at Rte. 40 where the nearest legal place to leave your car is at the roadside rest area about a half mile south of the river.

Hazards: None.

Water Conditions: Flow is dependent on the condition of the reservoirs. If the weather has been dry and Prettyboy and Loch Raven are down then do not look for any water in this section other than that fed by some small side streams. If the reservoirs are full then a hard rain during winter or spring can sustain runable levels for a week or more.

Baltimore City Reservoirs

Baltimore City's rules regarding boating on Liberty (North Branch Patapsco), Prettyboy and Loch Raven reservoirs vary from year to year but as on most municipal water supply reservoirs, boating is very strictly regulated. Presently canoeing and kayaking are permitted on Prettyboy only with Loch Raven being a future possibility. Seasonal permits, costing 25 dollars, are available on a quota basis. Applications can be obtained at the Liberty Dam office. For more details and up to date information call 301-922-6040.

Little Falls

Introduction

Not to be confused with its namesake rapid on the lower Potomac, this Little Falls is a delightful little brook rushing through the rich rolling countryside of upper Baltimore County to join Gunpowder Falls near Monkton. Endowed with lovely scenery and exciting whitewater, this stream makes an ideal extension to an upper Gunpowder trip or an excellent whitewater duo with the Prettyboy to Rte. 45 run on the Gunpowder.

Section 1. Parkton (Md. Rte. 45) to Gunpowder Falls

Gradient	Difficulty	Distance	Time	Width	Scenery	Map
20*	1-3	5.0	1.5	25-35	Good	44

*1 @ 50 fpm

Trip Description: This delightful trip begins at Parkton, a lovely little hamlet of vintage houses clustered about Md. Rte. 45. Immediately below, the creek rushes into a wooded gorge decorated by a variety of beautiful black rock outcrops and cliffs. The streambed is filled with boulders, and sometimes the downstream view is totally blocked; but, altogether, this section does not exceed intermediate difficulty. An old railroad grade along the bank provides good rescue or walk-out opportunity. The scenery opens up upon approaching White Hall, where a five-foot dam with a nasty reversal requires a carry. Below White Hall, the stream flows again into a pretty gorge that continues to the Gunpowder. One can take out at Blue Mount Road located a quarter mile above the mouth or continue on down the Gunpowder to Monkton Road or beyond (caution: Monkton Road is heavily posted with no-trespassing signs and no-parking signs, so please ask permission of the local property owners before using).
Hazards: Dam at upper end of White Hall that should be carried, possible fallen trees.
Water Conditions: Canoeable winter and spring within a day of hard rain.

Gauge

USGS gauge at railroad bridge just upstream of Blue Mount Road should read at least 1.7 feet. Also water should be at least up to the bottom of the arch on the Rte. 45 bridge at Parkton.

Western Run

Introduction

Western Run is a tiny, meandering brook flowing across a peaceful and genteel valley in upper Baltimore County to join Gunpowder Falls east of Cockeysville. It is a fairly unexciting but extremely picturesque run, best recommended for the lover of fine architecture, fine horses, and manicured landscapes.

Section 1. Dover (Mantua Mill Road) to Md. Rte. 45

Gradient	Difficulty	Distance	Time	Width	Scenery	Map
11	A-1	11.0	3.5	15-30	Good	44

Trip Description: Western Run is formed by the union of McGill and Piney runs. Put in on Piney Run at Mantua Mill Road about a hundred yards east of Butler Road (Md. Rte. 128). There is some very limited parking space on the shoulder of Butler Road. The creek is very tiny to Falls Road being initially only fifteen to twenty feet wide. It meanders about an open gently rolling valley, dotted by beautiful old farmhouses, horse farms, and huge mansions. The stream unfortunately tends to be bracketed by eroded mudbanks but they are low enough, often enough, to view the surrounding countryside. While not possessing any outstanding gradient, the creek still rushes over countless riffles formed by fine gravel and some rubbly rapids formed by washed away dams. Blackrock Run adds noticeable volume to Western Run just below Falls Road. About this point, the surrounding hills close in and the remainder of the cruise passes through an attractive, partially wooded gorge. Throughout the trip count on fallen trees, barbed wire, electric, and wooden fences to complicate navigation.

Much of this cruise is through an essentially residential neighborhood. Please make an effort to maintain a low profile and travel in small, quiet groups when paddling through. Considering how close this valley is to a big city, it is amazing (as of this writing) how few "posted" signs there are along this stream.

Hazards: Beware of strainers; barbed wire fences, electric fences, cattle fences, trees and log jams. The cattle fences here are loosely suspended in sections from a cable, thus forming a line of swinging doors that can be conveniently squeezed through. Watch out for one very hard to see barbed wire strand underneath the Cuba Road Bridge (steel truss below Falls Road).

Water Conditions: Canoeable winter and spring not more than two days after a hard rain.

Gauge

USGS gauge on downstream right bank at Western Run Road has an outside staff gauge nailed to a big beech tree just downstream of the station. A reading of 1.5 feet is low but very adequate for the creek from the gauge on down to Rte. 45 but due to the fast rising and falling character of this stream, probably 2.0 feet is needed to reflect minimal conditions at Mantua Mill Road, assuming that the river is dropping.

Little Gunpowder Falls

Introduction

Nestled along the border between Harford and Baltimore counties, this tiny stream dashes down a rocky fall line route to tidewater northeast of Baltimore. Though now just another little creek under the J.F.K. Expressway, the Little Gunpowder Valley was in colonial times a major center of commerce. At that time, the estuary floated ocean-going ships to Joppa, a booming tobacco port, while the upstream fall line gradient provided power for mills. But the harbor succumbed to siltation and the town to competition from the new port of Baltimore so that today the town of Joppa remains in name only, a bedroom community for Baltimore. The value of the stream is probably most appreciated by the opportunistic white-water paddler.

Section 1. Md. Rte. 147 to U.S. Rte. 40

Gradient	Difficulty	Distance	Time	Width	Scenery	Map
36	1-3	6.0	2.0	25-35	Fair	45

Trip Description: The Little Gunpowder is almost continuous action, dropping over gravel bars and rock gardens and, below Jerusalem Road, over a variety of interesting ledges. While generally an excellent intermediate trip, high water conditions here create big waves, frightening velocity, and vicious hydraulics that will thrill even the advanced paddler. The sharp drop behind the factory (Belko Co.) at Franklinville should especially be approached with caution. Although the stream flows through a typical wooded fall line gorge, the scenery is unfortunately degraded by trash, grafitti on rock formations, and residential developments. Take out at shopping center on U.S. Rte. 40.

Hazards: Fallen trees and, at high water, some of the ledges on this river form very powerful holes.

Water Conditions: Runable winter and spring within a day of hard rain. This is a small, narrow watershed with quick runoff.

Gauge

Canoeist painted gauge on upstream center pier of Rte. 40 bridge should read at least a half foot. At U.S. Rte. 1 bridge, a level of one foot roughly corresponds to six grooves down from the top of the left abutment.

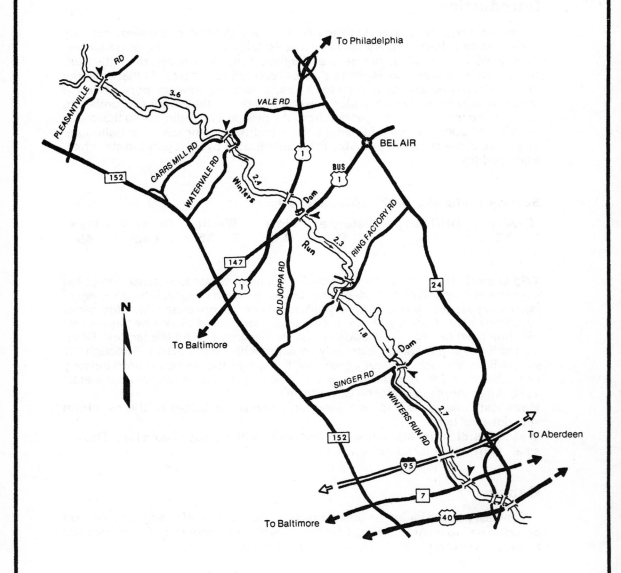

To Philadelphia

VALE RD

PLEASANTVILLE RD

3.6

152

CARRS MILL RD

WATERVALE RD

Winters

2.4

1

Dam

BEL AIR

BUS 1

RING FACTORY RD

147

1

Run

2.3

24

N

To Baltimore

OLD JOPPA RD

1.8

Dam

SINGER RD

WINTERS RUN RD

2.7

152

To Aberdeen

I-95

7

40

To Baltimore

WINTERS RUN

Winters Run

Introduction

Winters Run starts in the beautiful Piedmont hills, west of Bel Air, Harford County and rushes down a narrow wooded valley to the tidal Bush River. It is a graceful descent over the Atlantic Coast fall line, usually hidden away from the growing suburbia that it flows through.

Section 1. Pleasantville Road to Md. Rte. 7

Gradient	Difficulty	Distance	Time	Width	Scenery	Map
18	1-2	13.0	4.0	15-25	Good	46

Trip Description: Enter via steep banks at Pleasantville Road. The stream winds through a shallow wooded gorge filled with many beautiful beech trees, some of which unfortunately have fallen across the creek. There are continuous easy riffles of gravel bars and rock gardens and above Carrs Mill Road is a relatively steep, twisting rapid through the ruins of an old mill dam. Below here the scenery opens up and the gradient slows somewhat. At U.S. Rte. 1, there is a sloping four-foot high dam with a strong hole at the bottom which can be run by experienced paddlers. Below Rte. 1, the stream enters a gorge again, which except for the presence of a few attractive houses, is essentially wild. The white-water here is almost nonstop over a rocky bed with no real complications. Passing Ring Factory Road it enters the backwater of the narrow, attractive but silting-in Atkisson Reservoir. It is a two mile paddle across the lake to a sixty-foot high dam portaged on either side. Below the dam, the stream resumes its busy descent but the scenery degrades to a drab and trashy condition.
Hazards: Fallen trees, a dam above Rte. 1 with a powerful hydraulic, and the sixty-foot high dam that backs up Atkisson Reservoir.
Water Conditions: Only up within twenty-four hours of hard rain during winter and spring.

Gauge

None. Approximately nine inches of water over the dam at Rte. 1 should be adequate.

SUSQUEHANNA RIVER TRIBUTARIES

Chapter 5

The Susquehanna
River Basin

The Susquehanna River starts in the heart of New York State at Cooperstown and from there flows 444 crooked miles to the Chesapeake Bay at Havre de Grace. It has the largest drainage on the east coast covering almost 28,000 square miles in New York, Pennsylvania and Maryland. But only 254 square miles lie in Maryland. Nevertheless the Susquehanna may be Maryland's most important river and basin for its estuary is the Chesapeake Bay, probably the State's foremost natural resource. It is the Susquehanna's tremendous influx of fresh water (or sometimes the lack of it) that virtually determines the character and health of the Bay, affecting for example such diverse features as the abundance and quality of the Bay's renown seafood, silt deposition patterns that can affect navigation, and dispersion of any pollutants that enter these waters. The direct importance of this basin to the canoeist is that it remains a rural, still sparsely populated territory in the heart of a growing eastern seaboard strip city. It is a nice refuge that is still close to home for several million people.

The following streams are described in this chapter:
Susquehanna River
    Conowingo Creek
    Octoraro Creek
    Deer Creek

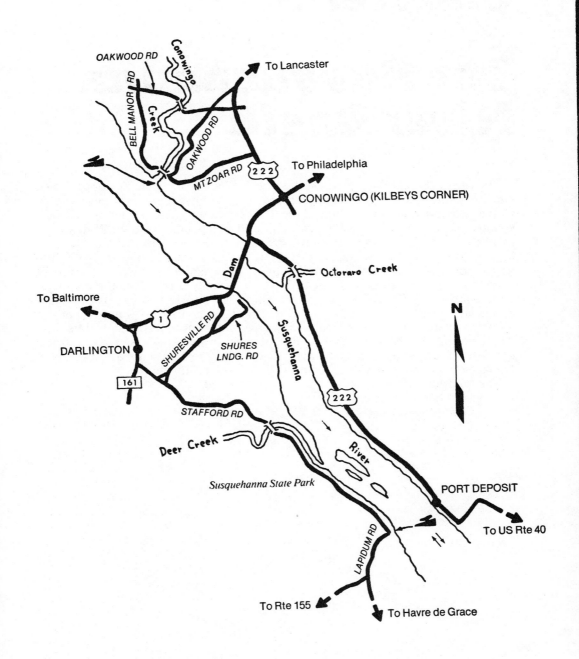

SUSQUEHANNA RIVER
CONOWINGO CREEK

Susquehanna River

Introduction

The Susquehanna stands out boldly in this state of small streams, for no other nontidal river in Maryland comes close to matching its nearly mile width. Although most of its long descent over the fall line to tidewater at Port Deposit has been reduced to a chain of pools behind hydroelectric dams, there are still a few free-flowing miles below Conowingo Dam that will interest the novice whitewater canoeist. Paddling this section, one cannot help but speculate on what a majestic and possibly exciting run the fall line of the Susquehanna might have been to the turn-of-the-century canoeist. But while whitewater paddlers might have once enjoyed the lower Susquehanna, it was bad news for commercial boatmen. During the nineteenth century, navigational interests wrote off the rocky river as a lost cause and bypassed it with canals on both banks from tidewater on into Pennsylvania. Ruins of the canals are still evident, where not inundated by the reservoirs, especially at Norman Wood Bridge (Pa. Rte. 372) near Holtwood, Pa. and along U.S. Rte. 222 above Port Deposit.

Section 1. Conowingo Dam (U.S. Rte. 1) to Susquehanna State Park

Gradient	Difficulty	Distance	Time	Width	Scenery	Map
3	A-1	5.0	1.5	2500-4000	Good	47

Trip Descriptions: One can put in at the tailrace of the powerhouse at the fishing access area on Shures Landing Road. If you are paddling down from points upstream, land at the south (right) end of the dam (steep, weed-choked exit with possibly debris-jammed approach but anyone who paddles this mile-wide expanse of deadwater obviously loves hardship), cross Rte. 1, enter the visitor center at the powerhouse and request portage assistance. Philadelphia Electric Company will truck you and your boats to the fishing area below, free of charge. This same public service incidentally is offered at Holtwood and Safe Harbor dams, upstream in Pennsylvania. For the next four miles, the river drops gently over an incredibly ledgey and jagged bottom. At low water this creates a rocky maze, without parallel, that not only demands good water reading ability but also requires the boater to have an intuitive sense (to decipher where, in a three thousand-foot wide panorama of pure rock, enough water gathers to float a boat). Higher water simplifies the river to a lot of fast water, spotted with rocks, eddys, little waves and little holes. Due to the difficulty of rescue, novices should avoid this section in cold weather or if the water level is high. These rocks and riffles, which bear the impressive title of Smith Falls (this is as far as Capt. John Smith got in his exploration of the Chesapeake Bay and Susquehanna River), end at the upstream side of Port Deposit. From there it is about a mile paddle across tidewater to the Susquehanna State Park launching ramp (right), at the foot of Lapidum Road.

Hazards: Rapidly fluctuating water levels, varying as much as eight feet at the trailrace launching area, so heed the warning signals. Conversely, the conclusion of power generation can leave the hapless paddler stranded high and dry in a sea of wet rocks, so check the generating schedule before launching. The width of this river makes cold weather paddling risky to the unskilled and winds can plow up some boat-swamping waves or just plain blow you away.

Water Conditions: Flow on this section is frustratingly variable depending on the flow in the river above, power generation at three upstream plants, level of Conowingo Lake and of course power generation at Conowingo. Generally, most or all of your water will be coming from the powerhouse. As a rule, if the Susquehanna is not high above the reservoirs, the powerhouse runs only during peak demand periods, i.e. Monday through Saturday in the afternoon. Water on Sunday during summer is not very dependable.

Gauge

None. An on-the-spot inspection and check of the generating schedule will tell you everything.

And Furthermore

Any river as big as the Susquehanna just has to be important. It was a major path of travel and trade even before the first Europeans arrived in the valley and has been so ever since. The river and its tributaries carved natural passageways through the formidable barrier of the Allegheny ridges and these have been exploited by every form of land and water transportation. The canal building era of the first half of the 19th century brought a series of canals, locks and channel alterations that allowed navigation up the river as far as Nanticoke, Pa., 180 miles above its mouth. The Susquehanna and its tributaries, Swatara Creek and the Juniata River also formed the central link in an amazing cross-Pennsylvania canal project which allowed passage by water, except for one stretch over a portage railroad, from Philadelphia to Pittsburgh. The canals' arch enemy and ultimate conqueror, the railroad, also followed these same routes and today, major lines of the Penn Central running along the mainstem and the Juniata are among the busiest in the country.

The Susquehanna is capable of gathering up a heckuva lot of water by the time it reaches Maryland. During the great flood of 1936 over 800,000 cfs poured past Conowingo and Hurricane Agnes topped that in 1972 with 1,100,000 cfs. Now Conowingo Dam can pass up to 80,000 cfs just through its turbines and for the occasions when there is an excess there are thirty huge spillway gates to accommodate it. In spite of all that capacity there were still some tense moments when Agnes' waters threatened to top the dam. About the only thing worse than floodwaters is floodwaters with ice. The excessive width of the Susquehanna allows great quantities of ice to form in the winter and if there is a quick early thaw or heavy winter rains, this ice can transform into a frightening floating glacier that can scrape away almost anything that stands in its path. Understandably, towns close to the river face each spring with great apprehension.

The Susquehanna once supported a great fishing industry based on the harvesting of shad. Shad, like salmon, is an anadromous fish, that is it migrates from the sea to the river to breed. The construction of Conowingo Dam and two more dams upstream totally blocked this migration and shad ceased to visit the river. Currently the Pennsylvania Fish Commission is experimenting with portaging the shad around the dams by tank trucks. If the experiment is successful permanent fish ladders may be constructed and perhaps someday the annual shad run will once again become a regular feature of life along the river.

Conowingo Creek

Introduction

Conowingo Creek is a small stream that flows peacefully out of Lancaster County, Pennsylvania into Cecil County, Maryland, only to end its journey with a violent plunge into the Susquehanna River upstream of Conowingo Dam. It is best classified as a quick, cheap thrills run; ideal as a chaser to any of the other neighborhood streams, when water is up.

Section 1. Oakwood to Susquehanna River

Gradient	Difficulty	Distance	Time	Width	Scenery	Map
50*	1-5	2.0	1.0	20-30	Very Good	47

*gradient reaches 200 fpm

Trip Description: Put in on road branching due west off U.S. Rte. 222 at Oakwood, Md. You have about three quarters of a mile to warm up, as riffles progress to easy rapids to medium difficulty rapids and onward and upward. Then comes a four-foot dam, runable through a breach on the right, after which the creek gets down to serious business. From here to the end, it is one steep, complex, snaggle-toothed rapid occasionally filtered through a fallen tree. At best there are only postage stamp eddys and they exist only at minimal levels. At higher levels, the run is one long uncontrolled flush. Do not attempt this run without scouting every inch between the dam and the mouth on foot, most importantly to identify any tree hazards. As of this writing, there is only one downed tree and it is negotiable with care. Take out at launching ramp on backwater of Conowingo Lake.
Hazards: The whole run is a hazard with special attention given to trees.
Water Conditions: Winter and spring within 24 hours of hard rain.

Gauge

None. Judge while scouting.

Past Prosperity

Nearby Conowingo Creek is the site of the Line Pits. This is an abandoned chromium mine that operated between 1828 and 1880 and which during its first twenty-two years of operation was the source of most of the world's chrome supply. This of course is not necessarily saying much since the two major uses for chrome, for electroplating and as an ingredient of stainless steel, had not been developed yet. Nevertheless a substantial market must still have existed as other chrome deposits were also worked during that period around Rocks State Park in Harford County and near Soldiers Delight in upper Baltimore County. The industry died when its overseas market turned to richer deposits discovered in Asia Minor (Turkey).

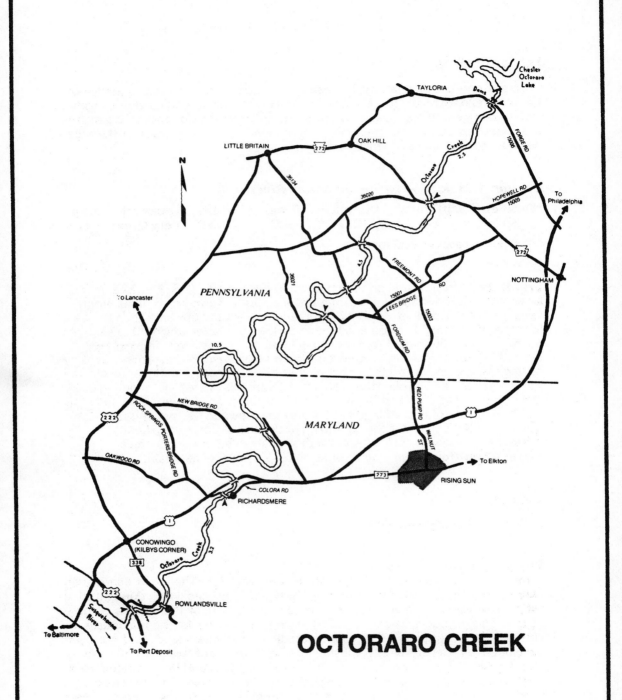

OCTORARO CREEK

Octoraro Creek

Introduction

Octoraro Creek drains the rolling, prosperous farm country of southern Lancaster and Chester counties in Pennsylvania. Formed by the confluence of the East and West branches, beneath the waters of Chester Octoraro Lake, the creek rushes (Octoraro is Indian for "rushing waters") through nineteen twisting miles, mostly in a wooded gorge to the Susquehanna River below Conowingo Dam.

Section 1. Chester Octoraro Lake to U.S. Rte. 222

Gradient	Difficulty	Distance	Time	Width	Scenery	Map
12	1-2	18.5	6.0	30-50	Good	48

Trip Description: Start at the covered bridge immediately below the reservoir. The first half of the trip to Horseshoe Bend, a large loop stradling the Mason-Dixon Line, is a rather slow coast down through flat water and easy riffles past attractive fields and woodland. Just above the bend, the stream enters a shallow wooded gorge that is quite pretty and, with the exception of one huge gravel pit, fairly wild. There is a boy scout camp, Camp Horseshoe, on this loop at which the creek drops over a runable three-foot rubble dam, followed by about a mile of interesting rock gardens. Below here to U.S. Rte. 1, the current is swift except for the backwater of a four-foot rubble dam that is runable but scratchy. The scenery along here is unfortunately degraded by summer homes. The final three miles comprise the liveliest portion of Octoraro. Those wishing to just run this section can put in at the right end of the Colora Road bridge at Richardsmere, just downstream of Rte. 1, provided that you do not have more than a few vehicles to park there. The stream rushes through a fairly isolated gorge over numerous rapids, formed by rock gardens, gravel, and small ledges. A few powerline crossings mess up the scenery which is otherwise wild. The gorge ends at Rowlandsville, once a busy nineteenth century industrial village that manufactured iron and paper. Take out just below at a side road that branches off of Rte. 222 toward Rowlandsville about a thousand feet west of the bridge over Octoraro Creek bridge.
Hazards: None.
Water Conditions: Runable winter and spring within two days of rainfall provided that this has been preceded by enough wet weather to fill Chester Octoraro Lake, a water supply reservoir for West Chester, Pa., to overflowing.

Gauge

Painted canoe gauge on U.S. Rte. 1 bridge center pier. Level of six inches is minimal level.

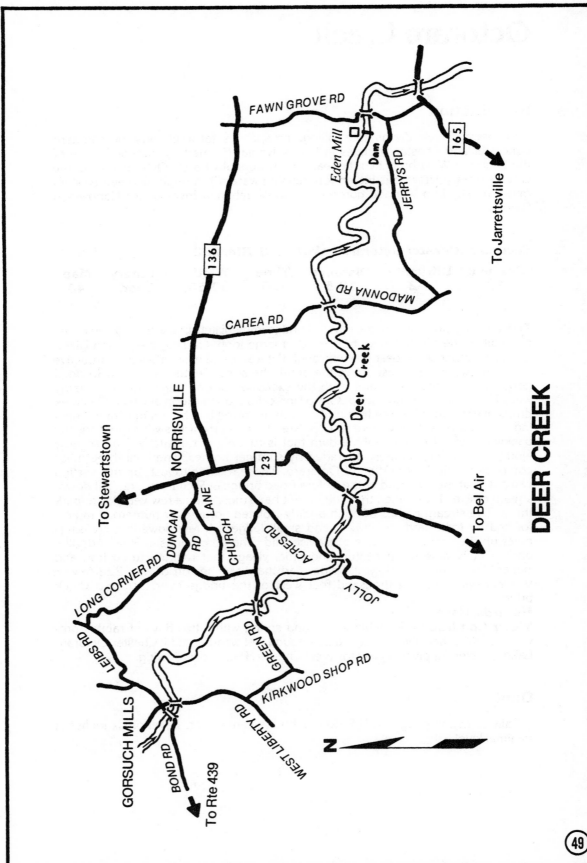

DEER CREEK

49

Deer Creek

Introduction

Deer Creek rises in the pasturelands of York County, Pa. and from there wanders across a corner of Baltimore County and the width of Harford County to join the Susquehanna River below Conowingo. Comprised of a pleasant mixture of woodlands, working farms and country estates, there is no prettier countryside in Maryland. Unfortunately this is also very prized, high priced and jealously defended real estate which means that there is a lot of posted land, especially at many potential access points. So when running this popular stream please be on your best behavior and be sure to obtain permission before crossing private land.

Section 1. Gorsuch Mills (Bond Road) to Fawn Grove Road

Gradient	Difficulty	Distance	Time	Width	Scenery	Map
15	1-2	13.5	4.5	15-50	Very Good	49

Trip Description: This far upper portion of this long stream offers the most pleasant cruising on Deer Creek. Just large enough to get a canoe into at Bond Road, the creek starts out by twisting about a flat agricultural bottomland fringed by pastoral or forested hillsides. Then at Green Road the hillsides converge and for the remaining miles Deer Creek rushes through a chain of wild wooded ravines. Though interrupted by two summer camps and a few roadbridges these miles offer the paddler plenty of quiet and solitude, a fascinating display of unusually sharp, jagged rock formations, cool hemlock shaded bends and assorted fond memories. The creek is always in a hurry, rushing over numerous riffles and easy rapids formed by gravel, rock gardens, boulders and ledges with swift current in between. One particularly boulder constricted rapid below Green Road should be scouted by novices. Fences come and go on the civilized parts of this section and occasional fallen trees, especially on the first few miles, will require carries. The run concludes at Eden Mill which in contrast to most long abandoned crumbling relics about the state stands well-preserved and was still operating, grinding local corn, as recently as 1965. Eden Mill Dam backs up water for about three quarter miles and is easily portaged on the left.

Hazards: Strainers include fences on the first two miles and fallen trees which decrease in frequency as the stream grows. There is a low-water bridge below Jolly Acres Road requiring a carry and the twelve-foot dam at Eden Mill should be carried on the left (has been run by at least one adventuresome sort).

Water Conditions: Runable winter and spring after a hard rain. Most reliably passable within day of rainfall but if ground is really wet then it may last two or three days.

Gauge

There is a yellow flood gauge on the right upstream end of Bond Road Bridge. Six inches is zero canoeable level.

Section 2. Fawn Grove Road to Stafford Road

Gradient	Difficulty	Distance	Time	Width	Scenery	Map
11	1,3	29.0	9.0	25-40	Good	50

151

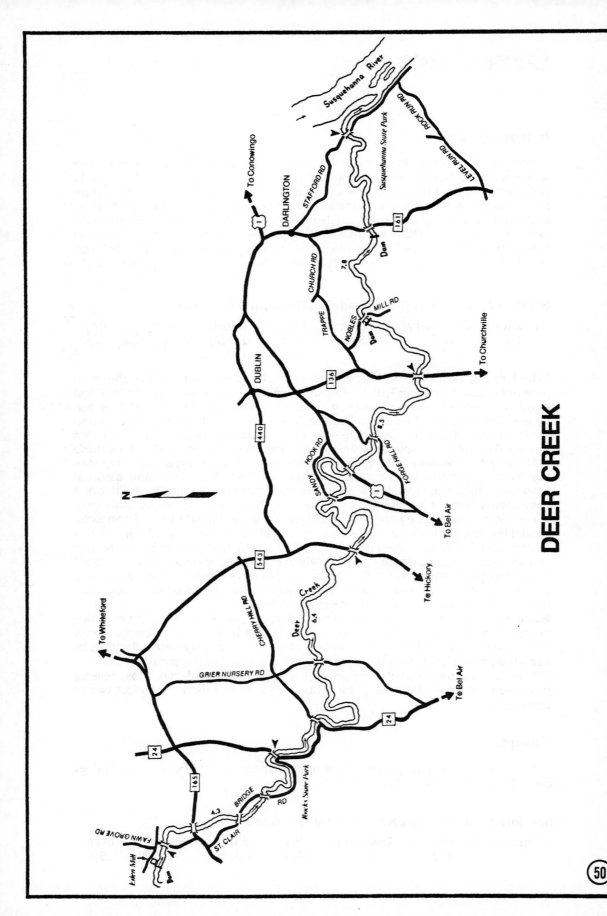

DEER CREEK

Trip Description: One can start at Fawn Grove Road or better yet, just upstream at the rustic Eden Mill. The initial miles to Rocks State Park are over swift flat water spiced with some gravelly riffles and sometimes with an ill-placed tree or fence. The creek winds about a narrow rural valley, views of which are unfortunately often blocked by eroded mud banks. At Rocks, Deer Creek breaks through the hard crystalline mass of Rock Ridge and tumbles down a short violent series of narrow chutes. Considering the broaching potential and the sharpness of the rocks novices are advised to take advantage of the nearby highway and carry. After decelerating through a stretch of gentle rock gardens the creek then settles down once again to an easy pace as it weaves through hilly countryside. However there is still a lively rock garden-filled wooded gorge below U.S. Rte. 1 and a riffly gorgelike section approaching Stafford Bridge to add variety. Also there is a three and a half-foot dam above Nobles Mill that should be carried at high levels and a sloping three-foot dam at Wilson Mill which is runable anywhere with a clunk. Possibly the finest quality of Deer Creek though is that through most of these miles the banks have remained undisturbed by vacation cottages, shacks and other eyesores that plague so many otherwise beautiful creeks in this area.

This section can be broken down into any number of comfortable-lengthed runs with the best combinations including the passage through Rocks or the gorge below Rte. 1. Access points that are presently unposted and offer some degree of parking space include Md. Rte. 165 (mile 1.0), along Md. Rte. 24 (mile 4.5 to 6.0), Grier Nursery Road (mile 9.0), Md. Rte. 543 (mile 12.5), Sandy Hook Road (mile 16.5), Md. Rte. 136 (mile 21.0) and Stafford Road. You can also continue another mile past Stafford Bridge to a muddy take-out at the mouth. If you do paddle down to Stafford or below be sure to stop at Susquehanna State Park and check out its old furnace and restored mills.

Hazards: Dam at Nobles Mill can be run on right at low water but is best avoided at high water. The sloping dam at Wilson Mill can be run anywhere at moderate levels. Finally fences and newly fallen trees are always a possibility on narrow rural streams as this.

Water Conditions: Canoeable winter and spring within week of rainfall.

Gauge

USGS gauge along Md. Rte. 24 at the lower end of Rocks State Park should read at least 4.5 feet to scrape through the rock gardens.

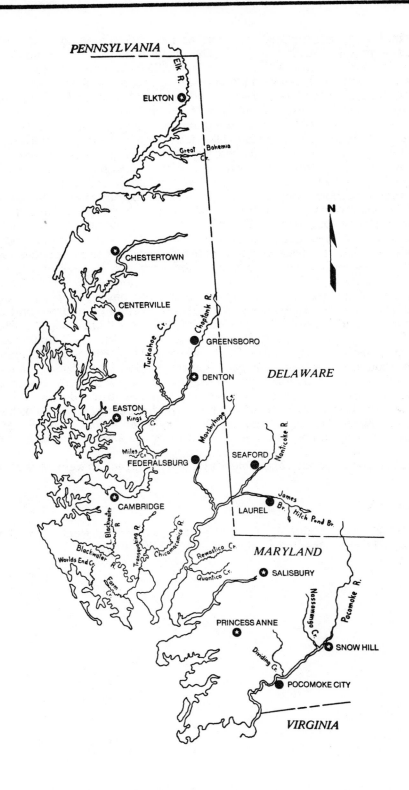

EAST CHESAPEAKE BAY TRIBUTARIES

Chapter 6

Rivers of the Eastern Shore

The "Eastern Shore" is generally used to describe an entity comprising Maryland east of the Chesapeake Bay but here it is used to describe in addition that portion of Delaware draining to the Bay. This is a flat low-lying area dedicated to agriculture and harvesting the Bay's seafood treasures. When you talk about rivers and creeks around here, you are usually talking about tidal estuaries. There is rarely enough time or room for enough branches to gather and grow to a canoeable-size stream before tidewater is reached. Still a few streams have managed to acquire enough size to be navigable to the swamp-loving river rat and one borderline creek, the Big Elk which enters the head of the Bay and might not be considered an Eastern Shore stream by the purist, even offers pleasant whitewater cruising.

The following streams are described in this chapter:

Big Elk Creek
Great Bohemia Creek
Choptank River
   Tuckahoe Creek
   Kings Creek
   Miles Creek
Worlds End Creek
Farm Creek
Blackwater River
   Little Blackwater River
Transquaking River
   Chicamacomico River
Nanticoke River
   Hitch Pond Branch and James Branch
   Marshyhope Creek
   Rewastico Creek
   Quantico Creek
Pocomoke River
   Nassawango Creek
   Dividing Creek

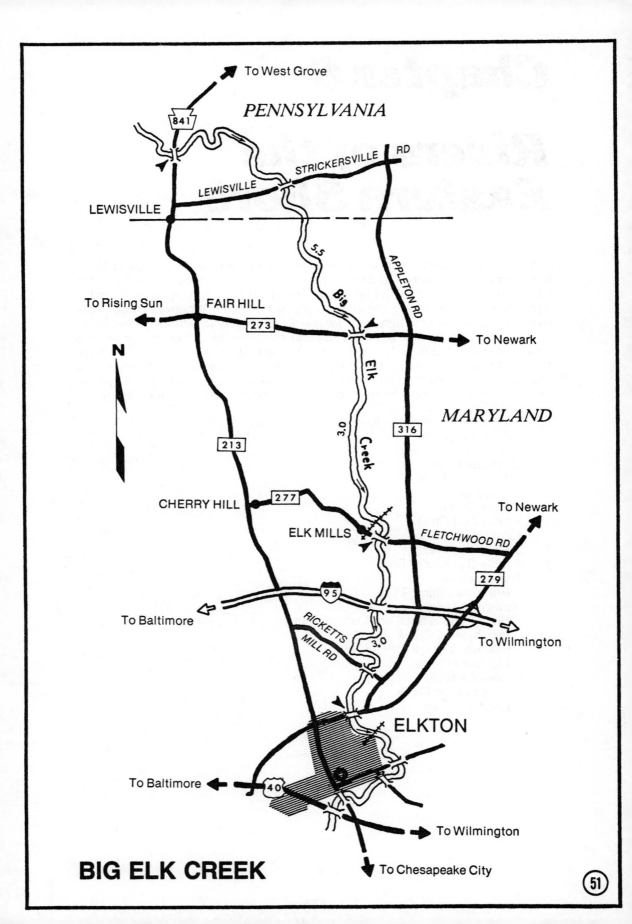

BIG ELK CREEK

51

Big Elk Creek

Introduction

Big Elk Creek flows out of the rolling Piedmont of southern Chester County, Pa. It drains a small narrow pastoral valley and accordingly is difficult to catch up more than twenty-four hours after a good rain. Much of the run down to Elk Mills is through the huge DuPont Fair Hill estate, now owned by the State of Maryland. This allows one to enjoy a remarkably serene, manicured, unlittered and practically unpopulated landscape in the heart of the great eastern seaboard megalopolis.

Section 1. Pa. Rte. 841 to Elkton, Md. (Md. Rte. 279)

Gradient	Difficulty	Distance	Time	Width	Scenery	Map
15	1-2	11.5	5.0	15-30	Good	51

Trip Description: Put in at Pa. Rte. 841 north of Lewisville. There is a dirt side road at the southeast end of the bridge where one can fit a few cars. Except where your view is blocked by high mudbanks the scenery is of rolling pastures and wooded hillsides. As on many other stream valleys in this corner of the state the hillsides are forested with some beautiful stands of beech trees. There are numerous riffles and small rapids of a rock garden nature that at low water are quite tedious but not dangerous. Hazards on this section include a fallen tree or two, one low-water bridge and woven wire fences. Most of these fences, used to facilitate fox hunting on the Fair Hill Estate, are washed out with only the supporting booms or cables remaining. But one troublesome fence remains intact except for one canoe-size breach at low levels. At higher levels the breach would be impassable and since the high and very difficult to scale fence continues on both banks the paddler should seriously consider carrying a strong pair of wire cutters. At Elk Mills there is a two-foot high wooden dam under the railroad bridge; run on right. Below Elk Mills the topography flattens out and the scenery becomes rather drab but the riffles are numerous to the end. Take out on the downstream left at the Rte. 279 bridge.
Hazards: All described above. The woven fence under the bridge warrants special attention as at high levels it blocks all progress downstream.
Water Conditions: Paddleable winter or spring within twenty-four hours of a hard rain.

Gauge

None. Judge at put-in and at Rte. 273 bridge.

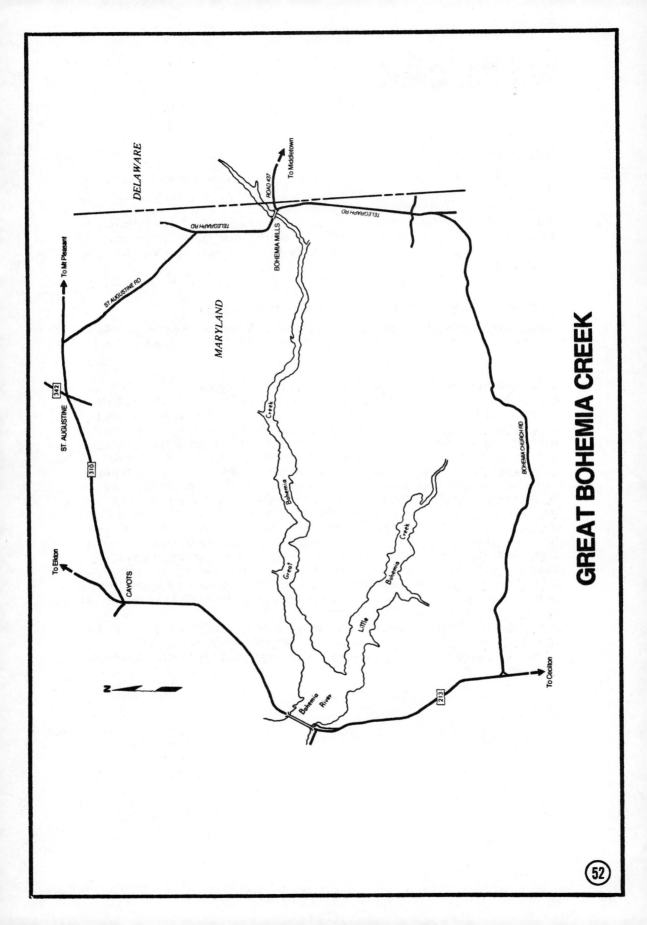

GREAT BOHEMIA CREEK

Great Bohemia Creek

Introduction

The upper Chesapeake Bay presents a superb mix of land and water that would charm just about anyone. Unfortunately that charm combined with proximity to Washington, Baltimore, Wilmington and Philadelphia has lured thousands of individuals into building their homes, estates and vacation retreats along hundreds of miles of its shoreline. There remains very little waterfront bearing the wild beauty that so impressed Captain John Smith almost four centuries ago and which would be of the most interest to the touring paddler today. However there are fortunately a few pockets of if not wild at least fairly undeveloped tidal creek on the upper Eastern Shore and the Great and Little Bohemia creeks are two of them.

Section 1. Telegraph Rd. to Md. Rte. 213

Gradient	Difficulty	Distance	Time	Width	Scenery	Map
0	A	5.5	2.0	15-2000	Good	52

Trip Description: If the tide is high it is possible to put in at Telegraph Road, Bohemia Mills, but once again, only if the tide is high. Even at such times a little bushwacking and perhaps a little dragging may still be necessary, but this soon gets you out to a shallow, narrow but floatable creek meandering through a freshwater marsh. In about a half mile Sandy Branch joins from the southeast and the head of navigation for even low tide conditions is reached. The problem with this creek is that it has been choked with silt over the years, leaving only a narrow channel over most of its length bracketed at low tide by either mud flats or four inch deep water. The channel through its unusually murky waters can often be quite elusive and will test your depth finding intuitions. If you arrive in this neighborhood at low tide, cancel your one-way trip plans and just put in at Md. Rte. 213 and then paddle as far up the creek as you like and return. A short side road at the foot of the south approach to the bridge provides easy access.

The creek cuts through a rolling countryside graced by attractive grain and horse farms. The shores, especially the south shore, tend to be wooded and sometimes break away into low eroded bluffs. There are narrow sandy beaches along the lower creek and narrow marshes along the upper and middle reaches. The usually wooded north shore is broken by views across farm fields and is dotted by a few attractive houses, barns and docks. It is a really nice and peaceful place to spend your time.

A pleasant side trip can be had by poking up Little Bohemia Creek. The Little Bohemia is even prettier and less developed than the Great. On its upper reaches are bluffs clothed in hemlock, a relatively uncommon sight on the Eastern Shore. Unfortunately this creek is even more silted in than the Great Bohemia and at low tide it can only be ascended about a mile and a half above its mouth.

Hazards: Being stuck in the middle of a black gooey bottomless mud flat on an ebbing tide.

Water Conditions: Tidal and thus canoeable all year except when frozen.

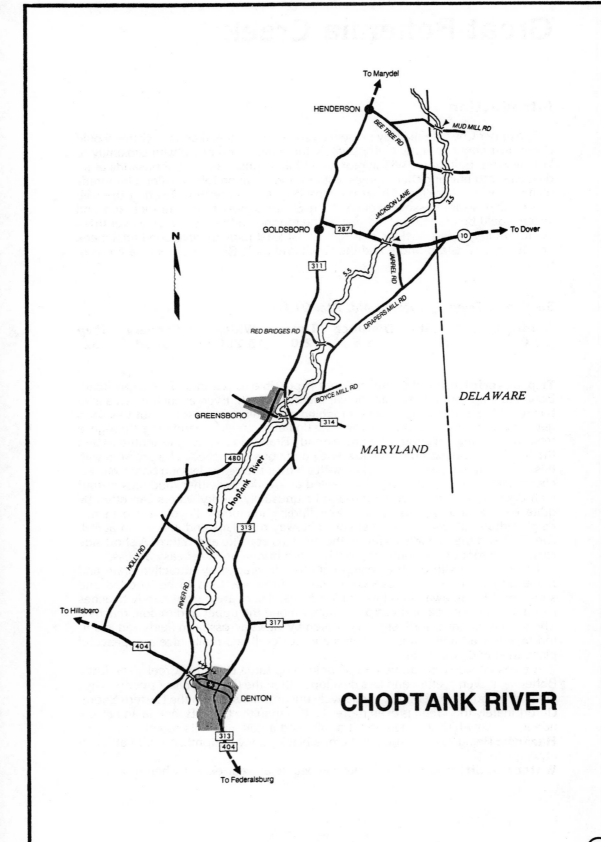

To Marydel

HENDERSON

MUD MILL RD

BEE TREE RD

JACKSON LANE

3.5

GOLDSBORO 287 To Dover 10

311

5.5

JARREL RD

DRAPERS MILL RD

RED BRIDGES RD

BOYCE MILL RD

DELAWARE

GREENSBORO 314

MARYLAND

480

Choptank River

8.7

313

HOLLY RD

RIVER RD

To Hillsboro

317

404

DENTON

313
404

To Federalsburg

CHOPTANK RIVER

N

53

Choptank River

Introduction

The Choptank River starts in Kent County, Delaware, west of Dover, winds its way through swamp forests to tidewater at Greensboro, Maryland and sloshes still onward to the Chesapeake just west of Cambridge. This is a typical swamp river above Greensboro with typical swamp hardships and one must be truly dedicated to the outdoors not to mention slightly crazy to subject oneself to this sort of masochism even if it is a lovely place to visit. Less athletic seekers of solitude will most prefer the segment to Denton while only those paddlers not discouraged by wide waters, built up shores and pesky winds will venture below.

Section 1. Mud Mill Road to Greensboro, Md. (Md. Rte. 313)

Gradient	Difficulty	Distance	Time	Width	Scenery	Map
4	A-1	9.0	8.0	10-40	Good	53

Trip Description: Mud Mill Road is the technical head of navigation only. Put in here and you subject yourself to a cellulose hell; logs, trees, bushes, vines, thorns, poison ivy, etc. without end. It is almost nonstop wrestling with this mess. Do yourself a favor and put in a mile downstream at Bee Tree Road. There are still a lot of deadfalls but at least you get a chance to paddle in between. As you progress downstream obstacles become fewer and by the end it is pretty easy going. Also with each mile downstream the scenery improves, the surrounding swamps widen and the trees get bigger. One interesting feature is the unusual number of holly trees along this river. Also some of the adjacent land has some elevation so that there are some pretty beech covered hillsides and interesting clay cliffs. Finally, last but not least, there is some elementary whitewater in the form of gravel bar riffles below Red Bridges Road.
Hazards: Trees
Water Conditions: Passable late fall, winter and spring except after drought.

Gauge

Staff gauge at Red Bridges Road. Level of 2.2 feet is about zero.

Section 2. Greensboro (Md. Rte. 314) to Denton (Md. Rte. 404)

Gradient	Difficulty	Distance	Time	Width	Scenery	Map
0	A	8.0	4.0	100-1000	Good	53

Trip Description: While this section lacks the intimacy of the upper Choptank it also lacks the hardships. Once beyond Greensboro it offers relative isolation amidst both high and swampy wooded banks. Access is plush; a nice fairground by Rte. 314 in Greensboro and a boat ramp and park by the Rte. 404 bridge, Denton.
Hazards: None
Water Conditions: Tidal and hence canoeable all year.

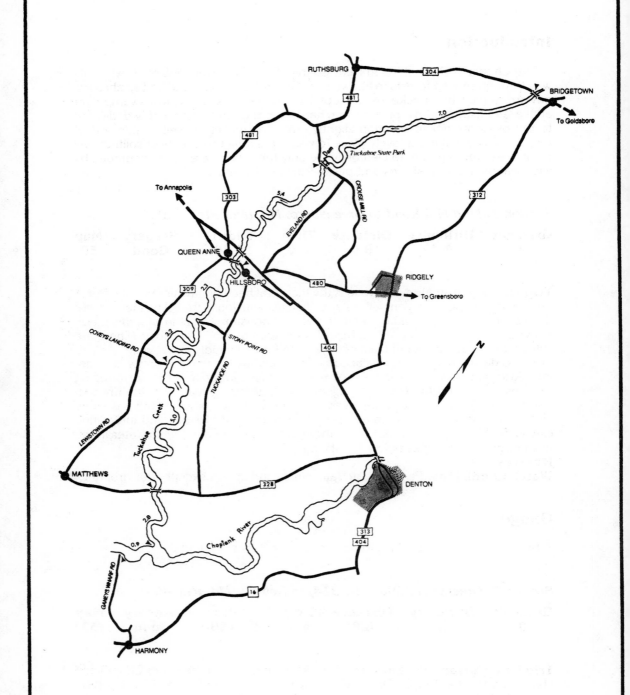

RUTHSBURG

304

BRIDGETOWN

481

To Goldsboro

481

7.0

Tuckahoe State Park

303

To Annapolis

5.4

CROUSE MILL RD

312

EVELAND RD

QUEEN ANNE

309

480

RIDGELY

HILLSBORO

2.1

To Greensboro

COVEYS LANDING RD

3.2

STONY POINT RD

TUCKAHOE RD

404

Tuckahoe Creek

5.0

LEWISTOWN RD

MATTHEWS

328

DENTON

2.8

313

404

Choptank River

0.9

GANEY'S WHARF RD

16

HARMONY

N

TUCKAHOE CREEK

Tuckahoe Creek

Introduction

Tuckahoe Creek forms the twisting border between Caroline and Queen Annes counties. Tiny, tangled and swampy above Rte. 404 and wide, placid and tidal below, it offers a satisfying escape from the congested nearby megalopolis.

Section 1. Crouse Mill Road to Hillsboro (Alt. Rte. 404)

Gradient	Difficulty	Distance	Time	Width	Scenery	Map
2	A	5.5	5.0	15-40	Good	54

Trip Description: Much of this run is within the bounds of Tuckahoe State Park. It is possible but not recommended to put in seven miles upstream at Md. Rte. 304, Bridgetown on the Mason Branch. The first two miles are now, thanks to the magic of the Soil Conservation Service, an ugly straight channelized ditch. This is followed by about three miles of tangled woody jungle followed by two miles of pond, most of which is flooded swamp forest. The paddler would find it much more worthwhile to put in on the pond at Crouse Mill Road, paddle upstream to observe the tremendous flocks of waterfowl that winter there and then proceed downstream. This also gives one the opportunity to run the three and a half-foot dam at the end of the pond. Below Crouse Mill Road there are still plenty of fallen trees to negotiate but you now have some time to paddle and enjoy the scenery. However things may improve even more in a few years as the State Park has ambitions to cut a canoe trail through this maze. The surrounding forest is deep, dense and contains a lot of really big beautiful trees. The water is fairly clear, slightly stained and fairly swift almost to the end of the trip which is on tidewater.
Hazards: Fallen trees and a sharp dam which can be run at center.
Water Conditions: Winter and spring except after prolonged dry spell.

Gauge

There is a staff gauge on the downstream right pier of the Crouse Mill Road bridge. One foot is minimal and about 1.25 feet is desired to run the dam.

Section 2. Hillsboro (Alt. Rte. 404) to Md. Rte. 328

Gradient	Difficulty	Distance	Time	Width	Scenery	Map
0	A	10.5	4.5	100-1500	Good	54

Trip Description: More suited for the leisurely paddler, this section meanders placidly past large tracts of marsh and mostly high wooded banks touched by little development. Embark at the small public ramp in Hillsboro. Rte. 328 concludes the best of the lower Tuckahoe as the last two miles to the Choptank are more built up. If you go the whole way, take out a mile down the Choptank at Ganeys Wharf.
Hazards: None
Water Conditions: Runable all year except when frozen.

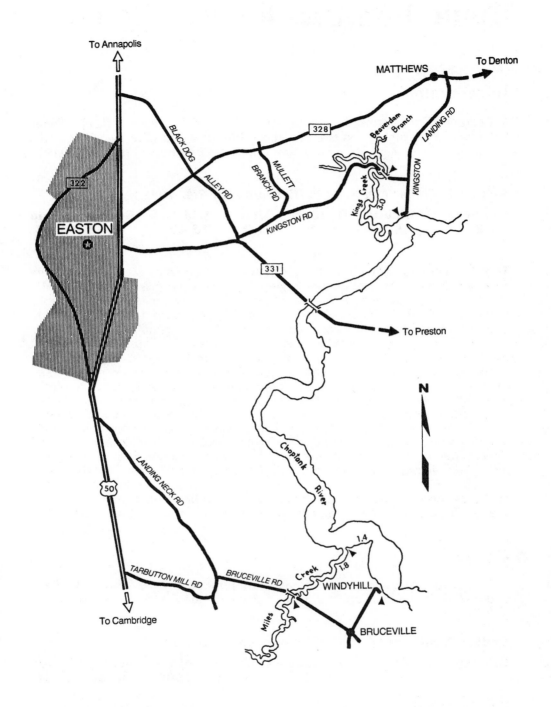

To Annapolis

MATTHEWS   To Denton

328

Beaverdam Branch

LANDING RD

BLACK DOG

ALLEY RD

MULLETT BRANCH RD

322

EASTON

KINGSTON RD

Kings Creek

3.0

KINGSTON

331

To Preston

N

Choptank River

50

LANDING NECK RD

1.4

Creek

1.8

WINDYHILL

TARBUTTON MILL RD

BRUCEVILLE RD

Miles

BRUCEVILLE

To Cambridge

KINGS CREEK
MILES CREEK

55

Kings Creek and Miles Creek

Introduction

They seem to usually hide the best rivers. In the mountains they hide them down in deep canyons and on the Piedmont fall line, down in narrow gorges. And out on the flat open Eastern Shore they hide them out in the middle of soybean fields and off of broad estuaries where you could cruise right by five times without noticing their mouths. They hid the two tiny Choptank tributaries called Kings Creek and Miles Creek out on the eastern edge of Talbot County but now we are letting the creek out of the bag.

Section 1. Kings Creek. Kingston Landing to head of river

Gradient	Difficulty	Distance	Time	Width	Scenery	Map
0	A	5.0	2.5	15-200	Very Good	55

Trip Description. This is a most beautiful watery byway. The paddler will see few structures from the water and only a few farm fields hint of the intensely cultivated land beyond its high wooded banks. Expansive marshes surrounding the mouth of this creek shrink as you progress upstream. After passing Kingston Road swampy shores just about replace the marsh but there is still always a thin fringe of cattails and reeds. If you have time, a short side trip up Beaverdam Branch treats you to more undisturbed marsh and forest. Heading further upstream Kings Creek gradually narrows until the end is suddenly reached in a tangle of fallen trees. You can start on Kings Creek near its mouth by putting in at Kingston Landing a half mile up the Choptank or half way up the creek where Kingston Road crosses. Watch your approach as the turnoffs to Kingston Road and Kingston Landing Road are poorly marked.

Section 2. Miles Creek. Windyhill to head of river

Gradient	Difficulty	Distance	Time	Width	Scenery	Map
0	A	5.5	3.0	50-250	Good	55

Trip Description: Miles Creek is not as pretty as Kings Creek for it is more developed in spots. Like Kings Creek it can be approached from near its mouth via Windyhill public boat ramp on the Choptank and midway via Bruceville Road. The lower creek winds through broad wetlands while the portion above Bruceville Road begins bumping a lot against high wooded banks. This upper section of creek becomes quite shallow so just how far up you ascend depends on whether the tide is in or not.
Hazards. None
Water Conditions: Tidal and hence always navigable. High tide is recommended for the upper reaches of these streams, especially Miles Creek.

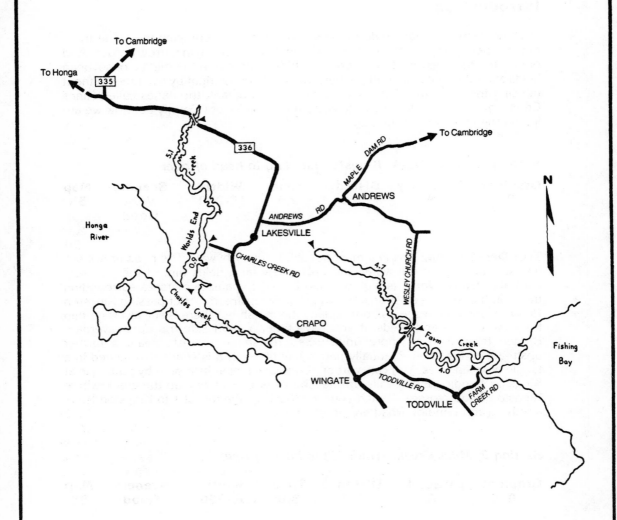

To Cambridge

To Honga

335

336

5.1

Honga
River

Worlds End

0.9

Charles Creek

Charles Creek

CHARLES CREEK RD

LAKESVILLE

ANDREWS RD

MAPLE DAM RD

ANDREWS

To Cambridge

N

WESLEY CHURCH RD

4.7

CRAPO

Farm Creek

4.0

Fishing
Bay

WINGATE

TODDVILLE RD

TODDVILLE

FARM CREEK RD

WORLDS END CREEK
FARM CREEK

Worlds End Creek
and Farm Creek

Introduction

There is probably no wetter place in Maryland than the southern half of Dorchester County. The roads down there wind almost as much as the ones in the mountains do but here they carefully thread a trail from one precious high ground to the next, linking little places like Honga, Crapo, Bishops Head and Crocheron to the higher and drier world beyond. It stands to reason that this is the right place to take a little boat to. And if you follow these long winding roads down to Farm Creek or Worlds End Creek, surely you will agree.

Section 1. Worlds End Creek. Md. Rte. 336 to Charles Creek

Gradient	Difficulty	Distance	Time	Width	Scenery	Map
0	A	6.0	3.0	20-1500	Excellent	56

Trip Description: Worlds End Creek is a perfect way to survey that unspoiled expanse of intimidatingly titled wetland called Hell Hook Marsh. This is one of those rare creeks where you can stand up in your canoe and look out across a vast area and see nobody nor any sign of them. The major portion of Worlds End Creek remains a terribly twisting thread down the middle of ever widening salt meadows bounded by an unbroken wall of forest. While this may be a lonely canoe trail today, old rotting black piles and timbers protruding from the bank muck at low tide remind one that this was once an important artery of local commerce in the pre-automobile era. The creek widens suddenly at about the five mile point to an estuary fringed by tall pines whose skyline as viewed from a boat eventually vanishes in the distance and then returns as a mirage. Public access to this beauty is limited to the narrow Rte. 336 right of way. The marsh is private property as is the landing at the foot of Charles Creek Road. Please respect this and only consider this creek as a circuit tour unless you can secure permission to cross private land.

Section 2. Farm Creek. Toddville to head of creek

Gradient	Difficulty	Distance	Time	Width	Scenery	Map
0	A	8.5	4.0	30-400	Very Good	56

Trip Description: Beginning as a pond in the heart of wild Beech Ground Swamp, tiny Farm Creek follows the crookedest path possible to its meeting with Fishing Bay. Start your journey just above the mouth at the public boat ramp on Farm Creek Road near Toddville and head upstream. As far as Wesley Church Road the narrow channel is usually hemmed in by tall reeds and hence that is most of what you see. However above there the reeds disappear, affording a wonderful panorama of wide green marsh meadows and dense pine forests. The trip climaxes in a shallow wilderness pond and then it is time to turn back.
Hazards: None
Water Conditions: Tidal with upper sections best at high tide.

BLACKWATER RIVER
LITTLE BLACKWATER RIVER

Blackwater River and Little Blackwater River

Introduction

The area surrounding Fishing Bay in southern Dorchester County is Maryland's convincing immitation of the Everglades. If you care to survey it by foot, bike or automobile, follow the road to Elliott Island. If you want to see it from a boat, follow the Blackwater system. The Blackwater and Little Blackwater drain much of Dorchester County south of Cambridge. This is a markedly low area where the difference between wetland and terra firma is often only two or three feet. Much of the Blackwater passes through lands or wetlands protected by either a national wildlife refuge or a state wildlife management area and those remaining areas that are privately owned are so remote that nobody has ever bothered to post them. In fact there are only two points of access to the whole 28 miles of the Blackwater and only two on the relatively civilized Little Blackwater.

Section 1. Blackwater River. Md. Rte. 335 to head of river

Gradient	Difficulty	Distance	Time	Width	Scenery	Map
0	A	6.0	3.0	15-500	Excellent	57

Trip Description: This is the best of the Blackwater and it must be handled as a circuit paddle. The still relatively wide river zig-zags into the wilderness of Moneystump Swamp. Civilization back here consists of a few duck blinds, some wildlife refuge markers and one improbable footbridge. In general the river passes through forests of almost pure pine fronted by freshwater marsh. The Blackwater, which now lives up to its name, eventually narrows on past the footbridge and finally dissolves into a vast cattail-filled marsh. The river's upper reaches support a beautiful floating garden of water lilies which in summer will delight you but also probably block upstream progress short of the true head of navigation. There is parking for about six cars at the Rte. 335 bridge.
Hazards: None
Water Conditions: Tidal so there is always water. Daily tidal fluctuations are slight up here but longer term effects due to sustained northwesterly or southeasterly winds driving water out or in can influence your success in shallow stretches.

Section 2. Blackwater River. Rte. 335 to Shorters Wharf (Maple Dam Road)

Gradient	Difficulty	Distance	Time	Width	Scenery	Map
0	A	10.0	6.0	150-6000	Good	57

Trip Description: This is not an easy section to deal with. First of all most of it flows within the Blackwater National Wildlife Refuge which is closed to river traffic from October 1 to April 1. This means that except for April and maybe early May you must endure the peak of the bug season to tour this place. Remember that in bad years even the locals are driven to distress by the little vampires. Besides being potentially tormenting it is against the rules to feed the wildlife. Incidentally the boating restrictions were not made with malice to canoeists. You see the refuge is an important avian rest stop on the Atlantic Flyway which is a goose's version of the New Jersey Turnpike. While some birds winter here, the major crush hits in late fall and early spring on their way through. The refuge's goal is to keep as many birds as possible within its boundaries during that busy period. This is so that during hunting season they do not get shot and at other times to assure that these feathered locust do not descend on neighboring farmers' fields and devour the newly sprouted winter wheat, etc., thereby incurring great wrath. And so boating and other backcountry travel is prohibited to avoid spooking the nervous honkers and quackers, causing them to prematurely flee to the troubled world beyond the refuge.

The other problem with this stretch is that to navigate it is an exercise in aquatic orienteering. Do not even consider venturing below Rte. 335 unless you have a good sense of direction and good eyesight. The entire reach from Rte. 335 to the confluence with the Little Blackwater is, contrary to what the topographic maps show, a huge lake. The lake is plenty deep where the old river flowed but where the islands and marshes once lay is now only a few inches deep. Of course to the uninitiated it all looks the same, just a big lake. Much of the channel on the eastern half of the lake is marked by sticks protruding from the water. These often require sharp vision to see and sometimes more than one channel is marked. You should bring along the Golden Hill and Blackwater River USGS 7½ minute quadrangle sheets and a compass to try to follow the old channel by map, using the twiggs to then verify your estimates. There are few markers in the first two miles. Generally that part of the channel describes a gentle arc from the Rte. 335 bridge, off of the southern tip of Spriggs Island by 1000 feet and across Raymond Pond. You will find sticks beginning to appear approximately 2000 feet north of Bull Point. The mouth of the Little Blackwater is marked by a yellow refuge sign instructing you to "Maintain Speed for Next Mile." This is because this is a bald eagle nesting area, so please obey the signs and do not land or linger. The rest of the channel to Shorters Wharf is easy to follow. Reed grass on this section is usually low, especially in the spring after winter fires have leveled much of it, so wide open views are plentiful.

Hazards: Getting lost in plain view of where you are headed.

Water Conditions: Tidal. Ideally an extraordinarily low tide might be an asset as the shallows would be exposed, thus revealing the elusive channel.

Section 3. Blackwater River. Shorters Wharf to Fishing Bay

Gradient	Difficulty	Distance	Time	Width	Scenery	Map
0	A	12.5	6.0	150-500	Good	57

Trip Description: This section passes through a vast beautiful marsh that is dotted with waterfowl filled ponds and sloughs but alas the tall riverside reeds block your view of it. So unless you go ashore now and then you will not see very much, though admittedly it is still a fine form of solitude. There is no access to the mouth so you can either turn around, forge across Fishing Bay to Elliott Island (risky), ascend the Transquaking to Bestpitch or paddle about five and a half miles down the west shore of Fishing Bay to the boat ramp at Toddville. All of these options will exercise you well. Wesley Road, a mass of mud and ruts, might get you out on Raccoon Creek but it is not recommended.

Hazards: None

Water Conditions: Always runable.

Section 4. Little Blackwater River. Key Wallace Drive to head of river

Gradient	Difficulty	Distance	Time	Width	Scenery	Map
0	A	7.0	3.5	20-800	Good	57

Trip Description: Unlike the wild Blackwater the Little Blackwater is a wide winding river coursing through attractive farm country. There are spots of woods between farms and still plenty of marshland but you will seldom be out of sight of someone's house except on the more remote upper reaches. The two and a half mile section below Key Wallace Drive partly flows through the refuge so it also is subject to the seasonal use restrictions and in addition the same navigational challenges as found on Section 2 of the Blackwater. A better way of seeing this lower section is from the observation tower on the scenic drive. Midpoint access to the upper river can be had via Maple Dam Road where it crosses Hughs Dam Creek.

Hazards: Watch out for spikes in old trestle pier near head of creek.

Water Conditions: Always runable.

Tides and Tide Tables

There are four changes of tides evenly spaced in any 24 hours. The tide coming in from the sea is called the flood tide, going out is the ebb tide and the pauses in between are called slack water. You can know in advance when these phases are to occur by consulting a tide table. You can purchase tables directly from the U.S. Coast and Geodetic Survey in Washington, D.C., from the Md. Dept. of Natural Resources (for a Chesapeake Bay Table only) or from your local marine supply store. While formats may vary, they all include the same basic information.

To understand the use of a tide table, let us take an example; say you want to paddle up the Smyrna River from its mouth on May 1, imaginary year. First you consult a table that gives the tide schedule at the nearest major point, in this case the entrance to Delaware Bay, on given days of the year (tide tables are annual publications). The chart has a column for time of slack water, time of maximum current velocity and maximum current velocity. The velocity column also indicates the tide's direction, ebb(E) or flood(F). So checking out May 1 you determine that maximum flood tide will be at 1110 (they use military time) and 2331 and that slackwaters preceding these tides are at 0812 and 2021 respectively. Now if you want to paddle by daylight, you would choose to time your trip to the first tide and start on the slack at 8:12 A.M., figuring to have a maximum favorable current at 11:10 A.M. and dead slack about six hours after you put-in (remember, four tides per day). But wait; this is the schedule of the tides at the Delaware Bay entrance. What about the Smyrna River mouth 45 miles up the Bay? It takes longer for the tide change to reach up here so you now consult another table which lists various points up and down the Bay and then lists the time difference between that point and the entrance. The lag times vary slightly between ebbs and floods since there is always a net flow down the Bay due to the Delaware River's inflow. So looking up Smyrna River entrance in the table you see the time difference at just before flood is +1 hour 48 minutes and for maximum flood is +1 hour 42 minutes. Therefore you add these to the schedule at the entrance and now you know that on May 1 of this example year you should start at 10:00 A.M. (8:12 + 1:48) and be moving fastest around 12:52 P.M. and should be hitting slack again around 4:00 P.M. Since further lags occur as you ascend the Smyrna, you may be able to keep going with the tide past 4:00 P.M. This is just the minimum that you can learn from a tide table but it is enough to canoe by.

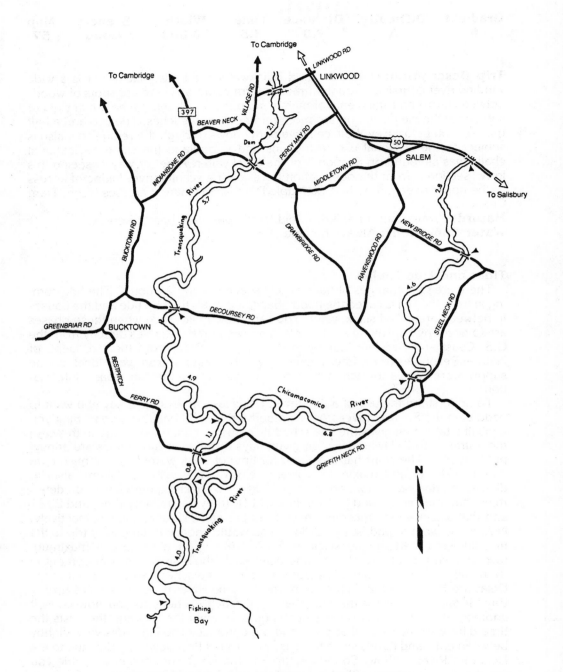

TRANSQUAKING RIVER
CHICAMACOMICO RIVER

Transquaking River

Introduction

The Transquaking River provides a serene tidal trail through the heart of flat, oh so flat, Dorchester County, Maryland. Although beginning only a few miles south of busy U.S. Rte. 50, thoroughfare of thousands of shorebound vacationers, the Transquaking meanders into one of Maryland's true geographical backwaters. This is some of the most thinly populated territory in the state with most people situated along a few narrow roads that thread through vast expanses of impenetrable swamp, marsh and on the higher grounds, corn and soybean fields. The river is in mild weather quite suitable for novices. However if you possess the skill and knowledge to handle cold weather paddling, winter and early spring are the recommended seasons as minimal motorboat traffic and absence of bloodsucking insects allow one to most enjoy this quiet land and water scape.

Section 1. Drawbridge Road to Bestpitch Ferry Road

Gradient	Difficulty	Distance	Time	Width	Scenery	Map
0	A	11.5	4.0	100-300	Good	58

Trip Description: As on most tidal waterways the put-in is arbitrary, depending on which way the tide is flowing. Starting at Drawbridge Road, where there is the luxury of a public launching ramp, parking and pit privies, you are just below the head of navigation which is Higgins Millpond Dam. It is possible to paddle upstream to the dam, lift over and then explore the two mile length of this pretty pond. Heading downstream from the put-in, initially the river courses past swampy shores broken by occasional solid ground and a few lonely farms. The black stained water provides a deep channel. About four miles downstream marshlands replace the swamps and these marshes gradually widen to one to two miles. In winter these broad meadows turn golden brown, contrasting boldly with the gray forests crowned by stately green pines that form the distant skyline. The claustrophobic paddler will revel in this Maryland version of the big sky country. Bestpitch Road pops up rather suddenly and offers easy exit via another public launch area.

There are still three to seven miles of river (depending on choice of routes) below Bestpitch through even grander and vaster wetlands. However there is no access to the mouth so the paddler then has the choice of either doubling back, or if one is a good navigator, find the mouth of the Blackwater River and ascend that stream to Maple Dam Road or finally if you are a strong competent paddler with a good assessment of the impending weather, cross the vast Fishing Bay to Elliott.

Hazards: Wind and mosquitos the size of B-52s.

Water Conditions: Navigable all year except when frozen.

Gauge

None.

Chicamacomico River

Introduction

The Chicamacomico River (pronounced Chi'·ca·ma·com'·i·co; say it fast five times) is a slightly longer and slightly prettier version of the Transquaking River to which it is a tributary. It has its origins in a handful of insignificant trickles and drainage ditches located about five miles east of the Transquaking's similarly humble beginnings and matures to a navigable stream only upon reaching tidewater a short distance south of U.S. Rte. 50.

Section 1. U.S. Rte. 50 to Bestpitch Ferry Road

Gradient	Difficulty	Distance	Time	Width	Scenery	Map
0	A	15.0	6.5	15-500	Good	58

Trip Description: It is possible to put in at U.S. Rte. 50 just below Big Millpond IF you are a truly dedicated hardcore swamp rat. That little ten foot wide and two inches deep trickle jammed with fallen trees and debris can get you where you want to go. Honest. Just walk west from the Rte. 50 bridge along the guardrail and about a hundred feet past the end of the guardrail you will observe a little five foot wide side channel that runs along the foot of the embankment and then bends off into the woods. Put in there. The channel immediately rejoins the main flow and for about the next two hundred yards this shallow rivulet rushes over a sandy bottom, twisting and turning through a gauntlet of low limbs, bushes and toppled trees. With a low profile boat such as a kayak or with a lot of skill in an open canoe one can wriggle through this mess with only a few carries. Others will probably fare worse but because the surrounding jungle is so dense and tangled, the creek route still beats trying to carry or drag through the woods to easy waters. Tidewater is soon (in distance if not in time) reached and the paddler can now settle down to a peaceful journey down a quickly widening and still twisting route through a swamp forest. In summer the dark waters will be bountifully decorated by water lilies. Unfortunately the river remains quite shallow for these first few miles so one must be constantly alert for the best channel. Less adventurous boaters will choose to start at New Bridge Road. The swampy shores continue on for a few more miles, interrupted now and then by a farm or cabin. Below Drawbridge Road the marshes take over and widen dramatically and you will be out in the wide open spaces. Since the river generally trends in a west to southwestward direction, this is a good section to avoid late on a sunny afternoon as the glare will be brutal. The take-out is a mile down the Transquaking at Bestpitch.
Hazards: None
Water Conditions: Most of the river is tidal and thus suitable to cruise all year. But the short nontidal stretch just below Rte. 50 needs extra water and should only be considered after wet weather.

Gauge

None

Nanticoke River

Introduction

The Nanticoke gathers its waters from the swamps and extensively cultivated flatlands of Sussex County, Delaware, and then cuts an imposing swath across Maryland's lower Eastern Shore. Unfortunately, most of it is a wide windy tidal estuary which, while very pretty, should only be attempted by paddlers armed with tide tables, lots of energy and ample bug protection during summer. Meanwhile, back in the headwaters, the U.S. Soil Conservation Service has done its best over the years to channelize all of the creeks in the neighborhood into drab, quick-draining, scum-filled straight ditches. But, somehow, they missed a few of the best ones and have left we canoeists the upper Nanticoke and its tributaries, the upper Marshyhope, James Branch and Hitch Pond Branch.

Section 1. County Road 545 to Seaford, Del. (U.S. Rte. 13)

Gradient	Difficulty	Distance	Time	Width	Scenery	Map
3	A	9.5	3.5	20-100	Good	59

Trip Description: It is not easy to find the starting point for this trip, as the put-in road is poorly marked by an unobtrusive yellow sign on Rte. 13A, 404 just south of Bridgeville, Del. and by a sign to a landfill on U.S. Rte. 13. There is no reason to start above here as the river has all been channelized. The river reverts to its natural channel at this point and commences winding through a pretty swamp, only occasionally marred by views into the surrounding farmland or by timbering scars. The most pleasant facet of this run is that it is relatively easy to negotiate. Unlike many other swamps, downed trees block the way with only moderate frequency and often there is a way around them. The stream turns tidal a few miles below the confluence of Gravelly Branch (left) but with the right tide you can enjoy a strong current well past Middleford, after which the stream widens out into a slow estuary with residentially developed shores. The choice of take-outs is a poor one. You can carry up the steep embankment to busy Rte. 13, you can continue one mile downstream to the confluence of Williams Pond at the community hospital, or you can continue a half mile further to a public launching ramp above the DuPont plant.
Hazards: Fallen trees and snags.
Water Conditions: Runable late fall, winter, spring and during a wet summer. Higher levels are desirable to increase options for bypassing trees.

Gauge

A USGS gauge is located at the put-in. Levels between 5.0 and 5.5 feet are excellent.

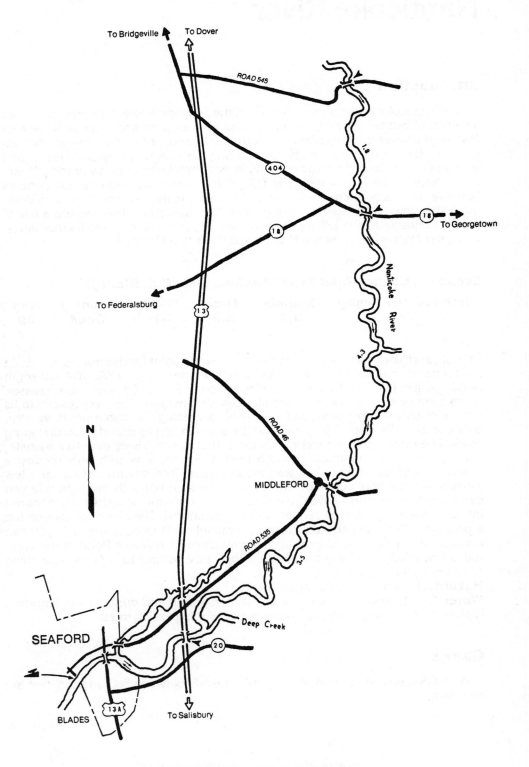

NANTICOKE RIVER

JAMES BRANCH
HITCHPOND BRANCH

Hitch Pond Branch and James Branch

Introduction

Whoever coined the adage "good things come in small packages" might have been inspired by this remote little swamp run. Canoeable streams just do not come any smaller, Delaware streams do not come any wilder, and on top of all that you do not need a chainsaw to get down it.

Section 1. Trap Pond State Park to U.S. Rte. 13

Gradient	Difficulty	Distance	Time	Width	Scenery	Map
4	A	5.5	2.5	5-25	Very Good	60

Trip Description: This trip begins at the foot of the spillway at Trap Pond Dam in Trap Pond State Park. This park offers fine camping facilities and makes an excellent base of operations for exploring lower Eastern Shore rivers. The stream immediately rushes off into a deep, dark, dank, and dense swamp forest that usually completely blots out the endless farms and fields that lie just beyond. Initially the creek is only five to eight feet wide but additional tributaries swell it to sufficient width that you cannot broach your boat between the banks. Hitch Pond Branch flows into James Branch below the first roadbridge from which point on there is plenty of elbow room. Amazingly, there are only a few trees blocking the course, partly because in years past the Delaware Department of Parks cleared the stream for canoeists. But the most outstanding feature of this swamp is its rich growth of cypress trees. Some surprisingly big trees still remain and the weird grotesque shapes of their unique trunks will never cease to fascinate. The trip ends too soon on the civilized Records Pond where a state launching ramp offers easy exit.
Hazards: Trees and overhanging limbs.
Water Conditions: Runable all winter and spring and often in wet summers.

Gauge

USGS gauge at the Trap Pond spillway. Level of 2.0 feet is excellent.

Trussum Pond

One should not visit this neighborhood without at least a short visit to Trussum Pond. Formed by an old dam across James Branch just above its confluence with Hitch Pond Branch, this is the closest thing to a bayou in Delaware. Access is via Rd. 72 at a small state park parking area. Trussum is more of a swamp than a pond. Graceful cypress protrude anywhere and everywhere from its black lily pad dappled waters, creating a bit of a challenge to navigation. While a main channel is often difficult to identify, a variety of routes and some persistence in pursuing them can lead you almost a mile and a half above the dam. This place is really special in late autumn when the cypress stand like great rusty mops against the now bare hardwood forests.

178

Marshyhope Creek

Introduction

Marshyhope Creek oozes out of Kent and Sussex counties, Delaware, and through Caroline and Dorchester counties, Md. to join the Nanticoke River below Sharptown. The upper river has been devastated by channelization but there still remains over nine miles of prime swamp cruising between Woodenhawk, Del. and tidewater at Federalsburg, Md. and easy wide open boating below.

Section 1. Woodenhawk, Del. (Del. Rte. 404) to Federalsburg, Md.

Gradient	Difficulty	Distance	Time	Width	Scenery	Map
2	A	9.5	4.0	20-30	Good	61

Trip Description: Do not be distressed by the dredged channel that you find at the put-in. A few hundred yards downstream, it abruptly ends and, after a brief introductory tangle with some trees, the creek begins its narrow, winding and sometimes subtle route through a very wet swamp forest. Like the Nanticoke, the going is *relatively* easy as fallen trees do not occur too often, compared to most small coastal plain streams, that is. Fortunately, the flooded nature of the surrounding woods often allows a bypass route. This is a pretty swamp without too many civilized inroads except for a large gravel mining operation below Noble Road. The take-out is a small public fishing access area on the Denton Road, (Md. Rte. 630) at Federalsburg, about a half mile above the town center. The best way to recognize this spot from the river is that it is the only spot below Noble Road that you are likely to encounter fishermen. Below here the river enters a dredged flood channel.
Hazards: Fallen trees and snags.
Water Conditions: Late fall, winter, spring and wet summers. Higher water increases options for avoiding fallen trees.

Gauge

None

Section 2. Federalsburg (Md. Rte. 318) to Nanticoke River

Gradient	Difficulty	Distance	Time	Width	Scenery	Map
0	A	16.5	8.0	100-700	Good	61

Trip Description: The tidal Marshyhope should have been named the "Swampyhope" as it flows for much of its length past wild and wet wooded fringes. Scattered patches of high ground are usually private and built upon. Together these characteristics make this mostly attractive river rather difficult to cruise as there are few places that you can stop along the way. Put in at the public marina above Rte. 318 and take out one mile down the Nanticoke at Riverton or at any bridge in between.
Hazards: None
Water Conditions: Tidal and always navigable.

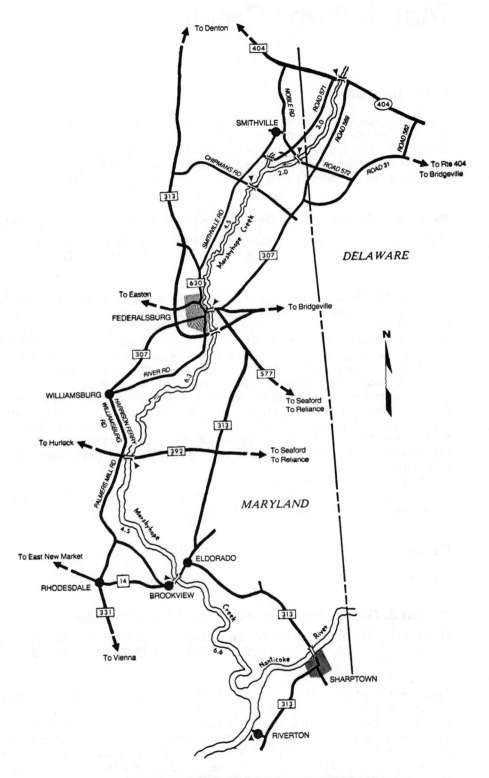

MARSHYHOPE CREEK

Rewastico Creek and Quantico Creek

Introduction

Rewastico and Quantico creeks are tributaries of the broad windswept lower Nanticoke River, diverging from almost a common mouth to wind their way back past marsh, forest and farm to headwaters only a dozen miles east of downtown Salisbury. These can be difficult waterways to explore as there is access only at their upper ends, meaning that it takes a fairly long trip to explore their entire lengths and this may include battling the wind and tide in addition.

Section 1. Rewastico Creek. Athol Road to Nanticoke River

Gradient	Difficulty	Distance	Time	Width	Scenery	Map
0	A	6.5	3.0	30-400	Good	62

Trip Description: The put-in is at the head of tidewater at the old crumbling gray mill and earthen dam forming Rewastico Mill Pond. This requires crossing private property so be sure to ask permission first. The creek quickly widens from the little dark pool at the mill but never really grows very big. The route is generally pretty with marsh-fringed shores backed by often wooded high ground but too many houses and farms occupy the surrounding high ground to generate a very remote atmosphere. Gradually though the marshes widen, farms disappear and by the time you reach the mouth you should feel far from anywhere. And in a way you are as the take-out is way back where you started or if you are really energetic it is a short hop down the Nanticoke and then a long haul up Quantico Creek to Rte. 347.

Section 2. Quantico Creek. Quantico (Md. Rte. 347) to Nanticoke River

Gradient	Difficulty	Distance	Time	Width	Scenery	Map
0	A	11.0	5.5	15-500	Good	62

Trip Description: Public access is available only off of the Rte. 347 right of way through a mess of mud, briars and brambles to a shallow and narrow little creek. Since the first 100 yards are complicated some by snags and deadfalls you might consider getting permission to put in across private property down an unnamed side street on the river right. The creek continues narrow and shallow for less than a mile, but now at least without obstructions, through woods until like Rewastico Creek it widens to modest dimensions. Quantico Creek proves to be quite pretty as unlike Rewastico there are few buildings crowding it, leaving mainly a tour of broad lonely wetlands and deep pine woods. These woods possess an understory of cedar and holly whose wonderful greenness will be most appreciated in winter when they so contrast with the golden marshes.
Hazards: None
Water Conditions: Runable all year but upper Quantico is marginal at low tide.

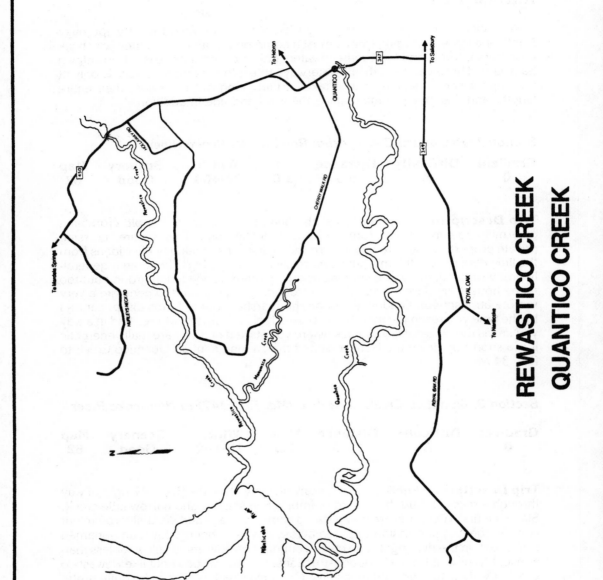

REWASTICO CREEK
QUANTICO CREEK

Pocomoke River

Introduction

The Pocomoke drains out of a big swamp in Sussex County, Delaware to eventually reach the Chesapeake Bay at the Maryland-Virginia line. What you see now is what remains of a once huge cypress swamp forest that has long since succumbed to lumbering, draining and massive fires. The swamp was for a long time lumbered to supply a thriving cypress shingle industry that was replaced by the use of redwood. Then in 1930 a fire ravaged the swamp (supposedly started by an exploding moonshine still) burning out not only trees but more importantly several feet of very slowly deposited peat. Even the river has been changed under past channelization efforts. But time has softened the scars, the forests are growing back and wildlife and waterfowl abound. This is now probably the best opportunity in the State for the novice paddler to escape the civilized world.

Section 1. Md. Rte. 346 to Whiton Crossing Road

Gradient	Difficulty	Distance	Time	Width	Scenery	Map
1	A	8.0	2.5	15-35	Good	63

Trip Description: This part of the Pocomoke has long been channelized and one has the feeling of paddling down a canal, not a river. However the banks are now densely wooded as is the surrounding swampy territory so one enjoys a feeling of remoteness. There is initially a strong current but this slows down considerably as the river widens.
Hazards: None
Water Conditions: All the time except for dry summers.

Gauge

None. Most marginal conditions are found at the put-in.

Section 2. Whiton Crossing Road to Snow Hill City Park

Gradient	Difficulty	Distance	Time	Width	Scenery	Map
2*	A	10.5	4.0	15-200	Excellent	63

*except for tidewater

Trip Description: The channelization ends below Whiton Crossing Road and the river commences twisting through a deep swamp forest. It is a forest of holly trees, maple, sweet gum and best of all, cypress. Even with all the past devastation some of the trees have survived to a giant size. The canoeist is carried through this wilderness by a remarkably fast and powerful current of dark tea-colored water (Pocomoke is Indian for "black water"). The path is mostly unobstructed as most fallen logs have been cut away to lessen flooding during high water (as an alternative to channelization). Below Porters Crossing the river becomes tidal but is still relatively narrow and easy to paddle. Cypress continue to line the dark waters but reeds and other still water plants now decorate the scenery. Take out

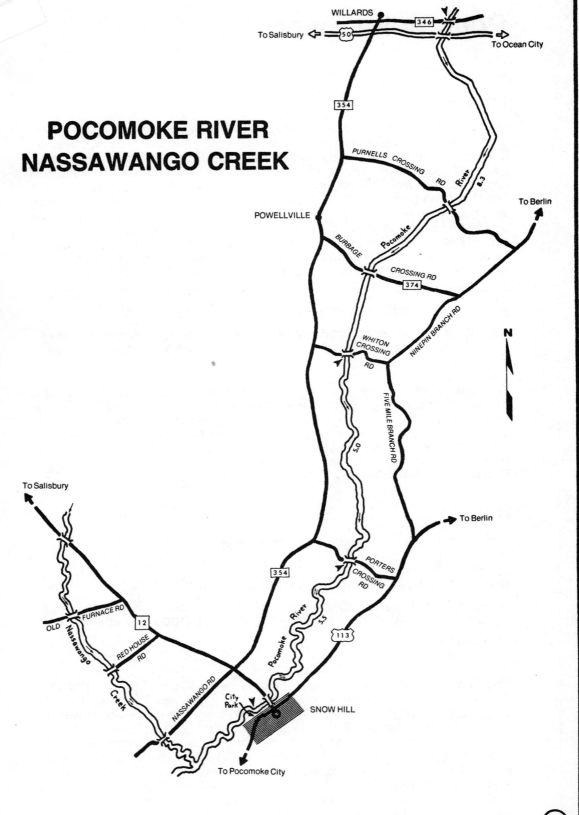

POCOMOKE RIVER
NASSAWANGO CREEK

WILLARDS

To Salisbury ← 50 346 To Ocean City

354

PURNELLS CROSSING RD

Pocomoke River 8.3

To Berlin

POWELLVILLE

BURBAGE

Pocomoke

CROSSING RD

374

NINEPIN BRANCH RD

WHITON CROSSING RD

FIVE MILE BRANCH RD

5.0

N

To Salisbury

To Berlin

PORTERS CROSSING RD

354

OLD Nassawango

FURNACE RD

12

RED HOUSE RD

NASSAWANGO RD

Pocomoke River 5.5

113

Creek

City Park

SNOW HILL

To Pocomoke City

at Snow Hill City Park which is on the left about a half mile below the Md. Rte. 12 bridge. For those wanting to avoid tidewater take out at Porters Crossing Road the roadsign for which is missing at its junction with Rte. 454, the probable shuttle route.

Hazards: None

Water Conditions: All year except during prolonged dry periods.

Gauge

None. Tidal below Porters Crossing.

Section 3. Snow Hill City Park to Pocomoke City (U.S. Rte. 13)

Gradient	Difficulty	Distance	Time	Width	Scenery	Map
0	A	13.5	6.0	250-900	Good	64

Trip Description: This is a very convenient and attractive piece of the Pocomoke to paddle. Still relatively narrow, the river rolls past wild tangled cypress studded swamp interrupted here and there only by a few farms and houses and facilities of two state parks. You are more likely to see motorboats on this section than above and you may even have to dodge an oil or gravel barge. There is a variety of access points at Pocomoke City; the park under the south end of the Rte. 13 bridge, a mile upstream at Winters Quarters Landing or a mile downstream of Rte. 13 at the Williams Street boat ramp.

Hazards: None

Water Conditions: Tidal and exceptionally deep.

Section 4. Pocomoke City (U.S. Rte. 13) to Shelltown

Gradient	Difficulty	Distance	Time	Width	Scenery	Map
0	A	15.5	7.0	250-1000	Good	64

Trip Description: This section of the Pocomoke would be the least interesting to the paddler. The river as far as Rehobeth still remains narrow as it continues past wild cypress swamp. However there is much more high ground along this portion and most of it is built upon. Past Rehobeth the cypress disappear and marshes begin to bracket the river with scattered farms occupying the solid ground just beyond. You can take out at Cedar Hall Wharf upstream of a lovely old colonial style house or at the ramp in Shelltown. The mouth lies two miles beyond Shelltown where the Pocomoke rounds the sandy tip of Williams Point on aptly named Fair Island into big blue Pocomoke Sound. This little island is probably the nicest feature of the lower river.

Hazards: Give commercial shipping a wide berth.

Water Conditions: Tidal

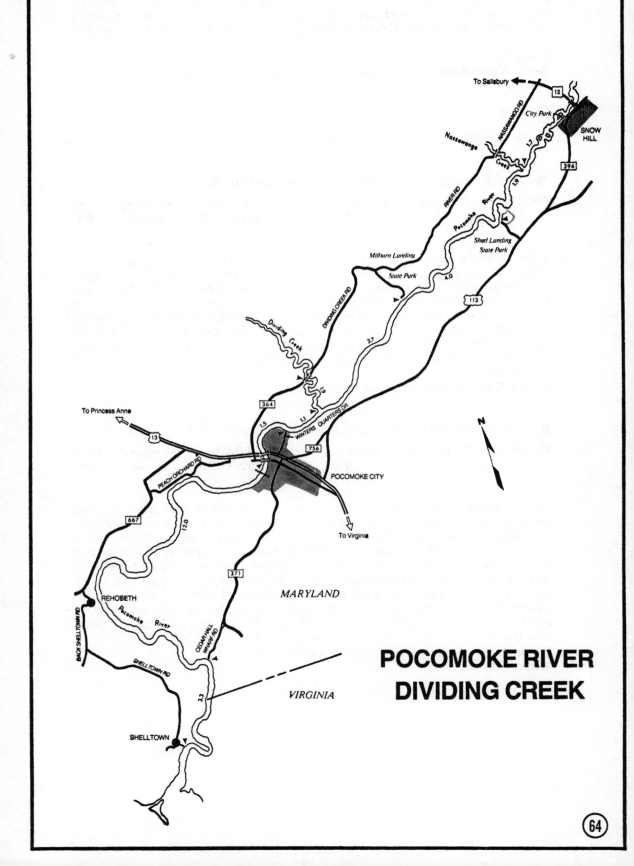

To Salisbury

City Park

NASSAWANGO RD

12

SNOW HILL

Nassawango

Creek

RIVER RD

1.7

Pocomoke River

1.9

394

Shad Landing State Park

Milburn Landing

4.0

State Park

113

DIVIDING CREEK RD

Dividing Creek

3.7

1.0

364

1.1

WINTERS QUARTERS DR

To Princess Anne

1.5

13

756

PEACH ORCHARD RD

POCOMOKE CITY

To Virginia

667

12.0

371

N

MARYLAND

REHOBETH

Pocomoke River

BACK SHELLTOWN RD

CEDAR HALL WHARF RD

SHELLTOWN RD

3.3

VIRGINIA

POCOMOKE RIVER DIVIDING CREEK

SHELLTOWN

64

Nassawango Creek

Introduction

Nassawango Creek is the Pocomoke's largest canoeable tributary, entering the Pocomoke about a mile and a half below Snow Hill. It is tiny but usually carries enough water to float a canoe through its lovely cypress swamp.

Section 1. Md. Rte. 12 to Nassawango Road

Gradient	Difficulty	Distance	Time	Width	Scenery	Map
2	A	6.0	5.0	10-60	Excellent	63

Trip Description: What you see at Rte. 12 seems awfully small but you will notice that there is a good bit of water flowing over the gauging station weir under the bridge and that is enough to float you. Like the Pocomoke, the water flows swiftly and clearly but stained dark brown by tannic acid leached from decaying vegetation. Like the Pocomoke it flows through a deep lovely cypress swamp forest. Unlike the Pocomoke, nobody came in and cut away the fallen trees. So it is rough going but well worth it. The stream below Red House Road is tidal, easy to paddle and still quite pretty.
Hazards: Fallen trees.
Water Conditions: Fall, winter and spring except after a prolonged dry spell and after heavy rains during summer. Tidal section is always boatable.

Gauge

USGS staff gauge at Rte. 12 should read at least 2.0 feet.

Beware of Fowl Play

One of the greatest natural resources of the Eastern Shore is its waterfowl. Located in the middle of the great Atlantic flyway, the Delmarva Peninsula is the wintering grounds or stopover point for tens of thousands of geese, swans, ducks and other migratory birds. Laced with waterways and wetlands, spotted with cornfields and normally subject to a fairly temperate winter climate; what more could a goose or duck want? There are four national wildlife refuges situated here to provide safe accommodations for the wandering fowl. They are Bombay Hook east of Dover, Delaware, Prime Hook southeast of Milford, Delaware, Eastern Neck south of Rock Hall, Maryland and Blackwater south of Cambridge, Maryland. At Blackwater there is a staffed visitor's center with interpretive exhibits inside and usually outside you can count on a few docile birds to strut around the yard for close observation.

Dividing Creek

Introduction

Dividing Creek is an aquatic gem known to but a few while so suitable for all. It provides an intimate hidden path into the twilight recesses of the vast Pocomoke Swamp. While it possesses a remote atmosphere as fine as is found anywhere in Maryland, it is easily accessible from nearby Pocomoke City. Being tidal, Dividing Creek is always runable, except maybe in the deepest iciest months of winter. It needs no shuttle; in fact it has none. The creek is remarkably deep and narrow and consistantly so for an unusually great distance. Study a map of the Delmarva Peninsula and you will find few if any estuaries with these combined characteristics. The upper reaches of this creek and swamp are targeted by some politicians and the eager engineers of the U.S. Soil Conservation Service for channelization to reclaim its "worthless" swamplands, so go enjoy it now before it becomes the Dividing Creek Canal.

Section 1. Pocomoke River to who knows where

Gradient	Difficulty	Distance	Time	Width	Scenery	Map
0	A	5.0	2.5	15-25	Excellent	64

Trip Description: Unlike most streams, start Dividing Creek at the bottom. The nearest convenient put-in is a public launching ramp on the Pocomoke River located in a park at the foot of Winters Quarters Drive in Pocomoke City. Paddle upstream on the Pocomoke past some houses on the right, cross to the left side of the river (northwest bank) and then when the last house begins to fade from view about a mile above your put-in, watch for an unimpressive looking break in the cypress on your left. Enter, for that is your creek. The stream winds in an unspoiled manner until it approaches and passes beneath Md. Rte. 364, Dividing Creek Road. There are a few houses here but the dark waters quickly burrow back into the deep swamp. The swamp forest is a combination of cypress and hardwoods. There is little solid ground touching on the creek so plan lunch and rest stops accordingly. Most of the going is easy and unimpeded by fallen trees, a rare luxury when it comes to exploring swamps. Do not worry too much about tides as the current is relatively moderate. As you reach the final stretches of navigability the creek begins to shallow somewhat and you will encounter forks to test your sense of direction. If you choose correctly you will stretch a few hundred extra yards out of the trip. Finally and rather suddenly the channel dissolves into the sodden no-man's land and it is time to turn back.
Hazards: None
Water Conditions: Canoeable all year.

Gauge

None

Chapter 7
Christina Basin

The Christina River Basin covers about 500 square miles of northern Delaware and southeastern Pennsylvania, emptying its waters into the Delaware River. It is drained by a few small streams rising in the Pennsylvania Piedmont and rushing to tidewater at or near Wilmington. The basin varies from headwater areas that are mostly and peacefully rural, the midlands which mixes farmland with prosperous and tasteful outlying residential areas and finally the lowlands covered by the busy and crowded urban and industrial complex of the Wilmington-Newark corridor. One who paddles these streams will see it all along with a fascinating exposure to three hundred years of history that is so intertwined with these waters.

The following streams are described in this chapter:

Christina River
   White Clay Creek
    Red Clay Creek
   Brandywine Creek

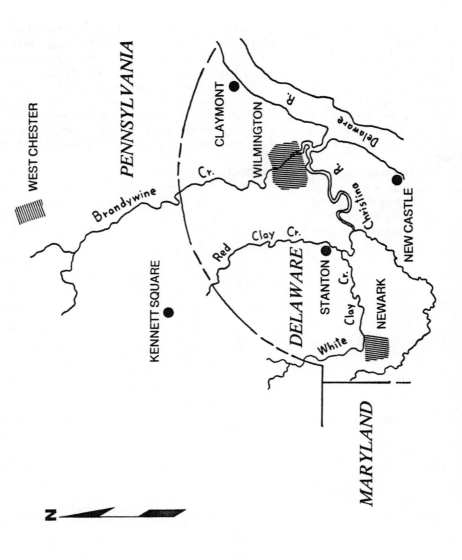

CHRISTINA RIVER TRIBUTARIES

Christina River

Introduction

The Christina River is a pathetic little dribble extending over three states, starting in some pastures west of Strickersville, Pennsylvania, cutting across a small corner of Maryland and then spanning New Castle County, Delaware to join the Delaware River at Wilmington. This is not the type of river that one travels great distances for. Hemmed in by mudbanks, plagued by deadfalls and flowing through average woodlands the Christina does little to be called outstanding. However time and place make the little Christina shine for as an intimate woodland canoe trail that carries fairly reliable water levels by the doorstep of 400,000 people, it must be regarded as no less than a precious natural resource. Novices will find this run at reasonable levels quite safe and suitable to attempt.

Section 1. Purgatory Swamp Road to New Churchman Road

Gradient	Difficulty	Distance	Time	Width	Scenery	Map
3	A-1	12.0	5.5	20-40	Fair	65

Trip Description: Put in at the crossing of the rather unsavory sounding thoroughfare called Purgatory Swamp Road. That teeny murky brook all of fifteen to twenty feet wide is your "river" and it quickly meanders off into the forest. Unfortunately that forest seems to initially be a forest of high voltage power lines, power lines and more power lines. Eventually the more traditional woodland decor of wall to wall trees takes over broken only occasionally by some encroaching homes or a road crossing. Except for the inescapable drone of distant roadways, the atmosphere is almost wild. The creek is generally entrenched in four to six-foot mudbanks which oddly, by restricting one's field of vision to the adjacent jungle, tend to enhance the illusion of remoteness. Of course in the tradition of all small coastal plain streams the Christina bristles with snags, fallen trees, logjams and overhanging vegetation. Quite remarkably though most obstacles can be bypassed, bumped over or squeezed under. Also it appears that some logs and limbs have been sawed away, perhaps by some considerate canoeists. The creek has no rapids, just frequent gentle riffles over bars of pea gravel or sand. As one proceeds, little tributaries subtly trickle in and the creek soon swells from teeny to tiny. Below Walther Road (sand and gravel operation on right) the stream really broadens as it enters Smalleys Pond which is formed by a six-foot dam easily carried on the right. Tidewater begins shortly below the dam. The banks now become increasingly developed but stretches of still primitive swampy and marshy shores prevail and thus these last few miles will still appeal to some.

Hazards: A six-foot dam at Smalleys Pond and snags and fallen trees.
Water Conditions: Late fall, winter and spring except after prolonged dry spell.

Gauge

USGS Gauge at Purgatory Swamp Road should read at least 3.5 feet.

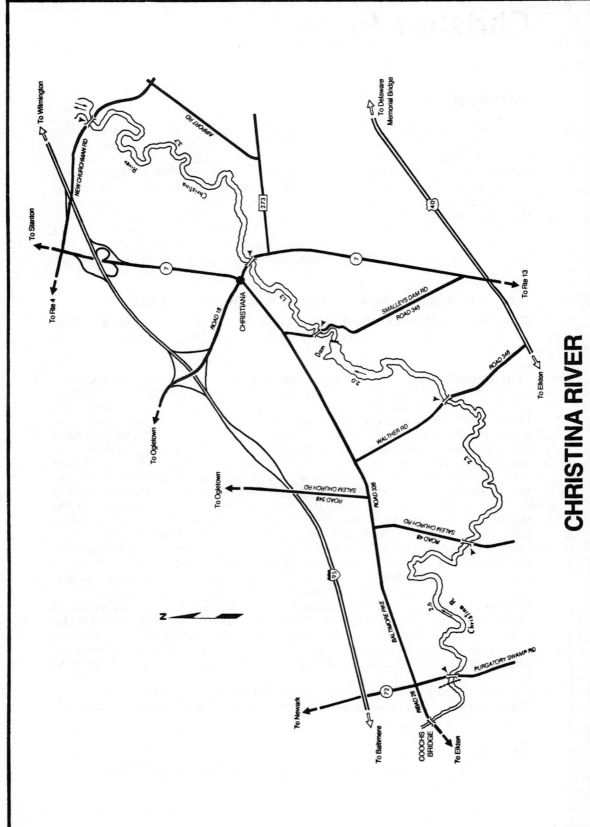

CHRISTINA RIVER

White Clay Creek

Introduction

The lands along the great arc of the Delaware-Pennsylvania line are remarkable in that they transform in just a few miles from one of the nation's foremost industrial areas, a vast sea of refineries, chemical complexes, power plants and shipyards, to a serene, sparsely populated landscape of old farms and country estates. White Clay Creek is born and matures in this rolling countryside but then finishes its short career in the fringes of the great sprawl of the northeast urban corridor. Somehow even through those lower reaches it does an admirable job of gerrymandering a fairly pleasant path amongst the scattered remaining patches of fields and woods all the way to Stanton. While hardly special enough to warrant driving great distances for, this creek fits the bill just perfectly for the local paddler desiring a quiet day floating through the countryside.

Section 1. London Tract Road to Stanton, Del. (Del. Rte. 7)

Gradient	Difficulty	Distance	Time	Width	Scenery	Map
10	A-1	14.0	4.5	10-40	Fair	66

Trip Descriptions: The cruise starts on the tiny West Branch a few miles inside of Chester County, Pennsylvania. It is a miserable put-in with barbed wire at both ends of the bridge and marginal parking space for not more than two cars. The stream zigzags down a mostly forested narrow valley and through short ravines. Like most other streams in this area the surrounding woods are graced with some beautiful beech trees. The creek moves along nicely, dropping over plenty of gentle rock garden and gravel riffles and may be blocked once or twice by fallen trees. Adding some spice to the run are a two-foot rubble dam early in the trip and a rough rubble dam at the water intake above Newark (run left of center). Further down a sloping six-foot dam located about a mile above Del. Rte. 72 is too scrapey to run but has a great playing hydraulic at the foot at moderate levels. White Clay almost sneaks by Newark, now a college town but once very much dependent on the falling creek to power its grist and paper mills. There is a sloping four-foot dam at Rte. 72 that can be run anywhere. Rte. 72 is at mile 6.5 and most people will prefer to take out here. Below Rte. 72, the stream works its way onto the coastal plain and past considerably more civilization including apartment houses, roads and the busy Penn-Central Railroad line. Still the majority of the passage is through open space or woods and there are still many riffles, two runable small dams each about two feet high and one sharp three-foot dam about a mile above Rte. 7 (carry) to keep things interesting. A short, steep, muddy exit on the right marks the trip's end at Rte. 7.
Hazards: Fallen trees and dams mentioned above, some of which form powerful hydraulics at high water.
Water Conditions: Usually must be caught within a day of a rain during winter or spring.

Gauge

None. If there is enough water to smoothly slide over the dam at Rte. 72, then the level is adequate.

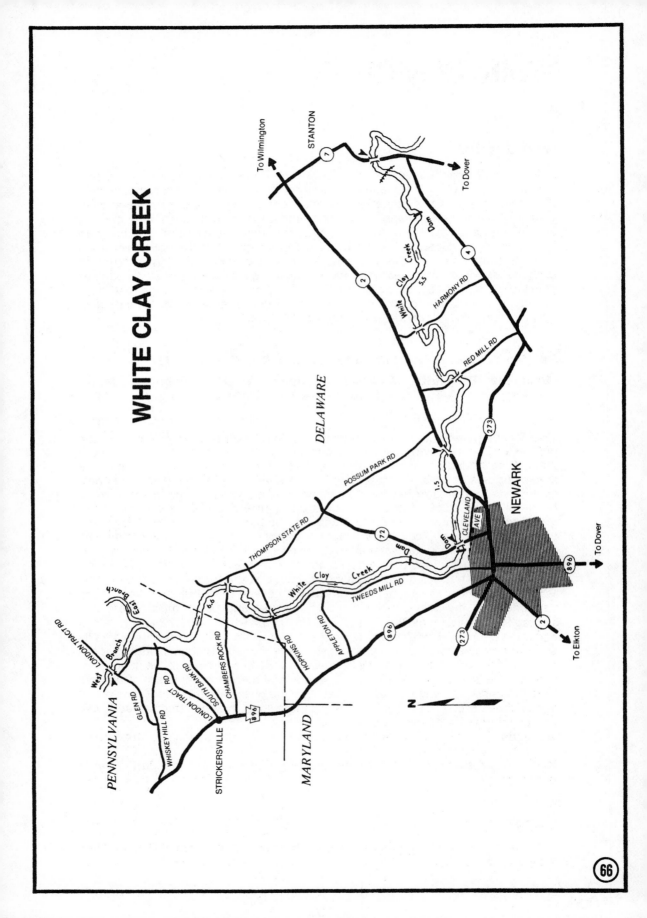

WHITE CLAY CREEK

PENNSYLVANIA

MARYLAND

DELAWARE

NEWARK

STANTON

To Wilmington

To Dover

To Dover

To Elkton

N

STRICKERSVILLE

London Tract Rd
West Branch
East Branch
Glen Rd
Whiskey Hill Rd
London Tract Rd
South Bank Rd
Chambers Rock Rd
Hopkins Rd
Appleton Rd
896
896
Tweeds Mill Rd
White Cloy Creek
6.6
Thompson State Rd
Possum Park Rd
72
Dam
Dam
1.5
Cleveland Ave
273
273
2
896
Red Mill Rd
Harmony Rd
White Clay Creek
5.5
Dam
2
4
7

Red Clay Creek

Introduction

Red Clay Creek gathers its waters from the hilly countryside surrounding Kennett Square, Pennsylvania and then winds down through northern New Castle County, Delaware to join White Clay Creek midway between Wilmington and Newark. The course is set mostly on the Piedmont and on the fall line, passing through a semi-rural, semi-suburban landscape in an old and affluent neighborhood. Needless to say the human influence is strong, but really quite pleasant, manifesting itself in the form of covered bridges, ancient stone and stucco buildings, old mills and a touch of Victorian gingerbread. The stream is punctuated by numerous old dams which testify to the former water-powered industrial might of this now peaceful valley. Today industry still thrives but the most important and famous industry is very subtle and easy to overlook. It takes place in dozens of big drab mysterious sheds that dot the surrounding countryside and is carried on in the dark. It is the growing of mushrooms, tons and tons of them, to smother the nation's steaks, to compliment its sauces and to generally please its palates.

Section 1. Marshall Bridge Road to Del. Rte. 41

Gradient	Difficulty	Distance	Time	Width	Scenery	Map
14	A-2	10.5	3.0	25-45	Good	67

Trip Description: Red Clay Creek is born at the confluence of its East and West branches just above Marshall Bridge Road. It is possible for the dedicated paddler to put in further up on the West Branch though it is pretty small. If you decide to do so, there is a four-foot dam just above Marshall Bridge Road that can be run down the middle. It is hardly more than a half mile to the next dam, a sloping four-footer run anywhere with enough water. Shortly downstream, the creek winds through the village of Yorklyn with its sprawling fibers plant and some dank and pungent odors wafting through the air from the mushroom sheds across the stream. There is a very gently sloping four-foot dam in Yorklyn run anywhere. From Yorklyn on down, for most of the way, a railroad track and various roads follow near the creek. However traffic is generally light on both, thus maintaining the quiet nature of the run. The creek flows through alternating stretches of wooded gorge and narrow grassy valleys and since the banks range from medium to low, the paddler sees most of whatever is going on. The dams do not stop at Yorklyn. Just below Yorklyn, above a railroad trestle is the fourth dam, a sharp five-footer that should be carried. Less than a half mile and the fifth dam is encountered, a sharp four-footer that also should be carried. It is over a mile and a half to the next dam, five feet high and unrunable, located on a pretty wooded loop above Mount Cuba. About a mile further is a sharp four-foot dam that should be carried. Except for the short pools behind the dams, most of the stream down to Lancaster Pike (Del. Rte. 48) is characterized by plenty of gravel-formed riffles and swift current. But then below Rte. 48, Red Clay begins to display a little spunk as it dashes over some short exhilerating rapids formed by boulder patches and rock gardens. There is an old broken out dam on this section that can be run on the left but scout first as the breach tends to be complicated by debris. Unfortunately just as things start really becoming enjoyable, the take-out at Rte. 41 appears (the bridge 200 yards upstream affords a much easier exit). It should be noted that easy rapids and endless riffles do continue well past Rte. 41. However,

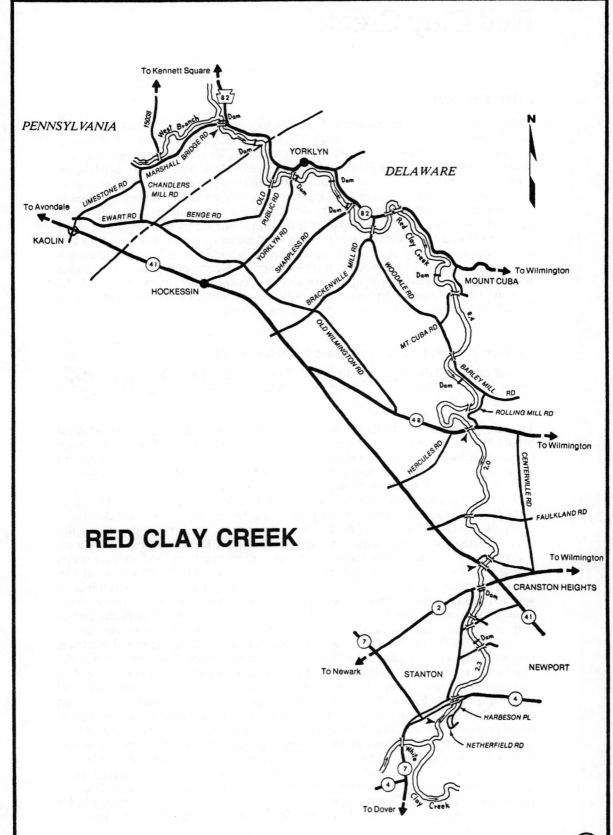

RED CLAY CREEK

67

industry, shopping centers, houses, noise, trash cluttered mud banks and poor selection of take-outs tend to offset the rewards of some extra whitewater. Also there are two more dams to portage, a six-footer under the Rte. 2 bridge and an eight-footer under the high Chessie System railroad bridge. For those who want to paddle the final two and a half miles below Rte. 41, a small park at the end of Netherfield Street, located just above the mouth, is the best take-out. Do not continue below here unless the tide is going out, as the tidal currents in lower White Clay Creek and the Christina River are horrendous.

Hazards: Nine dams described above, the lower seven of which require portages. Also the creek is spanned by several railroad trestles whose multiple piers could easily function as deadly strainers at high levels.

Water Conditions: Canoeable winter and spring within a day of hard rain.

Gauge

A government gauging station at Rte. 48 bridge has no staff gauge but you can use the concrete weir as a reference. You want enough water to cleanly clear the middle of the weir to make it over the rockier riffles far upstream.

Other Information

The clay for which Red Clay Creek was named shows in enough of the beautiful houses of the neighborhood but much more important is the product after which its sister stream was named. White Clay Creek received its name from the extensive local deposits of white kaolin clay, possibly the richest deposits in the nation. The clay traditionally was the raw material for fine china but today the bulk of it finds its way into a wide variety of industrial applications. The largest customer now is probably the paper-making industry which uses it as a filler in the manufacture of fine paper.

Maryland and Delaware managed to mostly avoid the brunt of the action during the Revolutionary War. The Christina Valley became one exception when in September of 1777 British General William Howe sailed up the Chesapeake Bay, landed his troops at the head of the Elk River (now Elkton) and marched northeastward across the valley to Philadelphia. They skirmished with a small Continental detachment at Cooch's Bridge on the Christina and then proceeded on to the Brandywine at Chadds Ford were they met the main American forces under General Washington. However twelve thousand American troops were no match for eighteen thousand British and Hessian troops plus a thick fog that Howe used to his advantage. Washington's forces were badly beaten thus opening the way for the subsequent British occupation of Wilmington and then Philadelphia.

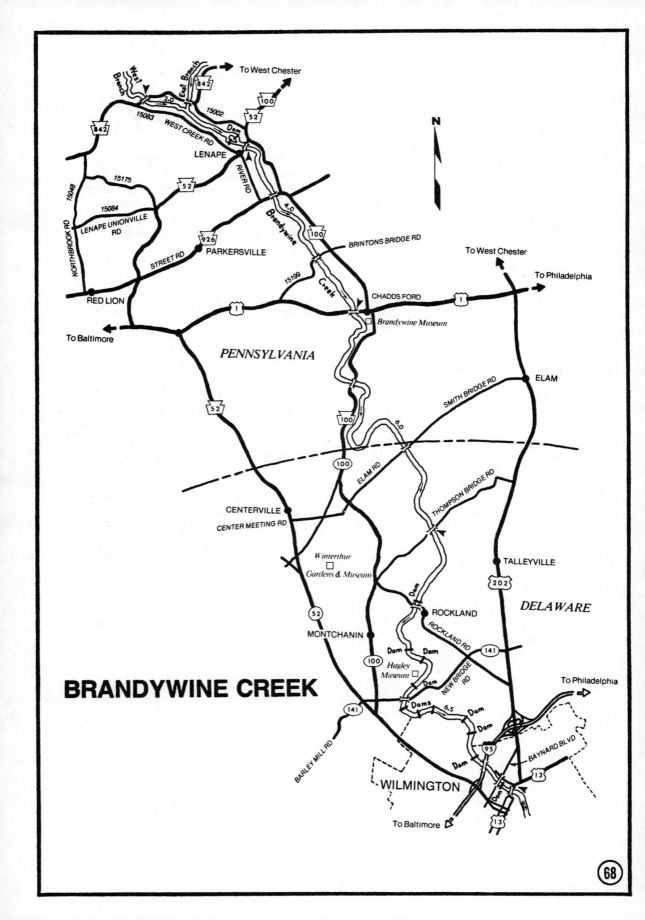

BRANDYWINE CREEK

Brandywine Creek

Introduction

Brandywine Creek drains the heart of Chester County, Pennsylvania and New Castle County, Delaware, emptying into the tidal Christina River in downtown Wilmington. This is a valley with a long and rich history. Settled over three and a quarter centuries ago first by the Swedes, then the Dutch and finally the English, it did not take long for its residents to recognize the enormous energy potential of the Brandywine's steep fall line gradient. By the Revolutionary War, the lower valley had developed into the most important milling center in the English colonies. Appropriately enough, this area was fought over during the Revolution and George Washington even slept here. But the valley's real claim to fame arrived in 1802, when a French immigrant with the improbable name of Eleuthere Irenee du Pont de Nemours, also eyeing that beautiful falling water, established a powder mill outside of Wilmington. Needless to say the business was a success and over the years as one of the world's corporate superpowers duPont has brought prosperity to the valley and for that matter, as a manufacturer of plastic resins, nylon and Kevlar, may perhaps even be credited with having brought you your boat.

It is worth visiting the Brandywine not only as a paddler but as a tourist too. Among its attractions are the Hagley Museum which includes the restored duPont powder works, Winterthur, a duPont estate renown for its gardens and interior design, the Brandywine Museum featuring works of the Brandywine Valley's most famous artisan, Andrew Wyeth, and just over the hill in the Red Clay Creek Valley the Longwood Gardens. If you are an admirer of fine architecture, carefully landscaped grounds, or just plain like to see how the other half lives, then you will love shuttling on the Brandywine. The drive out Del. Rte. 100, Rte. 52 and various interconnecting lanes offers an incredible display of rolling manicured estates, beautiful and diversely styled mansions, and on a less pretentious level, dozens of old stucco, brick or stone farm and mill houses dating back into the eighteenth century.

Section 1. Pa. Rte. 842 to Thompson Bridge Road

Gradient	Difficulty	Distance	Time	Width	Scenery	Map
4	A-1	12.0	4.0	60-150	Fair	68

Trip Description: The put-in is on the West Branch Brandywine Creek, about a mile above the East Branch confluence. The West Branch flows through a pretty rural valley that unfortunately is mostly hidden behind high mud banks which also make access a messy affair. The current is strong but occasional riffles are the closest thing to whitewater. With the addition of the East Branch, the creek and valley widen and a high-voltage power line also unfortunately joins the creek and plagues the already only fair scenery to U.S. Rte. 1. Current is minimal as the creek's already meager gradient is mostly backed up behind three small dams. A three and a half-foot rubble dam about a half mile below the confluence with the East Branch can be run anywhere on the right side of the island but first scout, a four and a half-foot rubble dam about a mile above Rte. 1 can also be run after scouting and a two-foot dam just above Rte. 1 is run through a breach on the extreme right. Below Rte. 1, the valley narrows and the stream is lined by attractive wooded hillsides. A good current returns and occasional riffles break the surface. Take out at Thompson Bridge on the left.

Hazards: Three small dams described above which are all runable at moderate levels.

Water Conditions: Can be run much of winter and spring except after prolonged dry periods.

Gauge

None

Section 2. Thompson Bridge Road to Market Street

Gradient	Difficulty	Distance	Time	Width	Scenery	Map
20	A-3	6.5	3.0	100-150	Good	68

Trip Description: This is an excellent intermediate run but if you despise dams, then skip this section as there are eleven of them. The put-in at Thompson Bridge with its following mile and a half of flatwater is chosen because of the heavily posted nature of the more desirable Rockland put-in. The first dam is a jagged, sloping and probably runable barrier located just upstream of the Rockland Bridge. It is easily carried on the right but the portage involves trespass on land very explicitly posted against boaters, so proceed only at your own risk. Strong current and a few riffles carry you into the grounds of the Hagley Museum (also posted) and about three quarters of a mile below Rockland appears the next dam. This is only about three and a half feet high but because of an ugly roller, carry on the left. Not far downstream is a gently sloping five-foot dam best run to the right of center. This is followed by a long complex boulder-studded rapid that carries you past the old powder works. The right bank of the river here is lined by three-sided stone walled buildings of heavy duty construction which originally had a relatively flimsy fourth wall on the side facing the stream. The logic here was that if there was an explosion, the streamside wall would go, thus directing the force of the blast harmlessly (except for those workers in the building or any canoeist happening by) across the creek and thus saving the adjacent buildings from destruction. Shortly below and still on the Hagley property, is a vertical five-foot dam that should be carried on the left. An easy rapid and some strong current carries you past some beautiful old industrial structures and to the next dam, a rather coarse sloping five-footer, run toward the right. Not far below this is a classic sloping eight-foot concrete dam that is runable right of center. When apartment houses appear on the right bank, watch out for a dangerous vertical seven-foot dam with a tight carry on the left that would be dangerous to approach at high water. This is followed by an interesting long steep boulder-studded rapid that ends in a short pool by a huge old mill. The pool ends with a dangerous six-foot vertical dam with a carry on the concrete fish ladder on the left. This also would be dangerous to approach at high water. Not far below this is a runable sloping four-foot dam. Next comes a vertical four-foot dam with a nasty roller that is easily carried on the left. The final dam is below the high Baynard Street Bridge, a vertical three-footer that can be clunked over on the far right with caution. The dam is followed by a short rocky rapid, the annual site in April of one of the country's oldest white-water slaloms, which brings you to tidewater above Market Street. Take out on the left at the foot of the rapid.

Hazards: Eleven dams described above. Even those described as runable could be hazardous at high water. Finally, watch out for playful tykes, especially around Baynard Street, who love to toss rocks at passing canoeists.

Water Conditions: Runable winter and spring within two days of rain or right after heavy local summer showers.

Gauge

None. Rapids above Market Street should have at least a foot of runable water for a good trip.

Stalking the Elusive Shuttle Road

Once that you have selected a river to run and confirmed that it probably has some water in it, you still have to find your way there and shuttle your vehicles. An ordinary gas station road map should accomplish the former and the accompanying maps in this guidebook should take care of the latter. However the author has found that even the best of directions and maps can be rendered useless if you can not distinguish the names of the roads.

Shuttling the various rivers described in this volume may involve navigation of roads in as many as five states. In doing so, you will find your most valuable and essential landmark is the common road sign. While interstate, federal and state primary roads are almost always easily identified, figuring out the secondary roads can be confusing, due to the varying and sometimes subtle labeling techniques.

The system in Maryland is simple; secondary roads are named, not numbered and names are found on ordinary street signs mounted on high metal or wood poles at intersections. Delaware numbers its secondary roads on tiny white signs attached to the posts of stop signs at the intersections. The signs identify the road that you are on and the road that it is intersecting, each marked by appropriate arrows. The roads are also often, but not always, labeled on yellow warning signs that announce upcoming intersections. Northern Delaware in addition labels roads with names displayed on regular street signs. Pennsylvania is a bit confusing due to its inconsistency. State maintained secondary roads are sometimes only identified by five digit numbers displayed on small white signs about a foot square mounted on four-foot posts (sometimes hard to see) at intersections. In some counties, such as Chester, they are also identified by names, displayed on street signs. Township roads are named and/or numbered and one or both may be displayed on high or low wood or metal signs or concrete posts. Having the eyes of a hawk is most useful. West Virginia labels roads with names on common street signs or numbers on small green signs. Virginia is easy, identifying roads with three digit numbers (which all tend to look alike). They are displayed on small white signs that are usually conspicuously located and in addition the signs tell you if the road deadends and if so, how far.

Needless to say vandalism, exotic driving habits, and target practice take their toll on these friendly monuments, thus rendering at times this disertation useless. So an investment in a good topo map might be well worth your while.

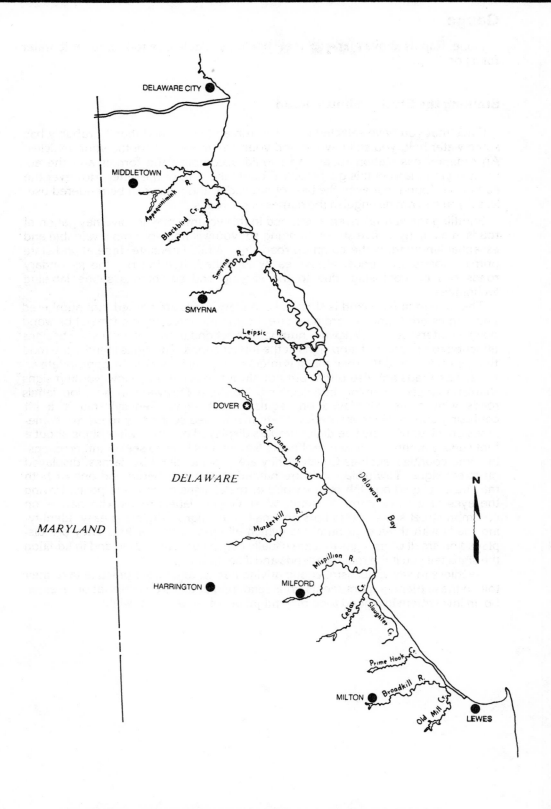

DELAWARE BAY TRIBUTARIES

Chapter 8

Delaware Bay Drainage

The edge of Delaware Bay is a beautiful ragged swath of vast marshes, tangled swamps and thin sandy beaches, periodically interrupted by narrow twisting tidal rivers that penetrate back almost to the centerline of Delaware. Long ago these rivers were centers of activity for this region. They were major commercial passages that made busy ports and shipbuilding centers out of now sleepy little towns such as Smyrna, Odessa and Frederica. But today the value of these waters is mainly recreational. If you have never visited here, drive down Del. Rte. 9 from Delaware City to Leipsic and you will quickly appreciate the beauty and canoeing potential of this slice of the state. To paddle here requires a minimum of canoeing skill but one must learn to use the tides as they can be fierce. Once you have figured the tides out you can ascend or descend a stream or descend one stream and then ascend a tributary or neighboring river or simply put in and paddle one way until the tide changes and then return, thus eliminating the need for a shuttle. The difference between a high or low tide can make the difference in whether you can peer across miles and miles of open marsh meadow or just stare up at a cellulose wall of cattails or spartina grass. Overall the paddling here is best during the cooler months when biting, stabbing and gnawing bugs are gone and motorboats are few. However all seasons are beautiful and with year round assured water, decide for yourself.

The following streams are described in this chapter:

Appoquinimink River
Blackbird Creek
Smyrna River
Leipsic River
St. Jones River
Murderkill River
Mispillion River
Cedar Creek
   Slaughter Creek
Broadkill River
   Old Mill Creek
   Prime Hook Creek

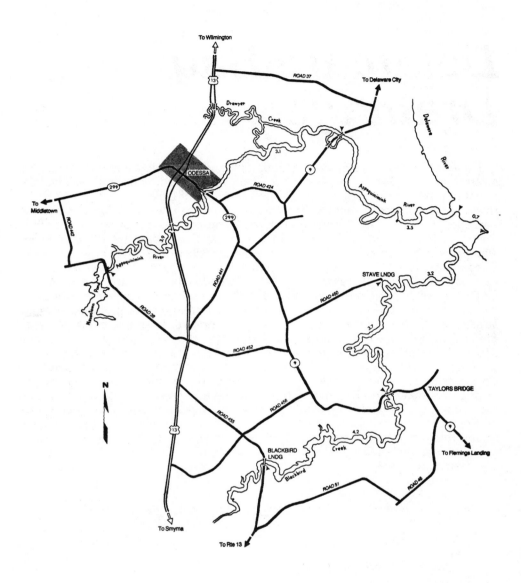

APPOQUINIMINK RIVER
BLACKBIRD CREEK

Appoquinimink River and Blackbird Creek

Introduction

The Appoquinimink River and Blackbird Creek, located in middle New Castle County where Delaware is skinniest, are the northernmost creeks of any length in this state's great band of tidal wetlands. Sharing almost a common mouth they enter the Delaware River just upstream of where it officially becomes Delaware Bay. Together these winding tidal waterways offer over twenty-three miles of exploring (not to mention getting lost on side channels) all within twenty-five miles of downtown Wilmington.

Both creeks unfortunately lack any good access to their mouths. So what this means is that if you desire to paddle the entire length of either creek you must also plan to tack on three to six extra miles, possibly against the tides, to reach a roadhead. Use the accompanying maps and plan accordingly.

Section 1. Appoquinimink River. Rd. 38 to Delaware River

Gradient	Difficulty	Distance	Time	Width	Scenery	Map
0	A	10.5	5.0	100-300	Good	69

Trip Description: Put in right by the spillway of the dike that separates freshwater Noxontown Pond from tidewater. The first quarter mile can be terribly shallow at low tide so at such times consider starting at Odessa. The river above Odessa winds through narrow marshy bottoms that are fringed by wooded higher ground while below it flows mainly through open marsh. The open marsh however tends to be closed, screened off by a cellulose curtain of riverside phragmites reeds. Thus, except for some occasional peeks out to the adjacent farmlands, you will be subject to hemmed in solitude.

Section 2. Blackbird Creek. Blackbird Landing (Rd. 55) to mouth.

Gradient	Difficulty	Distance	Time	Width	Scenery	Map
0	A	10.5	5.0	100-500	Good	69

Trip Description: Before going down, go up. The riverscape above Blackbird Landing is exceptionally pretty as the creek flows through swamps and past beech covered hillsides. The swamps part below Blackbird Landing and the rest of the creek's twisting path passes through the heart of lovely unspoiled marshlands. But as on Appoquinimink the paddler has limited opportunity to appreciate this beauty as he or she stares at up the endless towering wall of reedgrass (phragmites). However the graceful monotony of these reeds are regularly broken by clear and pleasing views out at the farmland perched on the adjacent high ground. Just go with the tides and you will have a good trip.

Hazards: Exceptionally strong current rips through the Rte. 8 bridge piers at Odessa on the Appoquinimink.

Water Conditions: Can be paddled all year except when frozen.

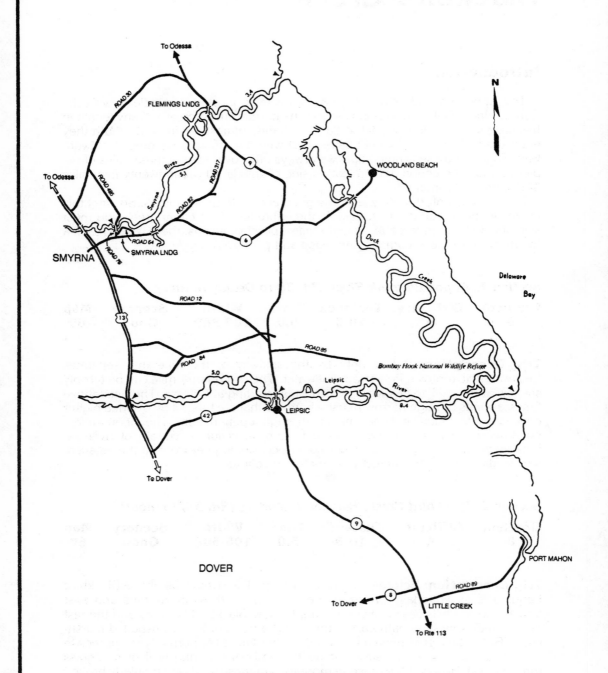

LEIPSIC RIVER
SMYRNA RIVER

Smyrna River and Leipsic River

Introduction

The Smyrna and Leipsic rivers are two rather similar tidal streams that flow through northern Kent County, Delaware. Until the late seventeenth century the Leipsic was a tributary of the Smyrna which then meandered for a long way parallel to Delaware Bay before finding an outlet near Port Mahon. It would still be possible for an energetic paddler to retrace much of this old route using what is now Duck Creek.

Section 1. Smyrna River. Smyrna Landing (Rd. 76) to mouth

Gradient	Difficulty	Distance	Time	Width	Scenery	Map
0	A	8.5	4.0	50-400	Good	70

Trip Description: It is possible to put in at Rte. 13 but highway noise, sumptuous views of fast food joints and a possible carry around the Rd. 76 bridge at high tide do not make it worth the trouble. The first mile and a half below Smyrna Landing runs past high wooded banks that appear to be man-made, probably dredge spoil from years past. But once beyond Mill Creek this becomes a marsh tour. The limited perspective of a canoe hurts here as the height of the riverside reeds often denies the paddler of an appreciation of the beauty and vastness of the wetlands that lie beyond. There is no access at the mouth so you can double back to Rte. 9 or if the wind and tide are with you it is an easy three and a half miles down the Bay to the town park at Woodland Beach.
Hazards: Jetty pilings at the south side of the river entrance can form a barrier at low tide.
Water Conditions: Paddleable all year except when frozen.

Section 2. Leipsic River. U.S. Rte. 13 to Delaware Bay

Gradient	Difficulty	Distance	Time	Width	Scenery	Map
0	A	13.5	6.0	50-500	Good	70

Trip Description: Put in at the Garrison Lake Fishing Access Area, north side. The first part of this run down to Rte. 9 is very pretty, wandering first through swamps and then through a narrow marsh. Below Rte. 9 the river is similar to the Smyrna in that it winds through the heart of a vast beautiful marshland of which little is visible because of the tall reeds. It is still pretty though and because it flows through Bombay Hook National Wildlife Refuge the lower part of this river is one of the few stretches in southern Delaware where you do not encounter duck blinds on every corner. Access to the mouth is also nonexistent on this river so you can either double all the way back to Rte. 9 or paddle nearly five miles down the Bay to the boat ramp at Port Mahon.
Hazards: None
Water Conditions: Tidal so there is always enough water.

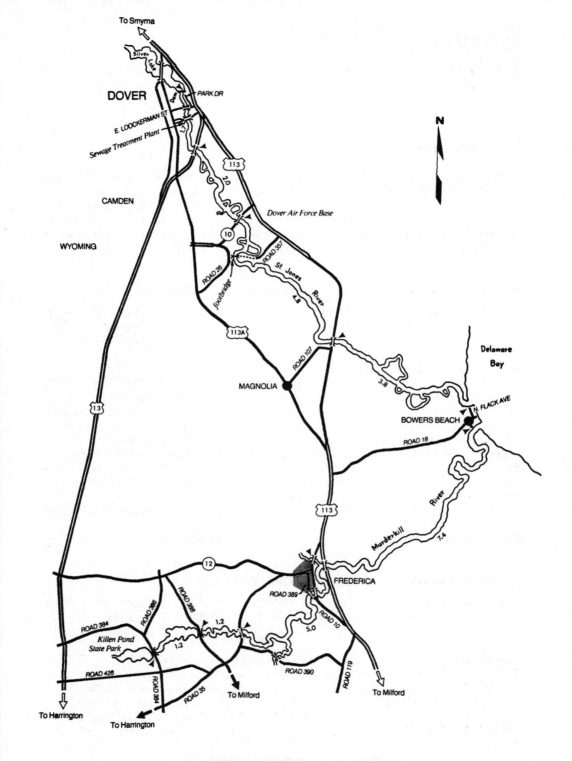

MURDERKILL RIVER
ST. JONES RIVER

St. Jones River and Murderkill River

Introduction

Please be assured that in spite of such bloodstained names as Murderkill, Broadkill and Slaughter Creek, Delaware a is very peaceful and friendly place to paddle.

The Murderkill and St. Jones rivers are almost tributaries of each other, entering Delaware Bay but a half mile apart at Bowers Beach. The former begins in the quiet farmlands between Harrington and Felton while the latter starts within the shadow of the State Capitol in busy Dover. This is another pair of streams where with favorable tides an extended two river journey can be conveniently had.

Section 1. St. Jones River. Dover (Silver Lake Dam) to Bowers Beach

Gradient	Difficulty	Distance	Time	Width	Scenery	Map
0	A	12.5	4.5	20-400	Good	71

Trip Description: If you care to explore upstream and paddle around on Silver Lake you need to secure a permit from the Dover Police Department to do so. The permit runs for a year, starting in February, and costs $5.00 for Dover residents and $10.00 for outsiders. There is excellent and free access to the creek at the foot of the Silver Lake spillway at the city recreation area reached by driving north off of East Loockerman St. on Park Drive. However three scrapey small drops in the first half mile may encourage some, especially those ascending the river, to skip this passage through a parcel of attractive manicured city parkland and put in or exit next to the town sewage treatment plant behind the corner of East Ave. and East Water St. The creek forges a narrow and swampy path through Dover and its suburbs and remains surprisingly attractive considering its location. Nevertheless buildings and trash do take their aesthetic toll here. But then again it is only on this section that one can best admire the St. Jones' most unique feature; it is on the approach path to Dover Air Force Base. The base specializes as the home for a huge squadron of gigantic jet transport planes. It is unlikely that you will ever see a larger flying object, except perhaps a Delaware salt marsh horse fly. Below the town, the planes and Rte. 113, the creek returns to a natural state, a winding channel through a soggy sea of reeds. Sadly, the mouth of this pretty river is marked by a small garbage dump. You can take out here, reached by North Flack Ave. or a half mile beyond on the Murderkill at the public boat ramp.
Hazards: None
Water Conditions: Tidal except for the upper half mile between Silver Lake and the sewage treatment plant, so runable all year.

Section 2. Murderkill River. Rd. 384 to Bowers Beach

Gradient	Difficulty	Distance	Time	Width	Scenery	Map
0	A	15.5	6.0	15-400	Good	71

Trip Description: Rd. 384 crosses the Murderkill on the dam that backs up Killen Pond. Protected by a state park, this is one of the prettiest and least developed ponds in Delaware and well worth exploring. The tiny outflow from the pond is actually nontidal and offers a short shallow run through the woods to the backwaters of Coursey Pond. This is also a very attractive pond with high wooded undeveloped shores. There is public access at the dam for both above and below, the foot of the dam marking the beginning of tidewater. The Murderkill next offers a forest-bound passage almost to Frederica, first bordered by high banks on one side and swamp on the other, then total swamp. Incidentally this swamp bears the wholesome name of Big Cripple Swamp. A few houses occupy some of the high ground along here. Approaching Frederica the marsh completely inherits the river for good, so reed grass is most of what you will see from here on down to the Bay. This section is fairly undisturbed except for a power line, the no trespassing signs and the ubiquitous duck blinds. If you decide to stop at Frederica the best access is found a few yards up Spring Creek at the Rte. 12 bridge. Access to the mouth is via a public boat ramp at Bowers Beach.

Hazards: Stay away from the spillways of Killen Pond and Coursey Pond dams.

Water Conditions: Tidal except for the short section below Killen Pond which may be too low in summer and early fall.

Gauge

None

Tidal Navigation Hints

While your typical tidal estuary usually gives the impression of substance and depth when viewed from the shore, the paddler soon finds that in reality these waterways are often only inches deep with only a narrow elusive channel suitable for even canoe navigation. However if you are cognizant of a few basic rules you can pick your way down these passages with all the confidence of a veteran waterman. First, channels on estuaries as on freshwater streams tend to hang to the outside of bends, especially on the lower reaches where bottom-scouring tidal currents are strongest. However be aware that on tight S-turns the channel often tends to diagonal across to the other side much sooner than on a free-flowing river. Next, look where the duck blinds are. Blinds are usually serviced by motorboaters who want deep water even more than you do, so the conservative navigator in shallow waters might choose to simply zig-zag from blind to blind. On the upper reaches of estuaries where the channels really start withering, look for strange sticks or clusters of sticks that seem to unnaturally protrude from the murky shallows. These are often some waterman's crude buoy system. Finally in the really upper reaches watch vegetative patterns. Lily pads, arrowhead plants, etc. usually only grow in shallows so watch for breaks and go for them. Finally if you still insist on messing up, do it at low tide. Then you just have to wait six hours and you get lifted off for a second chance.

Mispillion River, Cedar Creek and Slaughter Creek

Introduction

The waters of the Mispillion, Cedar and Slaughter all spill into Delaware Bay at a place called Mispillion Light. They share a common quality along with Broadkill, Old Mill and Prime Hook of remoteness, minimal development and variety of distracting scenery. Their marshes are exceptionally pleasant to explore as the grass is relatively short, allowing good views from the boat of this wet landscape. This is a good place to view all sorts of creatures, beautiful and strange. Walk the beaches at the mouth and you will find the sands littered with those living fossils, the horseshoe crab. Float through the marsh at low tide and see comical fiddler crabs scurrying for little holes in the muck as you approach. Of course there will be flocks of waterfowl, perhaps some muskrat and if you are dumb enough to paddle here in the summer, watch your bow partner be carried off by greenheads and mosquitos with six-foot wingspans.

Section 1. Mispillion River. Milford to Delaware Bay

Gradient	Difficulty	Distance	Time	Width	Scenery	Map
0	A	10.5	3.5	100-300	Good	72

Trip Description: The banks of the Mispillion in Milford are quite built up and often bulkheaded. As a result the best and one of the only entries is a public launching ramp located behind the town police station on the north bank about three-tenths of a mile above Del. Rte. 14 bridge. The first few miles pass by relatively high wooded banks. Some lingering development persists such as power lines, a marina and the Rte. 1 Bypass before the stream loses itself in the wide unspoiled marshes fanning out from the Bay. In summer this solitude is likely to be disturbed by the heavy motorboat traffic that frequents this waterway. For the indecisive, this river has two mouths, a man-made jettied exit at the lighthouse and a relatively new eroded break in the barrier beach about a hundred yards to the north. One can take out at the public boat ramp about three-quarters mile up Cedar Creek. Also if you are energetic and the tides are right it is possible to ride the strong ebb tide down the Mispillion, hit slack at Mispillion Light and then ride the swift flood tide up the Cedar to Rte. 1.

Section 2. Cedar Creek. Del. Rte. 30 to Delaware Bay

Gradient	Difficulty	Distance	Time	Width	Scenery	Map
0	A	9.5	3.5	100-200	Good	72

Trip Description: A steep sandy descent along the edge of the Swiggetts Pond spillway brings you to a pool of clear tea-colored water seeping off into the woods. The creek will demand for a short distance some tight maneuvering around sharp turns and under low-hanging limbs and deadfalls to reach open water. If you prefer to avoid these trials, put in at the old highway approach just above Rte. 1, but by all means paddle upstream as far as you can go before heading down to

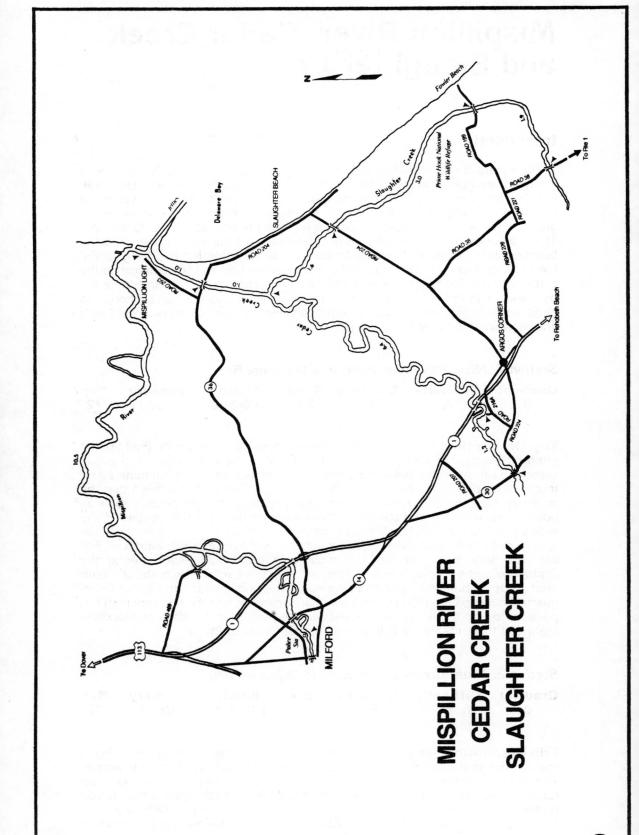

MISPILLION RIVER
CEDAR CREEK
SLAUGHTER CREEK

the sea. This segment between Rte. 30 and Rte. 1 is the prettiest on the Cedar for this is where it earns its name. Dense stands of fragrant white cedar envelope the dark still waters. This is swamp scenery at its best. You can enjoy it from a distance from the creek's deep main channel or poke up any of several side channels past the shaggy gray trunks.

Passing Rte. 1 the swampy fringe and cedars continue for a while but then this all opens up to a wide marsh lined by distant pine forest. There are a few summer homes scattered through here but generally the atmosphere is primitive. While the surrounding scenery is quite spread out, the creek is unusually narrow. The wild part of the journey ends near Rte. 36 as Cedar transforms into a long harbor for pleasure boats and commercial fishing vessels. The best take-out is a public boat ramp about a quarter mile below Rte. 36 on the left.

Section 3. Slaughter Creek. Rd. 38 to Cedar Creek

Gradient	Difficulty	Distance	Time	Width	Scenery	Map
0	A	6.5	2.5	50-70	Good	72

Trip Description: Much of this run is within Prime Hook National Wildlife Refuge so that during fall, winter and spring you should be rewarded with, if not the sight of waterfowl, at least a cacaphony of nearby and far away quacks, honks and whistles. It can definitely be the wrong place to be if you have a headache. This trip starts as a narrow ribbon of dark water weaving through a freshwater marsh bordered by dark tangled forests of pine and cedar. The creek is initially rather shallow but adequate to float a canoe, including on about a half mile of creek above the put-in. About a mile and a half downstream of Rd. 38, just short of Delaware Bay, the creek swings hard left and parallels the Bay following what appears in a very subtle way to be a man-made channel. Studying the map, it appears that Slaughter Creek formerly turned hard right and emptied directly into the Bay. The lower creek flows fairly straight through vast unspoiled salt marshes, the view of which is partly obstructed by the dense vegetation that grows on the often slightly raised banks, further evidence that this is a dug channel. The vegetation is not all bad though as many of the little trees that you see are persimmons. If you paddle this creek after the first frost give this much maligned and misunderstood ping pong ball sized fruit a try, that is if the possums do not beat you to the punch. A road bridge to Fowler Beach crosses the creek and not far beyond an abandoned bridge crosses, both of which may lack clearance at high tide. For a little variety you can land at that first bridge and walk the quarter mile of road to a bayside lunch stop or hike on lonely Fowler Beach. After passing the village of Slaughter Beach the creek passes more wild marsh and joins Cedar Creek. Take out a mile and a quarter down Cedar Creek at the public boat ramp.
Hazards: None
Water Conditions: Tidal and thus runable all year.

Gauge

None

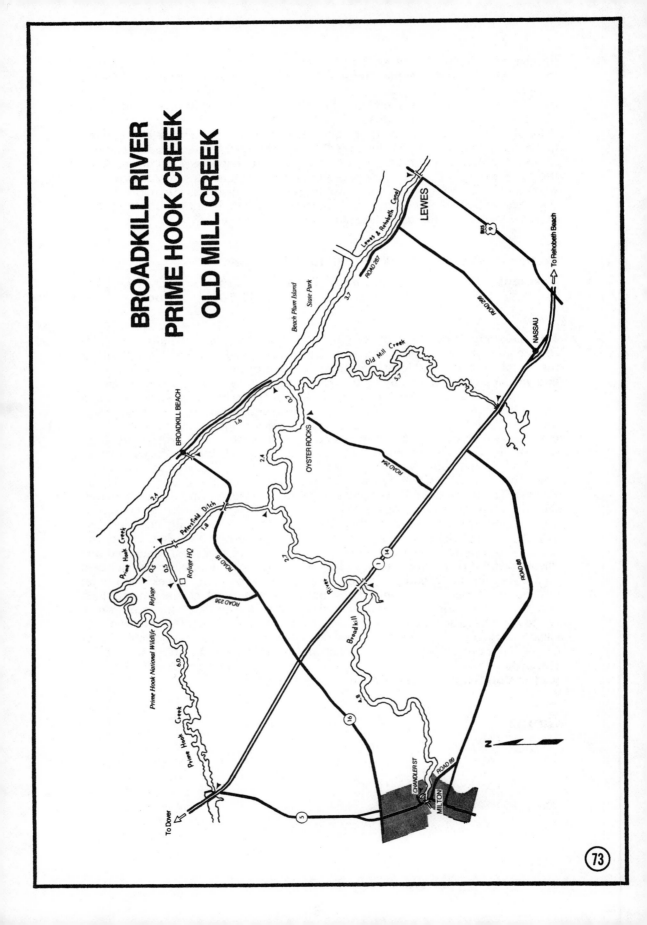

BROADKILL RIVER
PRIME HOOK CREEK
OLD MILL CREEK

LEWES

Lewes & Rehoboth Canal

ROAD 267

3.7

Beach Plum Island State Park

BUS 9

To Rehoboth Beach

ROAD 266

NASSAU

Old Mill Creek

3.7

BROADKILL BEACH

2.0

1.6

OYSTER ROCKS

ROAD 264

2.4

Petersfield Ditch

1.9

2.4

Prime Hook Creek

Refuge

0.5

0.5

Refuge HQ

ROAD 16

ROAD 236

2.7

River

14

1

Prime Hook National Wildlife

6.0

Broadkill

4.8

16

ROAD 88

Prime Hook Creek

5

N

CHANDLER ST

MILTON

ROAD 89

To Dover

73

Broadkill River and Old Mill Creek

Introduction

Broadkill River is the southernmost tributary of Delaware Bay, entering at the old port of Lewes. Like most Delaware Bay tributaries it is formed by a handful of unnavigable branches and ditches, many dammed to power long gone or crumbling grist mills. It is also fed by Old Mill Creek, one of the loveliest tidal creeks in Delaware and a highly recommended side trip. Either run combines nicely with a day of beachcombing at nearby Cape Henlopen or Beach Plum Island.

Section 1. Milton (Del. Rte. 5) to Oyster Rocks

Gradient	Difficulty	Distance	Time	Width	Scenery	Map
0	A	10.0	5.0	100-300	Good	73

Trip Description: There is a public launching ramp off Chandler St. in Milton located on the north bank. The dark waters meander for the first mile past pretty wooded mostly swampy shores. Here and there is the only high ground that you will see by the riverside on this cruise so enjoy its beech-dotted slopes while you can. All too soon the woods recede a bit and are replaced by a narrow margin of freshwater marsh. The marshes gradually widen and then turn to lush salt meadows which after Rte. 1 dominate the scenery. Except around Rte. 1 most of this passage is through undeveloped territory, if you do not count the numerous duck blinds. Oyster Rocks is a nice place to take out although a short downstream excursion to Beach Plum Island is recommended. Beach Plum, which is owned by the State, is a relatively wild stretch of beach that is part of a narrow spit diverting the Broadkill to its man-made mouth at Roosevelt Inlet. Those desiring to paddle to the bitter end will soon encounter built up shores, but if that does not bother you then proceed up the Lewes and Rehobeth Canal to the public take-out at Rte. 9.

Section 2. Old Mill Creek. Del. Rte. 1 to Oyster Rocks

Gradient	Difficulty	Distance	Time	Width	Scenery	Map
0	A	6.0	3.0	20-100	Very Good	73

Trip Description: Old Mill Creek has a lot going for it including its quaint name. It is narrow, intimate with its wet surroundings and first and foremost it is wild. This is one stream where six miles may seem entirely too short a run. The creek amounts to almost nothing at its put-in behind the old red mill at Rte. 1 so be prepared for some slogging if you do not depart on a high tide. Like the Broadkill this trip starts in the woods, here a wild and lonely swamp. Marsh soon takes over but this marsh's lawnlike uniformity is broken by pine and cedar covered hummocks, islands of solid ground in this sea of muck. The mouth dumps you about a half mile downstream of Oyster Rocks which unfortunately means a short fight against Broadkill's stiff tidal currents (still easier than going down to Lewes).
Hazards: None
Water Conditions: Canoeable year round.

Prime Hook Creek

Introduction

Do you seek smooth water to paddle on but not if it means dealing with wide exposed wind-swept rivers? And does getting those tides straight and enduring the exhausting long haul that ensues if you do not, make staying home and mowing the lawn even look good? Then maybe you should come on down to Prime Hook Creek. Hidden away in the soggy heart of a national wildlife refuge this is one of the nicest canoe streams in Delaware. This is one tidal stream that remains mostly narrow and is usually sheltered as it is snuggly entrenched in either forest or tall reeds. And although it is tidal, the range is small and the current relatively weak. You will never find a more forgiving stream near the shores of Delaware Bay.

Section 1. Del. Rte. 1 to Refuge Headquarters

Gradient	Difficulty	Distance	Time	Width	Scenery	Map
0	A	7.0	3.0	10-30	Good	74

Trip Description: The start is one of the most unpromising that you will see anywhere; for that eight foot wide dribble behind the tavern is what you just drove all this way for. But be patient, duck those low hanging limbs and in a few yards you will be gliding quietly across the head of a string of swamp-fringed ponds. The ponds invite poking and probing around their backwaters, a good way to see wildlife, but if you are in a hurry, generally bear left as you cross the ponds, except at the first island, and when far ahead you spot a white sign then paddle for it. If the sign says "To Blinds 27, 28" you are doing just fine, continue straight and in a short distance the last of the ponds will funnel into a tiny tea-colored creek. From here the route meanders initially through a swamp forest which then slowly evolves to a wooded facade that screens out a vast freshwater marsh beyond. While the place is generally quite primitive, the woods are peppered with little white signs, most of which point the way to public waterfowl hunting blinds. The blinds incidentally are located on little side channels which once again are the best place to spot wildlife. While the signs can be a bit of an eyesore, the ones saying "To Refuge HQ" can save the day for you (and maybe part of the night also) when you confront the confusing intersections with major ditches. Amazingly there are few deadfalls complicating this creek and those that exist have been sawed out. About a mile or so past Foord Landing, which is closed to public use, you can kiss the last tree goodbye as the creek burrows into a reed-lined corridor. To navigate here just continue to follow the signs which means that you will turn right at each of the two major intersections. Just for the record, the last two miles of this tour are not really on Prime Hook Creek but first on Petersfield Ditch and then on Headquarters Ditch.

Section 2. Lower Prime Hook Circuit Tour

Gradient	Difficulty	Distance	Time	Width	Scenery	Map
0	A	10.5	4.0	25-400	Good	73

Trip Description: All in all this is a nice paddle but after the upper creek it is a let down. Prime Hook Creek once dumped directly into Delaware Bay but storms and shifting sand blocked its path and now the creek has two outlets to the Broadkill River, an arrangement well suited to a circuit paddle. Arbitrarily starting at the Refuge Headquarters and arbitrarily going clockwise (in practice you should plan your direction and put-in point according to direction of wind and tides), head out Headquarters Ditch to Petersfield Ditch, turn left and head northwest for about a half mile to a fairly important looking ditch (with the "To HQ" sign pointed toward the channel that you are on) and turn right. You are now back on Prime Hook Creek, headed downstream. This stretch is quite shallow at low tide but passable and its narrow channel is squeezed within a corridor of towering twelve-foot phragmites. When you spot the houses of Broadkill Beach follow the deeper fork to the right and you will now be on Broadkill Sound which is just another ditch. To your right are nice views across salt meadows of the refuge while on your left is the sprawling clutter of Broadkill Beach, a bayside resort community. Upon entering Broadkill River turn right. As you ascend the river you will notice a white cone-crowned structure, probably a beacon. Petersfield Ditch, which is much larger than any others that have branched off of the north side of the Broadkill so far, lies on the right about a mile past this landmark. The ditch offers good views of the attractive marsh and has no complications except for a high tide carry necessary around the low Rte. 16 bridge. Turn left onto Headquarters Ditch at the second major ditch intersection past the bridge. This ditch is marked by a sign.

Hazards: None normally but two small dams are sometimes seasonally erected on Broadkill Sound and Petersfield Ditch and may in a few years become permanent. Their purpose will be to improve waterfowl habitat by flooding out the weed-like phragmites reeds with freshwater. These will add two short carries but on the other hand eliminate fighting adverse tidal currents which do indeed exist on this circuit tour.

Water Conditions: Tidal and hence almost always navigable. The occasional exceptions occur at unusually low tides.

Gauge

None

Chapter 9

Stormdrains and Flashfloods

Paddlers living amid the vast sprawl of the Washington-Baltimore metropolitan area will be pleased to know that there are dozens of runable whitewater streams right at their doorsteps. Disguised as mild-mannered trickles meandering about parklands, shopping centers, factories and houses, they can be almost instantly transformed by a summer shower into roaring raging whitewater wonders. These phenomena, often dubbed with the unflattering title of storm drain, are the products of extensive urbanization that results in almost complete and immediate runoff of any rain that should fall in that watershed. Riding such floods can be both thrilling and even aesthetically rewarding but it is essential that the paddler be aware that urban canoeing is also fraught with perils and peculiarities and should thus be prepared for some of the following problems before ever putting in.

First of all there are the obstacles. Of course, as on its country cousins, the ill-placed fallen tree, undercut banks and snags are an ever present problem but this situation is noticeably aggrevated by the highly errosive nature of these flash flooding monsters. Then many of these streams flow through developed parklands where numerous low footbridges hovering over high velocity current threaten to brain the unwary boater. Many streams have seen past development such as dams, sewers, bridge piers and retaining walls, which have long since washed, crumbled or dissolved away but often with ugly iron reinforcing rods still remaining. Camouflaged by the extremely muddy waters, these can often account for those mysterious gaping holes that suddenly appear in your "indestructo" boat. Not all of the obstacles stand still. By the time that you put in, the stream may have already flooded and receded back within its banks, but in the process accumulated such wealth as picnic tables, shopping carts, logs and in winter, ice flows. Remember, on a really small stream there is not always a whole lot of room to outmaneuver such tumbling, thrashing battering rams. Unidentified flying objects can also, on odd occasions, menace you as storm drains have been known to flow through golf courses, rifle ranges, archery ranges and past bored juveniles who love to toss rocks and bottles. Finally there are the hazards involved in the ultimate in urban storm drains, the concrete-paved channels. Scout every inch of these before attempting as the danger of all hazards described before are magnified by the inability to stop in these flumes. In addition, such channels are sometimes strained through concrete energy dissipators, narrow culverts, pipe crossings and some really exotic predicaments such as the "bottomless pit" on Little Falls Branch below Massachusetts Ave. in Montgomery County or the two mile long tunnel on Jones Falls under downtown Baltimore.

Next the paddler must be fully aware of the abysmal quality of the water that he or she is about to boat on and possibly bathe in. For you see that brown water roaring past you is not all just mud. Street runoff also includes such appetizers as motor oil, lawn and garden fertilizer, pesticides, doggy dung, garbage and anything else that lands on the ground. Furthermore, it is common practice to run sanitary sewers down stream valleys and even stream beds and these sewers often overflow, especially during storms. There is not much you can do about this except stay upright and keep your mouth shut in heavy whitewater.

Boating in highly populated areas can attract considerable attention which can create problems. Local police sometimes react unfavorably to the sight of some fool flushing down a swollen creek, interpret it as a self-destructive act and thus may move to save you from yourself by ejecting you from subject stream. A more substantial problem is that of attractive nuisance. Attractive nuisance means that just the sight of you causes trouble in the eyes of the law. Many storm drains are paralleled by parkways and highways where drivers can be easily distracted by your interesting activity, thus setting the stage for some really juicy accidents. You can argue that that is not YOUR fault but local administrators subsequently drafting regulations prohibiting boating on local streams may not see it that way. So keep a low profile and stay off such creeks during rush hour.

You have to be foxy just to catch these streams up. A creek draining a totally urbanized basin is purely dependent on rainfall intensity, i.e. it has to rain hard. You often must arrive at some of your smaller selections while it is still raining and a mere half hour afterwards could be too late. Locating an area of intense rainfall is difficult, as storms, even the widespread winter type, tend not to be uniform. With summer showers it can be pouring on your house but the sun may be shining a mile away. A telephone call to friends or relatives in the basin in question can be your scouting. Otherwise it is a game of chance.

Finally good luck and be careful.

Index